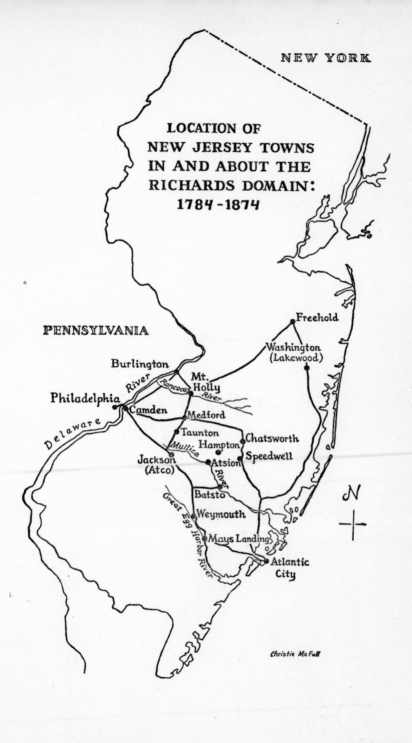

NEW YORK

LOCATION OF
NEW JERSEY TOWNS
IN AND ABOUT THE
RICHARDS DOMAIN:
1784-1874

PENNSYLVANIA

Freehold

Washington
(Lakewood)

Burlington

River

Rancocas River

Mt.
Holly

Philadelphia

Camden

Medford

Taunton

Hampton

Chatsworth

Mullica

Delaware

Jackson
(Atco)

Atsion

Speedwell

River

Batsto

Weymouth

Great Egg Harbor River

Mays Landing

Atlantic
City

N

Christie McFall

Rutgers University Press

New Brunswick, N. J.

Family Empire
in
Jersey Iron

The Richards Enterprises in the Pine Barrens

ARTHUR D. PIERCE

974.9
Pie

ACKNOWLEDGMENT

The author acknowledges with gratitude permission to quote from the
following: *Tocqueville in America* by George Wilson Pierson, published by
Doubleday and Company, Inc.; *Rebels and Gentlemen: Philadelphia in the
Age of Franklin* by Carl and Jessica Bridenbaugh, published by Oxford
University Press; *Days Off* by Henry Van Dyke, published by Charles
Scribner's Sons; and *Philip Vickers Fithian: Journal, 1775-1776*, published
by Princeton University Press.

The diary of William Richards is published by permission of the Historical
Society of Pennsylvania.

TO *Meta Richards Taylor*

*A dear friend and gallant inheritor of
the finest qualities of the Richards line*

Contents

Introduction

In southern New Jersey's pine country stands a monument to halycon days. It is a mansion, built in the plantation style, with tall columns along a broad veranda which reach to the roof above the second floor. Long windows open onto this veranda, those downstairs rising from the floor level. On top of the house is an "observatory," and on all sides oaks provide shade and a green setting. Although it was built by Thomas Richards, Jr., more than a hundred years after the birth of William Richards, founder of the Richards family, the mansion has become a sort of symbol of that family to the author.

Thomas Richards, Jr., built not only the mansion but also the town of Atco which eventually surrounded it. The house, the center of social life in the vicinity, was the scene of lavish entertainment. Liveried coachmen drove ladies, dressed in hooped gowns, and dashing gentlemen up the curving drive. There was dancing by candlelight in the drawing room with its high windows framed in rich brocade. And from the kitchens came the feast which was laid in the large dining room.

The mansion was the hub of the family. Off in the woods in which the mansion stood were ironworks, paper mills, glassworks, and other enterprises of the Richards family. In later years the mansion, through neglect, became shabby—with paint peeling from the walls and pigeons roosting in the upstairs bedrooms. But even then the inherent splendor of the place lingered. Some years ago the mansion was restored and remains a fragment of yesterday in a world of today.

Much of this picture was formed for the author, when, in his teens, he spent his summers in a cottage across the road from the mansion. The name Richards cast a spell then as it still does today.

William Richards was a physical giant. His offspring— 19 children, 40 grandchildren, and almost countless descendants in subsequent generations—were of all kinds, but strength was predominant. Yet even the strong had their failings. As one of their descendants, the distinguished Herbert DuPuy, put it, some of "those old duffers were great gin and whisky drinkers, as well as great borrowers and poor payers." Yet increasing acquaintance with the colorful cast of Richards characters has evoked the author's admiration, respect, and interest, plus a conviction that their story, insofar as facts are available, ought to be told.

The substantial influence which William Richards and

his family had upon the industrial development in the Delaware Valley from before the Revolutionary War until the Civil War has been inadequately appreciated. Their contributions to American financial, professional, and political life at that time are largely unknown. The Richards built not only ironworks but glass furnaces, cotton mills, paper factories, and brick-making establishments. They helped produce munitions for two American wars. They were lumbermen, merchants, inventors, and shipbuilders: the founding of Atlantic City, the "world's playground," was their brainchild. They led in establishing two of Philadelphia's largest banks, several of its foremost insurance companies, and numerous other institutions. Members of the family led in organizing the Camden & Atlantic Railroad, and one helped to establish its first competitor for seashore traffic. Three were members of the New Jersey legislature, one a member of the Pennsylvania legislature, and another a Mayor of the City of Philadelphia. Several were members of the bar in both Pennsylvania and New Jersey. And as a family, the Richards collectively were for many years among the largest landholders in the eastern United States—at the peak their properties totaled more than a quarter of a million acres.

The name Richards is of Welsh origin, and the family line dealt with here is but one of a number of the same name who came to America in the 17th and 18th centuries. Some of these Richards families seemed to favor the same Christian names. For example, during the American Revolution at least five and possibly more men in the Philadelphia area—apparently unrelated—were named William Richards. To complicate matters further, a German family named Reichart upon coming to Pennsylvania anglicized their name to Richards, and members of this family became active in the iron business as did so many of the Welsh Richards.

Within the family of William Richards the tendency to

duplicate first names was great. Place names and other devices are used together with Christian names for clarity in distinguishing between members of the Richards family concerned in this book because in four generations there are: eleven Williams, six Johns, five each of Samuel and Thomas, and four of Joseph. Within individual branches there was even further duplication. For his children William of Batsto, N. J. used four names twice: William, Joseph, Charles, and George Washington. Samuel Richards of Atsion had three boys named William, two of them with the middle name Smith. These and other repetitions occurred because the first possessors of the names died at early ages. The reader will observe similar duplication among the women's names also, particularly Mary, Sarah, Elizabeth, and Anne.

This story of the Richards family will be informal and not a genealogical treatise (A genealogical sketch will be found in the Appendix). For the generations covered it is as complete as the author could make it, but there are gaps which research has failed to fill. In the sketches which follow, however, the reader shall meet—one by one—the more rugged of the Richardses: William of Batsto, his two wives, a number of their 19 children, and even a few of their more colorful grandchildren.

NOTE: Where an asterisk (*) precedes a name it signifies that a biographical chapter appears later.

   * WILLIAM RICHARDS: Ironmaster, who built a fortune in 15 years through his Batsto Iron Works.

   MARY PATRICK: William's first wife, daughter of his first boss, mother of his first 11 children; from her portrait, a sweet person.

   ABIGAIL RICHARDS: First of the 11 children; took care of the big house at Batsto while her mother was having children; never married, and died six months before her mother.

   JOHN RICHARDS: Second child of William and Mary; associated with his father in the iron business; resided briefly in Philadelphia; died at the early age of 26; never married.

* SAMUEL RICHARDS: Ironmaster in his own right; owner of Atsion, Weymouth, Hampton, Martha, and Speedwell iron works; a man of character and warmth who amassed even more wealth than his father.

ELIZABETH RICHARDS: Fourth child; as the second wife of the Rev. Thomas Haskins she thereby became her brother Jesse's mother-in-law. He married the daughter of her husband's first marriage.

* REBECCA RICHARDS: Her marriage to John Sevier did not please her father; her husband was son of the first Governor of Tennessee.

WILLIAM RICHARDS: Sixth child and first of two sons to be named for his father; little known of him except that he was sickly and died at 21.

JOSEPH RICHARDS: Died at 19. According to family tradition, William and Joseph were tuberculosis victims.

* THOMAS RICHARDS: Married the granddaughter of famous naturalist John Bartram; built two glassworks; owned the famous Bonaparte mansion in Bordentown, N. J.; one of the founders of the Camden & Atlantic Railroad.

* JESSE RICHARDS: Succeeded his father as owner of Batsto.

CHARLES RICHARDS: Tenth child, he died in his third year.

ANNA MARIA RICHARDS: Eleventh and last of Mary Patrick's children, she married John White, of Delaware, for whom Thomas Sully copied his oil portrait of Samuel Richards of Atsion.

MARGARETTA WOOD: Second wife of William Richards, daughter of Isaac Wood, of Moorestown; by Margaretta—sometimes called Margaret and Marget—he had eight more children. Mary Patrick had died at Batsto, November 24, 1794. William and Margaretta were married January 18, 1797.

* BENJAMIN WOOD RICHARDS: William's 12th offspring, first by Margaretta Wood; one of the most distinguished of the Richards children; merchant, banker, Mayor of Philadelphia.

CHARLES HENRY RICHARDS: He lived but three years, about nine months longer than the first Charles whose mother was Mary Patrick Richards.

GEORGE WASHINGTON RICHARDS: His life was even shorter than Charles', a little over a year and a month.

AUGUSTUS HENRY RICHARDS: Fourth child by Margaretta; became a lawyer in Philadelphia; died at 36.

* WILLIAM RICHARDS: To be known hereafter as William III, third in line; most enigmatic member of the family; left almost no mark on Richards history, and many of his kinfolk never heard of him.

GEORGE WASHINGTON RICHARDS: William's deep admiration for the Father of Our Country was expressed for the second time when he named his 17th child; he became a merchant, cotton manufacturer, and influential figure in Philadelphia financial circles.

JOSEPH BALL RICHARDS: Named for his father's noted nephew, Little Joseph survived less than three months.

MARY WOOD RICHARDS: Her father was 77 when she was born; "Little Mary" was to brighten his life for seven years; never married; and her numerous brothers looked after her carefully.

JOSEPH BALL: Nephew of William Richards, manager of Batsto during the Revolution; ardent patriot; partner in various Richards enterprises; one of Philadelphia's wealthier men, and a friend of Stephen Girard, noted businessman and philanthropist.

JOHN RICHARDS: Grandchild of William's brother James; worked under William at Batsto; later associated as manager of Weymouth, Atsion, and Washington Furnaces, and as part owner of Gloucester Furnace near Egg Harbor, N. J.

Much of the material in this book is new and has never been published before such as the wealth of information in the Richards family archives, the old Weymouth Furnace book, and the extracts from subsequent record books of that once-great enterprise. The story of Jesse

Richards' embarrassing failure at Washington Furnace has not been told previously and there is new light on the remote ironworks at Hampton. Railroad buffs will encounter sidelights on the establishment of the Atlantic City Railroad. The antique-minded—and many more—may welcome the most extensive account to date of the life of Benjamin Randolph, famous as a cabinet-maker, devoted as a patriot in the Revolution, and puzzling as an ironmaster at Speedwell (which was later owned by the Richards family). Some discoveries were also made such as: the whereabouts of the furnace machinery at Etna, now Medford Lakes; the fact that a silk mill was established at Atsion and a woolen mill was located at Pleasant Mills which was so named in the 1790's; the two murders that occurred at Speedwell and Hampton; the story of the "lost forge" above Quaker Bridge; and particularly, the visit of Alexis de Tocqueville to Benjamin Richards.

For any interested in the strictly economic aspects of the various pineland enterprises, it should be noted that nearly all surviving furnace records—of Batsto, Weymouth, Washington, etc.—are time books, letter books, and store books; with a few exceptions, the account books have not yet come to light and may have been lost or destroyed.

Readers of *Iron in the Pines* by the same author may note specific discrepancies between this book and that one, because the information here is based on later and more conclusive research.

The author is always happy when he can work from manuscript records, and much of this book is based on them. He still recalls the evening when he was a dinner guest of Mr. and Mrs. Louis B. Taylor, and a treasure box of manuscripts was entrusted to him to help in writing this book. Another exceedingly useful cache of Richards records was made available by Benjamin Richards Townsend. Other documentary material of the Richards family has come from Mrs. Maud Richards; Susan Richards; the later Harriet Richards Jeter Robeson; Mrs. Harold Haines, nee Emily Richards; LeRoy Richards; Mrs. Arthur Devan; and Mrs. Reginald Forbes. To all these my best thanks, and the hope that I have not done too badly by their family.

Many more helped in preparation of *Family Empire in Jersey Iron*. I am particularly grateful to Mr. and Mrs. Arthur Becker, who loaned me their 1808-1810 Weymouth account books; to Captain Charles I. Wilson for the most generous possible help in research and cooperation; to his son, Charles I. Wilson, Jr., for his transcripts of the Atsion Furnace Books in the Burlington County Historical Society; and especially to my friend Howard R. Kemble, whose keen eye ferreted out much information which he kindly made available. Thanks are due also to Joseph J. Truncer and the New Jersey Department of Conservation and Economic Development for the Washington Furnace records and others in State possession; to Raymond and Mary Baker, always helpful friends; to Munroe W. Copper, Jr., owner of the old Weymouth mantels; and Dr. Henry K. Bisbee for use of his file of the *Mount Holly Mirror*.

Other aid has come from Mr. and Mrs. John Stewart, Carolyn Stewart, Andrew Stewart, M. Alice Stewart, Jack Boucher, Charles F. Hummel, Caro M. Larsen, Carter Larsen, John D. F. Morgan, Henry S. Ross, Mrs. Leonard G. Rundstrom, Harold Thompson, Dr. Harold F. Wilson, Mrs. A. K. Wolcott, and last but far from least, the late Charles S. Boyer, and Nathaniel Ewan.

Every cooperation has been given by the staffs of the following: Historical Society of Pennsylvania, New Jersey Historical Society; the Atlantic, Burlington, and Camden Historical Societies; the Savitt Library of Glassboro State College; the Lakewood, N. J. Library; the Henry Francis du Pont Winterthur Museum; St. Andrew's Episcopal

Church, Mount Holly, N. J.; St. Stephens Episcopal Church, Philadelphia; the Yale University Library; the Recorder of Deeds and Surrogates offices in Philadelphia as well as Atlantic, Burlington, Camden, Gloucester, and Monmouth Counties, and the Burlington County Detective Bureau.

Finally, what can an author say to a wife who has freely and fully contributed her assistance, encouragement, labor, and particularly her patience? "Thank you" seems dreadfully inadequate.

ARTHUR D. PIERCE

Cherry Hill, New Jersey, 1964

The Family Album

William Richards of Batsto

"*Its no use going back to yesterday,
because I was a different person then*"

—Alice, to the Mock Turtle

Eastern Pennsylvania's natural countryside in the 18th
century was a pleasant place for children. Beyond each
green hill were new discoveries: an unexpected brook rip-
pling and splashing; outcroppings of rock rich with iron
that were often shaped to spark a youngster's imagination;
strange lanes leading through dark forests; perhaps even a
cave. In addition to the natural surroundings, a child at
that time would also have had fun watching a nearby furnace or forge, for there were many scattered over the townships of Berks and Chester counties.

Here William Richards spent his childhood, but it was

soon over. For William Richards, aged 13, his childhood ended in January of 1752, when his father died.

The elder William Richards had been fond of his son and seemed to have sensed his great potentialities. Big for his age, the boy was a willing and able helper at farm chores, got along well with his father, and was affectionate in the family circle. If the boy had a nickname, it is not known, but that he had one is likely for while his name was William Richards, so was his father's name, and no less than three of his cousins had that name also. The name of the family of his mother, Elizabeth, is also unknown, but from her side came some of his great stamina and physical strength, and no doubt a part of his strong character as well. Now the family circle was broken. The elder Richards had been but 47, a fairly early age to die, even then.

When the will was read, young William turned out to be the residuary legatee. That will, dated December 26, 1751, and filed in Philadelphia, decreed that all of Richards' property be sold; and after minor bequests to six of his children*, his wife was to have use of the proceeds for life. There was the usual clause that "if she thinks proper to alter her condition, she shall have her thirds according to law"—legal language for discouraging a widow's remarriage.

The will made two specific provisions concerning young William: first, that he should "live with his mother for the space of one year, and then be put out to a trade which he likes"; second, that after his mother's death he should inherit any residue of the estate upon his coming of age.

The mid-18th century being what it was in rural Penn-

---

* Mary, who married John Ball; Owen, his oldest son, and Margaret each were given five shillings, suggesting that they had been given advances; Ruth and Sarah each was willed five pounds, and Sarah additionally a "chest of drawers at her sister Margaret Deweeses home"; James got ten pounds and a mare.

sylvania, young William had no formal education. What he learned came chiefly from his parents; yet somehow he became an enormously successful man. He lacked virtually all the advantages considered essential today. His closest approach to gymnasium facilities were farm fences and the stouter branches of convenient trees; and in lieu of a swimming pool, a likely spot along French Creek, which winds through eastern Pennsylvania, had to do.

By modern standards young William was a child laborer, apprenticed at 14 to an ironworks. Quite probably he welcomed that as an opportunity. Both his brothers and at least two of his sisters had married (one of his sisters was less than 13 when she married); and there he was at home, contending with three women. The ironworks presented a world filled with drama, excitement, and challenge to one of William's capacities and temperament. The smelting process is awesome and elemental with its earth-pounding hammers, roaring blast, and the climax in flowing, glowing, molten iron.

In the family there is a story that young William's apprenticeship was at the Coventry Iron Works. It was established about 1718 by an Englishman, Samuel Nutt. By the time of William Richards' supposed apprenticeship in 1754, Coventry had been expanded from the original forge to include a blast furnace, a steel furnace, a slitting mill, a bloomery forge, and a refinery forge. Nutt had died some years earlier and in 1754 the works was owned by his widow, Anna.

However, neither William Richards, nor John Patrick, who supposedly took William under his wing and taught him the iron business are in the Coventry records[1] for that period. Anna Nutt owned another important ironworks, Warwick Furnace,[2] not too far away from Coventry; and there one finds frequent references to John Patrick, from

1750 on. In the 1760's there is also repeated mention of other members of the Patrick family, including John Patrick's second wife, Abigail in addition to William. The following notes from the Warwick books may be of interest:

1765:	September	16	Michael Mick, purchase of molasses.
	October	4	William Dewees: 3 large 6-plate stoves.
	November	11	Abigail Patrick, provisions.
1766:	April	11	Samuel Patrick, purchase of paper.
	July	20	Abigail Patrick, 2 qts. molasses.
	September	20	Abigail Patrick, 12 lbs. of beef.
	October	21	Samuel Patrick, 46 lbs. of beef.
1767:	May	6	William Richards, 6d of sugar @ 9d.
	August	6	William Richards, 4 qts. of molasses.
	August	10	Abigail Patrick, rice.
	September	6	Abigail Patrick, 6 sheets paper, 6d.
	October	2	William Richards, 2 bushels rye meal.
	October	6	William Richards, pair of shoes, 7/6.
	October	21	Abigail Patrick, to repair garters, 8d.
1768:	February	17	William Richards, 14 yds. chk.
	February	26	Abigail Patrick, 1 quire paper.
	April	16	Samuel Patrick, a quarter of veal.
	April	25	William Richards, 42 days plowing 7-19-0.
	May	3	William Richards, by his part of the Castings due to estate of John Patrick 4-3-7.
1770:	January	21	Samuel Patrick, hauling 4 loads to Phila.; 2 tons Pig Iron to "pottsgrove," etc.
	March		Widow Patrick, acct. credited by Balance due to Jno. Patrick 196-16-10.

In these records is Michael Mick, whose family was to be active later at various Richards furnaces in New Jersey. As shown above William Richards alternated his work in the forges with plowing, and Abigail Patrick and her step-son Samuel were much given to letter-writing as indicated by their purchases of paper. Others at Warwick in those days, but not noted in the above extracts, were Thomas Mayberry, manager of an ironworks in Mount Holly and Taunton during the Revolution, and Aquilla (Equilia) Jones, who later followed William Richards to Batsto.

This background also shows that John Patrick was an important figure at Warwick Furnace, and that his family lived nearby. Beyond doubt, too, it was Patrick who in 1754 took young William in hand, at Warwick, not Coventry; and because Patrick liked and respected his young apprentice, William soon found himself on terms of close friendship with the Patrick family. That family included the son, Samuel, and two daughters, Esther and Mary; and since William appears to have been a steady lad not given to the carousings and binges common in furnace gangs, he was always welcome.

When William first arrived at Warwick, Mary Patrick was eight years old, and most likely a charming child to judge by the one picture there is of her. Gradually the Patrick household became something of a second home for William. And he and Mary became friends for she grew up into a captivating young lady. The only wonder in those days of early marriages is why William waited until she was 19 before he married her. Perhaps he felt he should be able to support a wife before he married or he may have had to wait until his apprenticeship term expired. In any case, when the wedding took place in 1764, the groom had worked at Warwick 11 years; and the bride had lived there all her life. A year later, in 1765, Mary Patrick Richards gave birth to her first child. She named her daughter Abigail after her stepmother of whom she was fond.

In the same year William was caught up in the mounting

tensions which preceded the American Revolution. 'Sixty-five was the year of the notorious Stamp Tax. That levy was resented throughout the American colonies. The persons who bore the brunt of the resentment were those appointed by the British to distribute the tax stamps in major American cities. In Philadelphia the royally-chosen stamp distributor was John Hughes, and a committee of seven called upon him to demand that he resign his appointment, as many other stamp agents had been "persuaded" to do. On that committee of seven were Robert Morris, James Tilghman, Archibald McCall, William Bradford, Charles Thomson (once called the "Sam Adams of Philadelphia"), John Cox, and William Richards. At this late date one cannot be certain that this was the William of Warwick Furnace but Cox and Thomson who were on this committee became his close associates in the future which is suggestive.

In Warwick Furnace records William Richards does not appear after May of 1768. The iron industry was slow at that time and a new furnace had "recently opened" in the New Jersey pinelands. Its name was Batsto, and experienced men were needed there. At some time in 1768 William Richards went to Batsto and there got a job—his first at the ironworks he was later to own. William left his family behind him at Warwick and appears to have worked probably as a founder until that year's blast was complete. Only after ice froze the furnace waterwheel and halted work did he go back to Warwick.

Five years later William Richards returned to Batsto, this time as manager for his friend Col. John Cox. Advertisements of 1773—one for woodchoppers, another for two "runaway Irishmen"—were signed "William Richards, manager at said Furnace," or "John Cox in Water street, Philadelphia." *

* Batsto had been purchased by Cox and Charles Thomson in 1770. Three years later Thomson sold his share to Cox.

An interesting letter of June 17, 1773 addressed to "Mr. William Richards, at Batsto Furnace" was written by his wife's brother, Samuel Patrick, then living at Andover Furnace (Pa.). The following extract, hinting for a job, also suggests how close-mouthed ironmasters were about their affairs:[3]

> This minute I received your Unsatisfactory letter; you say you can't come to see me, and it is not for want of affection. What is it for want of? Not time . . . unless you don't want me to come see you. A man out of employ can't afford to loose [sic] a week in a year to go see his relations.

> You didn't say anything about the Furnace. According to custom. . . . This week Andrew Miller dressed our Bellows, the Furnace is not Quite Clean, we have got some new ore to try next Monday, and if it don't do well I shall be very much disappointed. (Our F goes on Well) (a little more than you said). . . .

During this period Richards moved his family from Warwick to Batsto. With them came his nephew, Joseph Ball. And we are fortunate to have an intimate glimpse of life at Batsto in those years. It is provided by the observant Rev. Philip Vickers Fithian[4] in his Journal under the date of February 13, 1774. On a pineland preaching mission, Rev. Fithian visited the Pleasant Mills Church. He writes:

> After dinner I rode over to the Furnace and visited friendly and agreeable Mrs. Richards [Mary Patrick]. Towards evening with Mr. Richards, Mrs. Richards and Mrs. Ball I call'd in to see Mrs. Punner where we had some useful conversation.
> Evening. [Mrs.] Richards, Mrs. Ball, Miss Punner & Miss Richards [Abigail]—Mr. Richards, Mr. Ball, Mr. Hugh . . . Lusk and Myself all rode from the Furnace to Singing School. We had however not the greatest harmony.

Not given to merriment himself, the Rev. Fithian can hardly be expected to reflect the exuberance and gayety which must have marked such a songfest even as the sour notes floated through the pines. There must have been many such warm moments at Batsto in those days, and it is a pity that there are no other records of them.

William Richards remained at Batsto through 1774, and on November 8 he advertised:

> Left at Batsto Furnace on the 7th instant, a bay horse colt, about 4 years old, with saddle and bridle, supposed to be stolen. The owner is desired to come, prove his property, pay charges, and take him away.

In 1775 Joseph Ball succeeded his uncle as manager at Batsto because William Richards returned to Warwick and Chester County in Pennsylvania. Revolutionary War fervor was spreading. Soon William was commissioned as "Standard Bearer to the Second Battalion of Associators" in Chester County. The commission itself is now in possession of a member of the family. It reads:

IN ASSEMBLY

to William Richards, Gent. June 6, 1775. We, reposing Special Trust and Confidence in your Patriotism, Valour, Conduct and Fidelity, Do by these Presents constitute and appoint you to be Standard Bearer to the Second Battalion of the Associators in the County of Chester for the Protection of this Province against all hostile enterprises and for the Defense of American Liberty, etc.

Signed by Order of the Assembly
JOHN MORTON, Speaker.

One tradition in the family says that Richards was a colonel during the Revolution. No records have been found thus far to support that belief. More probably William was a private either in the militia or in the Continen-

tal forces. This is suggested also by a memorandum, probably in his wife's handwriting, which is headed: "Articles
sent Wm. Richards, when he went to Camp, Aug. 13,
1776." [5] The list follows:

1 bedquilt, 1 blankit, 1 pillow, 1 pare sheets an Pillow
cased, 2 knives and forks, 3 spoons, 1 tea-pot, 1 bole, 1 tin-
sugar-dish, 1 dish, 2 plates, 2 cups and sasers, 1 tin-cup, 1
table cloth, 3 towels, peaper case and Box and Clothes
Brush, 2 cote, 2 packets, 4 pairs briches, 5 stokes, 5 pare
thred stokin, 1 pare ditto worsted, 1 ditto yarn, 1 pare gaiters,
1 doble Morning gound, 1 small trunk, 1 vial camphire in the
till Rags, peper, all spice, 4 poket handkerchies, 1 nite cap,
1 Bible, 1 brisket beef, 1 box shaved ditto, 1 ganion, 1 box
wafers, pen, ink, sage, balm, sacepan, 1 gridiorn, 1 pewter
bason.

This document is fascinating not only in what it says,
but in what is left unsaid. It was given by William Richards' second wife to her grandson, Louis Henry Richards,
in 1848. The "articles" listed suggest that William would be
quartered in a place where he could set up housekeeping;
and the inclusion of a tablecloth, a morning gown, clothes
brush, and gridiron indicate that by the standards of those
times William was accustomed to comfortable life.

The location of the "Camp," the military unit involved,
and any hint of rank is not mentioned. Had William been
an officer, even a non-commissioned one, his status almost
surely would have been noted. The important camp at
that time was in the New York area where Washington was
building up the army which was to fall apart so tragically
after the Battle of Long Island. Had Richards been there, it
is probable that some record of his presence would have
come to light; thus it seems more likely that he was sta-
tioned at one of the militia centers in eastern Pennsylvania.

Another story that has been handed down places William Richards at Valley Forge during the terrible winter of 1777-1778. Again no records have come to light although a search has been made for them. He may have been there, perhaps as an "emergency man" as DuPuy suggests,[6] but he was not a colonel. The list of "articles" above could not have been sent to him there since the list is dated August 13, 1776, more than a year earlier. The one document which does possibly have a Valley Forge connection is the oath of allegiance which William took on May 30, 1778. During that month a number of officers and other army men took oaths of allegiance to "The United States of America" and formally renounced "any allegiance or obedience" to George III, king of England at that time. Richards' oath states that "William Richards of Whiteland [refers to a tract of 151 acres which Richards had purchased earlier in that year] hath voluntarily taken and subscribed the Oath of Allegiance and Fidelity, as directed by an ACT of General Assembly of Pennsylvania," and it is witnessed by "To. Taylor."

Never far from an ironworks, William Richards was living "Near Warwick Furnace" in 1781, for on January 4, of that year a letter was sent to him there by Charles Pettit, Assistant Quartermaster General and one of the owners of Batsto. It was an invitation to become again manager of that ironworks, which Pettit and Col. John Cox (also an Assistant Quartermaster General) proposed to improve. The text of the letter is interesting:[7]

Sir:
    From the favourable mention Colonel Cox has often made of you as a suitable person . . . I have for some time had it in contemplation to make some proposals to you respecting the management of Batsto Works, with which you are well acquainted. I have some time ago communicated this inten-

tion to Mr. Ball who has other matters in view for himself & therefore cannot long continue in charge of them. He tells me you were lately at the Works and that you intimated a willingness to engage in this Business. Col. Cox & I were there together within a few days past, and we have concluded to carry them on with vigor, in order to which we propose to erect a forge as speedily as may be at a place called the Old Mills [formerly Krips Mill], which will make the Works more extensive and convenient. If it be convenient for you to engage in the business I should be glad to see you here as soon as possible; not to exceed next week, & if you can come down by Monday or Tuesday I should like it the better, when I imagine I shall be able to offer you terms that may be satisfactory to you. If you cannot come so soon you will please to let me know by a Line.

CHAS. PETTIT

You will find me the north side of Market Street, next door below 4th Street.

Just when William Richards met Pettit is not known; but within a short time he was in charge at Batsto, although on this occasion he did not move his family there. Warwick was still "home," a fact clearly shown by the diary which he began keeping at Batsto. A fragmentary and often puzzling chronicle, it starts on April 17, 1781, and two days later there is this memo:

Left Batsto to go to Pena to see my family Shall leave 2 half Joes [about $8.80 in hard money] with W. Lash and two of State [New Jersey currency] Wm. Loviman for the hay.

Going home, the diary shows, was a two-day trip and he made the journey of eighty-odd miles a number of times. On this occasion he stayed the night of the 20th at the Black Horse Inn (location unknown), and spent the 21st "on the road."

Batsto's physical condition in 1781 may be visualized from its description in an advertisement which appeared two years later. June 26, 1783 offering the property for sale. The advertisement reads:[8]

A Furnace sufficiently large and commodious to produce upwards of 100 tons of pigs and castings per month. The metal is remarkably well adapted for castings, both of hollow ware and cannon, in which experience has sufficiently proved it to excel . . . The Furnace is furnished with an excellent sett of brass patterns for hollow ware, and may be put into blast in a short time. . . .

A Rolling and Slitting Mill, which, from the strength and construction of the works, and large head of water, is capable of great execution.

On the same dam are also a Saw-Mill and small Grist Mill. . . . A Forge with four fires and two hammers, nearly new, well constructed and in good order, now at work, distant about half a mile from the Furnace, on another well adapted stream; on which is also an excellent, newly built Saw Mill; and near the Forge are some tenements for workmen and a large new Coal-House.

Contiguous to the Furnace is a commodious Mansion-House, accommodated with a spacious, well-cultivated garden, in which is a well chosen collection of excellent Fruit Trees of various kinds, and adjoining it a young bearing Orchard of about 2000 apple-trees, mostly grafted.

A number of Dwelling-Houses for the accommodation of tradesmen and others necessarily employed about the works; which, together with the Store-Houses, Barns, Stabling, Smith's Shops, Nailery, Coal House and other convenient Buildings, form a considerable village; the whole of which, together with the various works are overlooked from

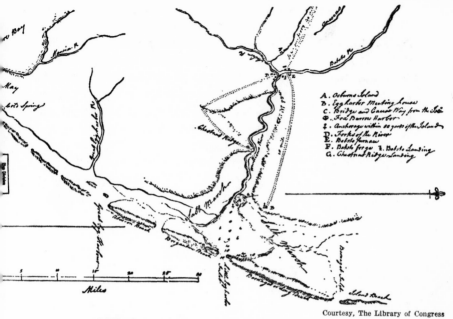

1778 Map of Batsto and the Mullica River Basin.

the door of the mansion-house, which stands on a pleasant eminence.

The river affords a good and easy navigation for sea vessels of burden within a mile, or thereabout, of the works, and for large scows to the Furnace bank . . .

Terms will be made easy to the purchaser. . . . Apply to *John Cox*, Esquire, at Bloomsbury, near Trenton, Charles Pettit, in Philadelphia, or Joseph Ball, managing owner at the said Works.

Against this background, William Richards' diary tells quite a bit. The mansion house referred to in the advertisement was on the "pleasant eminence" where the present mansion house is located (and portions of that early mansion can be found in the walls now standing).

The diary also says that Joseph Ball was still in residence there when Richards took over the management of the works. It may be wondered why Ball remained at Batsto, since Pettit's letter offering Richards the management said that he had "other matters in view for himself." These other matters were his extensive ventures in privateering, which he carried on with Batsto as his headquarters, often on his own account but sometimes in collaboration with Pettit and Cox. Ball had been engaged in privateering and speculation in captured cargoes for three years before Richards came to Batsto in 1781 and continued until the surrender at Yorktown knocked the bottom out of that business in 1781. Significantly, the name of William Richards appears nowhere in the privateering activities for which the Mullica River was the base.

It thus becomes clear why William Richards left his family back at Warwick. There may also have been some difficulty between William and his nephew for on April 26, 1782, little more than a year after Richards' arrival, his diary shows this note: "Left the manamint [management] of Batsto works to Mr. J. Ball." And there is no further note to the contrary. (This was undoubtedly a temporary arrangement.)

Richards' diary introduces a number of other people at Batsto and vicinity. It tells about the building of Batsto Forge and notes that in June 1781 the timbers were being erected by William Crooks "with his two sons." The Lusk brothers—Hugh and Robert—already mentioned at Batsto during William's stay in 1774, were apparently his right-hand men at the Furnace. Aquilla (Equilia) Jones, who had come from Warwick Furnace, was running the grist-mill. Timothy Leach, in June 1782, contracted to produce "four thousand three-foot shingles at six pounds, ten shillings per." Other Batsto employees listed during those years were: W. Lash, Joseph Hugh, John Greay (probably Gray), Michael Rogers, Daniel Morrison, David Howell, and Nathiel (sic) Jones, son of Aquilla.

Around Batsto also was found Captain Timothy Shaler, Ball's top privateersman; Even (sic) Anderson, another sloop captain; Richard Price, John Newland, James Dunwoodey; and among the ladies Mrs. Margaret Paschel and "Old Mrs. Leonard's mother." Naturally the names of Ball and Pettit appear frequently. From the diary it is learned that Richards bought hay from William Loviman, Charles Loveland, Joseph Estelle, and one Smith whose first name probably never will be known. Fish and salt were purchased from Samuel Suves, spirits from Isrel (sic) Whelton; six pieces of "Died Jeremy Linnens" from Col. Benj. Randolph, and a box of candles from Thomas Regroary (sic). On November 7, 1782, oxen were bought for 16 pounds, seven shillings six, but the vendor is not named.

Several other aspects of Batsto life appear briefly. There was a "Scool master" whose name was Mathers and in November 1782, he was paid one pound, 17 shillings six. On June 18, 1783, mention is made of a mason about to begin work, presumably on the furnace. There is also reference to quarrying stone and loading timber at "Olliphants and Hayneses" (probably in the vicinity of Medford, N. J.). Carters were hired from the town of Long-a-Coming (now Berlin). In August 1783, 20 bushels of lime were sent to the "Meeting House," which was Elijah Clark's "Little Log Meeting House," predecessor of today's Pleasant Mills Church. One touch of humor in the diary is the notation for October 31, 1781: "Lent a stub Pensil not returned to Mr. Wescoat. Present." This was probably Col. Richard Wescoat, who was then living in the Clark Mansion at Pleasant Mills.

The chaotic state of money in those days is sharply reflected in the diary. Some transactions are in pounds, shillings and pence; some in dollars; and a number in foreign currencies. Spanish coins have been found at Batsto and were in common use. The "Johannes" or "Joe" was a Portuguese coin worth approximately $8.81, and a "half-Joe" was thus about $4.40 in hard money (gold or tied to gold). Richards borrowed "nine pounds in gold from Joseph Ball," and repaid it in "Hard Money"; Loveland received "2 Half-Joes and four hard dollars." Wm. Roggins was paid in "Eight Dollars State" (New Jersey currency); Captain Anderson received "French Crowns," while Richards "gave Joseph Ball five bushels of Mault in exchange for Ten Bushels of Rye and Cash."

Although William was a manager of an ironworks, there is surprisingly little comment on iron production at Batsto in his diary. One interesting notation covers Richards' expenses for a trip to Mount Holly, N. J. on September 26, 1781, "to get Dementions [dimensions] for forge plate Pattrons." Richards does mention the name of his bellows-maker—"Kinnerd, Esq."—having stopped to see him on his way from "Home" to Batsto on November 21, 1781. The preceding June he had sold Mr. William Read "six Kittles—£6-0-0 [six pounds and no shillings or pense] and there remains Nine Pounds unPaid which is to be paid by the first of September." (It was paid in October.) On December 19 of the same year, Richards paid another visit to his bellows-maker, but not until October 8, 1784, is there further mention of the iron business: "Expenses after Forge Men at Hanes."

From other sources, especially the correspondence of Charles Pettit and Gen. Nathanael Greene, it is learned that with Richards arrival in 1781, Batsto began to prosper. By April 1781 the furnace was in blast again. "Two pairs of sixes" had been contracted for and cast, and although these cannon were "not yet dressed and bored out," their delivery was anticipated within a week.[9]

The forge at Batsto was built in the summer of 1781, and William Richards was in charge of the construction. The site chosen for the forge was about half a mile from the furnace on another stream Nescochague Creek. This was the site of earlier sawmills, and Pettit wrote that much of the dam remained only "wanting some additions." By May the foundations and tailraces had been dug, and some six to eight thousand acres of woodland had been purchased to assure additional and sufficient fuel. Importance of the forge was explained by Pettit to General Greene as follows:[10]

> Bar iron is necessary to the usefulness of the Slitting Mill— it is not to be had in that country by purchase—to buy it here adds too much to the transportation, which is very expensive. In carrying on the furnace, tho' we run as much as we can on guns & other castings, pigs will necessarily accumulate, which we must sell at an undervalue if we sell them there [at the furnace] & they will not bear land carriage to market. Thus a double advantage offers by having a forge to work them [the pigs] up on the Spot, and rod-iron [product of the Slitting Mill] has in some measure the force of hard money.

Batsto's new forge was hardly pounding away before Cornwallis had surrendered at Yorktown. The American Army had begun to melt, and the people prematurely turned their attention from the war to civilian pursuits. The change in conditions affected Batsto. Gaps in Richards' diary suggest prolonged periods when the furnace was not in blast. And soon the normally optimistic Pettit was ready to call it quits. Advertisements began to appear offering Batsto for sale. At first it was declared to be a great opportunity for investment in the iron business; by 1784, no buyers having appeared, fresh advertisements stressed Batsto as a site for gristmills! [11] But still no one was interested in it.

William Richards had been manager for four years. More than anyone else he knew the Batsto Iron Works, its strengths and weaknesses; its possibilities and its problems. Also, he was aware of the lost enthusiasm of its owners, and the extent of their eagerness to sell the works and salvage what they could of their investment. What Richards did not have was money; as things turned out, he did not need any.

William Richards bought the Batsto Iron Works not with gold, but with iron. Not iron which he possessed, but iron he expected to produce over years to come. On July 1, 1784, he apparently took title to the property; however, a private agreement shows his interest was then only one-third, although he was to be manager with a salary of three hundred pounds annually. The other two-thirds—in what was a newly-formed company—was divided equally between Joseph Ball and Charles Pettit. Half of Richards' own interest was purchased from Blair McClenachan, of Philadelphia, payment to be 1,750 pounds "in Bar Iron, Pig Iron and Iron Castings at certain stipulated prices." Within two years Richards had paid more than half of this debt—980 pounds, seven shillings and eight pence—in iron. He was to buy out Ball and Pettit in similar fashion until the ironworks was wholly his. Iron was his money. And in only ten years he had amassed what his son Samuel called "a sufficient fortune to make your mind easy about worldly affairs."

Part of the Richards-Pettit-Ball agreement of 1784 provided that Pettit was to be "Agent and Factor" in Philadelphia, handling the sale of Batsto products there. Among those products were four firebacks cast for George Washington, which were to be installed at Mount Vernon. Two of them are still there. (The story of this transaction appears in the Appendix.)

As late as January 1, 1789, Col. John Cox was also concerned in the Batsto ironworks although his connection with it is not clear. That such a tie existed is shown by a letter he wrote on that day to William Richards requesting, first, that his man "Sambo" be employed "in the Forge in

such a way as you may think best"; and, second, suggesting
that Richards line up his employes to vote for a Cox-
favored ticket in the notorious first New Jersey election
under the new federal constitution. Cox even proposed to
be on hand at Batsto on election day, but whether he
showed up is not known. In any case the candidates he
opposed were the eventual winners.

No documents have been found which show just when
William Richards acquired full control of Batsto. Probably
the date was about 1790. Shortly thereafter, Samuel Richards, William's son, took over the Philadelphia agency from
Charles Pettit.

William Richards seems to have stayed close to Batsto,
relying upon Samuel for information about market prices
and the kinds of iron products most in demand. No doubt
this close personal supervision of the furnace and forge
were major factors in Richards' success. He had rebuilt the
furnace in 1786, and over the two succeeding decades,
despite market slumps and yellow fever epidemics in
Philadelphia, Batsto's wares enjoyed a good and reasonably steady sale.

Batsto's products during that period were largely pig
iron, bar iron (from the forge), six, seven and ten-plate
stoves, and hollow ware such as pots, kettles, skillets, sash
weights, etc. Other castings were made to order. A number
of these were for pumps, for "square bar iron," and in
1806 for a special kind of stove called "Citchins" which
were popular, Samuel wrote his father, "as they save fuel
and labour and are said to bake meat equal to that which
is roasted." A further outlet for Batsto pig iron was assured
when the Richards acquired in 1805 a controlling interest
in the Eagle Iron Works, at Callowhill Street and the
Schuylkill River in Philadelphia. William and Samuel each
took a third in the venture, the other third being held by
the manager, Henry Foxall.

With all his financial success, William Richards was not happy at Batsto. Many tales have been told of old iron-masters living in princely splendor; entertaining foreign and domestic dignitaries; staging lavish entertainment, from balls and cotillions to band concerts, as well as exciting, colorful hunts with hares and hounds. This was not the case with William Richards. He was indeed "Master of Batsto" in terms of power over his big plantation and the workers living there; but socially there can be little doubt that his mansion house was an austere establishment, and his way of life was lonely and uncomplicated. One hint of this is given in a letter from his son Samuel. William, no doubt at the wish of his wife, had asked Samuel to purchase various articles including "figurd muslin." The reply was that he could find none to please him, and added: "They are so much out of fashion" that "only old shopkeepers had any," and what they had was "very homly."

William Richards was not a cultured man; his command of English was meagre as his diary indicates. Handsome he had always been. Standing six feet four, he had remarkably good health and a powerful physique, matched by an aggressive temperament and a capacity for leadership in a rugged and exacting industry. His success had been won the hard way, and in his youth he had not had much time for gaiety. One of the few light touches in his correspondence tells of the incident in 1802 when William won an election bet with Samuel; the payment was "a brown hatt."

Thus, as an adult William was a man of simple tastes, warm-hearted, affectionate, and kindly, with most of his interests outside the ironworks centered on his family. Nevertheless, he was weary of his life at Batsto and as early as March of 1794 his grumbling led Samuel to remark that "there is no necessaty for your confining yourself so much at home. It would make me perfectly happy to see you enjoy yourself visiting your friends and shaking off the Chare [sic] of business you have so long been burdened with." But William stayed put—and continued to complain.

There was much to sadden him besides loneliness in the pines. While his wealth had accumulated, tragedy became a dark commonplace at Batsto. His unhappiness began in 1789 with the death of his three-year-old son Charles. Four years later he lost his eldest son, John, at the age of 27. John had been employed by his father selling iron on commission in Philadelphia, although he had lived much of the time at home in Batsto. John Richards died November 3, 1793, and left his father one-half of the commission due him; two pounds to his mother; 50 pounds to his sister Abigail, and the residue to his brother Samuel, who was made sole executor. Then, less than six months later, on May 14, 1794, Abigail herself died. She was 29. William and Mary Richards had lost their two eldest children in such a short span of time.

Mary Patrick Richards had been ill much of the time following the birth of her last child, Anna Maria, on February 8, 1789. Previously she had borne ten children in 20 years, and she was 41 when Anna Maria arrived. In the fall of 1794 Samuel wrote his father that "Mama continues to be poorly." On November 24 of that year she died. It was a crushing blow and her husband's first reaction was to talk about selling Batsto, so that he might escape his rich wilderness, now lonelier than ever before. In five years William had lost three children and his wife.

Yet more was to come. William, Jr., his third son, died two years later, four days before Christmas of 1796; and the following March 26, the fourth boy, Joseph, passed away. William was 21 and Joseph 19. Both boys are believed to have been victims of tuberculosis. They had lived at Batsto.

In 1797 William Richards, hoping to escape his loneli-

ness, married Margaretta Wood, daughter of Isaac Wood
of Moorestown, a slim and charming young woman of 24.
Richards then was 59, but still handsome and vigorous.
The marriage took place on January 18 at St. Andrew's
Episcopal Church in Mount Holly, and was performed by
the Reverend Andrew Fowler.[12] On November 12 of that
year Margaretta's first child was born: Benjamin Wood
Richards, who was to become one of the most distinguished
members of the family. Less than 15 months later, another
child was born—Charles Henry. Two years afterward,
Margaretta's third child came, and was named for William's idol, George Washington. Charles Henry only lived
three years and died in April of 1802. Two months later
George died. This meant two funerals at Batsto in 1802.

The tragic family pattern was broken in 1803, after which
three more sons were born at Batsto: Augustus Henry, William, and another boy named George Washington. All three
were to survive their father.

William, nevertheless, was anxious both to leave Batsto
and to retire from an active role in the iron business. No
doubt he had made attempts to sell his ironworks, but it
was not easy to find customers prepared to pay what such
a valuable property was worth. Thus in 1809, when he felt
his son Jesse capable of managing the works, he moved
his family to Mount Holly and spent the rest of his life
there.

This move in itself was characteristic. His former partners Ball and Pettit had chosen to live in Philadelphia.
And Cox lived in his mansion, Bloomsbury Court* in
Trenton. They all became prominent in business and public affairs. In contrast to Philadelphia, Mount Holly, the
seat of Burlington County in New Jersey, was pleasant and
quiet. It appealed to Richards' simpler tastes; he was content and happy there, whereas he probably would have

* Now known as the Trent House.

been uncomfortable in the Quaker City with its more pretentious social circles.

William and Margaretta Richards enjoyed 14 years of married life in Mount Holly. Despite his age—he was 71 when he moved there—Richards continued to enjoy good health. While he was retired, he was far from idle. He still kept an eye on Batsto and he bought and sold real estate. He was a communicant and pew holder in St. Andrews Episcopal Church and donated land for its cemetery. He was active in Mount Holly affairs and he built the home which still stands on what was then called the Santo Domingo Tract. Here he spent his last years. In addition, he sired two more children: Joseph Ball, who survived less than three months; and, in his 77th year, Mary Wood, whom he affectionately called "my little Mary."

In addition to his home and Batsto, Richards owned the Pleasant Mills tract; three properties in Mount Holly*; the sprawling Sleepy Creek Cedar Swamp; Squan Bay meadows and Hog Island in the Mullica River; plus six properties in Philadelphia including a tavern on Fourth Street above Callowhill. The rents from these alone provided more than enough to live on comfortably. In addition there was income from Batsto and his share of Weymouth Furnace which he helped finance for Samuel in 1808. That William and Margaretta's house should be near "Iron Works Hill" in Mount Holly was pure coincidence. The ironworks there—owned by his old friend Colonel John Cox—had been destroyed by the British army back in 1778. And from all indications William, soon after 1809, had lost almost all active interest in iron.

On August 31, 1823, William Richards, 85 years old died in his Mount Holly home leaving his wife Margaretta and

---

* The Mount Holly properties were a house in School Alley; another house on the south side of Mill Street; and a house and stable on the north side of Mill Street.

three minor children: William, best known as William III since he was third in line; George Washington, and "little" Mary," then 9 years old.

In life, William Richards had warned his sons "not to raise one above another." In his will he followed that principle. After assuring the comfort of Margaretta with an annuity, he divided his estate equally among his children.[13] But while the estate was appraised at more than $200,000, some of the boys owed it more than $72,000 for advances their father had made them.

William was buried in St. Andrews Cemetery, not far from his big brick home. There a high marble "trunk tomb" bears his name in fast-fading letters. The bill for that tombstone reads:

The Estate of Wm. Richards Deceased

April 12th, 1824   To John Struthers, Dr.

To a Tomb Stone	$140.00
To Cutting 110 Letters	3.30
To Packing Boxes	4.00
To Fixing the Same	15.00
	$162.30

Samuel: His Richest Son

Husky, good-looking, dynamic, and enormously successful was Samuel, third child and second son of William and Mary Patrick Richards. Named for his uncle, Samuel Patrick, he was the first and most illustrious of the many Samuels in the Richards clan.

Although he liked to say that he was merely lucky, he was the only member of the family to surpass his father's outstanding success in the industrial world. He owned not one iron furnace but four, and three were money-makers. Samuel acquired Atsion Iron Works in 1819 and he turned this financial failure into a highly profitable enterprise. In real estate he was equally adept; and even when he swapped iron for land, the land turned out to be good. Some of his brothers envied his "Midas Touch," while his competitors respected his ability. In his personal relationships, Samuel Richards was warm-hearted, generous, and affectionate. Liked by his workmen, he was adored by his family.

Not much is known of Samuel's childhood. He was born May 8, 1769. There is doubt as to the actual place of birth. Some believe it was Valley Forge, but it probably was "near Warwick Furnace." He was only six when the Revolution broke out, and no family records of that period have come to light. After his father acquired Batsto in 1784, Samuel, 15 years old, began to learn iron-making. In six or seven years he learned so much that he was representing the firm in Philadelphia, while his father, off in Batsto listened to his advice even if he did not always follow it.

More than once Samuel sent discreet complaints to his father about the quality of some of the iron which was being shipped to him from Batsto. In October 1794 he notes that "the old Iron that is upon hand is very rusty which hurts the sale . . . I have mixed a good deal of it with the new and worked it off that way."

Family jealousies probably are inevitable and Samuel had difficulties with some of his brothers. In 1794, the deaths of his sister Abigail and brother John made Samuel the eldest child. For reasons not clear, his father at that time cautioned him to think in terms of "mutual services of the family . . ." and of "one not raising above another." Yet Samuel's ability and the fact that he was running the Philadelphia store made it difficult to obey such an injunction. In July 1796 there was criticism—by whom it is not clear—because as executor he had not been able to settle completely the estate of his deceased brother John. Said Samuel: "These reflections cut me to the heart." That same year his brother William, although seriously ill, com-

plained about Samuel to his father. Samuel replied:"I
wrote him my sentiments some time ago and made all the
offers in my power . . . to take him into partnership here,
or to give him this business entirely." (William was to die
only a few months later.)

Eight years later there was difficulty with brother
Thomas. The latter had gone to Baltimore "to purchase an
air furnace there, which I [Samuel] feel a little hurt at as
my friendly offer to him will be giving him the information
necessary to enable him to be a rival in that Business."
(Samuel was a partner at Eagle Iron Works, Philadelphia.)
Not long afterward the brothers worked together on plans
for some sort of partnership, but there is no record that
they materialized. In 1814 there was some difficulty with
brother Jesse, then in charge at Batsto. Samuel wrote him
bluntly in protest against Jesse's apparent cutting of prices
on iron "in the family." There seemed to be an agreement
among the brothers that one would not undercut another's
prices, and Jesse was undercutting Samuel's prices at Weymouth in violation of this agreement. The protest seems to
have had some effect for only a year later Samuel was lend-
ing money to Jesse on rather generous terms.

Despite the family differences, Samuel seems to have
had a rather free hand in spending his father's money.
The first and one of the most interesting of these transactions that Samuel conducted concerns the early days
of Pleasant Mills.* In August of 1796, Samuel wrote to his
father:

I have purchased Pleasant Mills from Mr. Ball and all his
Estate in that neighborhood including Mordica [Mordecai]
Swamp, Belanges Swamp towards Mays Landing, Sleepy

* Pleasant Mills plantation had been established in 1762 by Elijah Clark.
Clark sold it in 1779 to Richard Wescoat, and he in turn sold it to Edward
Black, who ran sawmills there. Black conveyed the property to Joseph Ball
in 1787 to satisfy a loan Ball had made him.

Creek Swamp and all his different tracts of Land in the neighborhood. When I see you I will inform you what they stand me in and if you have a mind you can take them off my hands. Since I purchased it I have sold Mr. C. [Clayton] Earle one half part of the Mill and estate belonging to it, not including any of the swamps nor G. Peterson's place. I am in hopes I have made a good purchase. . .

Until now there was a legend—better called a yarn—that Pleasant Mills was known as Nescochague until the cotton mill was erected there in 1822. Here is clear evidence that Pleasant Mills bore that name way back in 1796. At least two of the original mills were sawmills. But under Richards ownership a new kind of enterprise—a mill for reclaiming wool from used and worn fabrics—was established. This mill was operated, under lease, by B. W. Lord, who had invented machinery for the process of making new wool out of old. By 1804, however, the venture was in trouble. On January 2, 1804, Samuel wrote his father:

I have through a third person purchased all of B. W. Lord's rite [lease] to P. Mills . . . all the stock on hand of every kind as well as all the debts to said concern and the patent rites . . . I have thought it best to inform you by the Stage, so that you might suspend levying for rent. As soon as I get the papers, key and books I will forward them to you. In the meantime I will advise you to have a sharp look . . . as they may fly from the contract I have made which I consider a good one, if the property on hand is worth any thing like the estimate . . .

They do not seem disposed to carry on the mill. If you can get some person to take [over] it will be best as I consider it a "lowesy" [sic] business altho it may be a profitable one. [In an N. B. Samuel adds:] The purchase money is 750 dollars.

Trouble developed as Samuel had anticipated, and the following December both the lease and the patent were put up for sale in Philadelphia at Shannon & Paulls auction house. The auction ended in confusion when Carden, the successful bidder at $30, inquired if the lease was subject to arrears in rent. He was told that it was and then withdrew his bid. The auctioneers tried to force him to honor it and concluded the sale. Samuel, who attended, wrote William:

> I think they [the lessees] are compleatly on the stool of repentance, and all you have to do is look out for your rent and not let them remove anything if you can prevent them legally, but nothing by force. I would let them enter a week or ten days in the next year's rent and try to fix one more years rent on the expenses, by their not giving up the lease before the end of the year. You must look sharp as you have a Hawk to deal with.

Not that Samuel was not on the sharp side himself.

That the Richards came out on top is indicated by a note in February 1805 in which Samuel writes to Batsto: "I have sold the bags of wool sent up as well as all in the mill of the same quality to be delivered as soon as the river brakes up, at Nine Cents per M. The person that purchases says you may send it in olde Barrells or Hhds [hogsheads] or any packages that are convenient so as to keep it dry and clean." Since there are no further allusions to wool shipments, it is probable that no further effort was made to operate the woolen mill.*

Samuel was romantic but far from impetuous. He was to marry twice, and both his wives were widows. In 1794, he was thinking about getting married. He wrote his father, rather blandly: "I have had thoughts of settling myself and seeking a companion if I could find one that

---

* The subsequent story of Pleasant Mills is told in the author's *Iron In the Pines,* Rutgers University Press, 1957.

would please myself and all the rest of the family, tho I doubt my pleasing all. I mentioned something of my intentions to Mrs. M—— [Mrs. Mary Smith Morgan] but I have not made the attempt and am afraid it would be in vain." Two years later he wrote: "The hint I dropped you seems still as flattering as then but will not be too sanguine lest it should fall through. There is one great obstacle that I have yet to surmount. That is the old Gentleman." Not long afterward, Samuel seems to have found both tongue and courage. On November 18, 1797, Samuel, 28, married Mary Smith Morgan at the home of her father, William T. Smith, 77, on North Water Street. The ceremony was performed by the famous Rev. Ashbel Green, one of the two chaplains of the U.S. Congress.

William T. Smith, an "eminent and respected merchant" according to his newspaper obituary, was a very wealthy man, commonly known as "Old Silver Heels." At first Samuel's relationship with Smith was cordial and even cozy. Five years later Samuel was still bulging with good will, and when he and Joseph Ball decided to buy the White Clay Creek Mills in Delaware—a large four-stone gristmill and sawmill—Smith was included in the transaction as "an equal partner."

Not long after that Samuel made a big mistake. Trained to thinking in terms of family solidarity, he signed sizeable notes for two of "Father" Smith's sons, confident that when they matured Smith would honor them. But he would not, and Samuel was saddled with them.

Samuel's most earnest letters failed to make "Old Silver Heels," for all of his wealth, part with any silver. His businesses included Smith's Wharf on the Delaware and various other properties such as two sugar plantations in the Virgin Islands. Soon Samuel found himself short of money. Borrowing delayed matters, but that was all. By 1811 the situation had become so serious that Samuel planned to sell all the assets he had worked so hard to acquire. These included his interests in the Weymouth Iron Works, his share of the Eagle Iron Works in Philadelphia, and various other equities including his third part of the Delaware Mills in which Smith held another third.

An advertisement was drawn up for the sale of these holdings, but then came an unexpected rescue. Early the next year on February 23, 1812, "Old Silver Heels" died. There was a public ceremony, and he was buried in Christ Church graveyard. Soon afterward, the executors of Smith's estate—estimated at nearly $300,000—honored those notes which Samuel had signed and which Smith himself had contemptuously rejected. Oddly enough the executors were Samuel and Joseph Ball.

The bitterness engendered by this affair was to linger over the years, even long after Samuel's death. Mary Morgan Richards had passed away in 1820. Yet half a century later one of Samuel's granddaughters penned this note:

> Grandpa Richards was only about forty years of age when his wealthy old father-in-law was refusing to pay his Sons' debts for which Grandpa had endorsed—and so I found him [Smith's portrait] turned to the wall in the attic. I tugged and worked to carry Billy downstairs and when Ma discovered him, old black John, the waiter man, was sent groaning up the stairs with him. He had light eyes, a narrow foxy face, and looked penurious.

Prior to his marriage, Samuel's store was located at "17 North Wharves, Philadelphia." By 1798 he had relocated at 111 North Water Street, where the family business remained for nearly half a century. Samuel and Mary made their home nearby on Water Street, for some years; and while this was convenient for business, it placed them in the heart of the area devastated by yellow fever in the epidemics which occurred around the turn of the 19th century.

In October 1802 Samuel wrote his father that "we still remain in the country and God knows when we shall get back to our Home. . . . Yesterday a person died nearly opiset our House in Water st said to be with the fevour. This death is the third out of that family (Flemmings) and one other person is now sick in the same house . . . Our little family enjoy good health and our dear little boy [William Smith Richards] is growing finely and bids fair to be a comfort to us . . ."

A year later they were less fortunate It was on September 5, 1803, that Samuel wrote: "Our family consisted of six persons five of which were sick at the same time. Mrs. Richards & myself were both very ill and unable to attend to our dear little babe whom it hath pleased God to take from us [probably Samuel Patrick Richards, born February 19, 1802]. We have returned to our home in Water street. . . ."

During the period from July 17, 1799, to the summer of 1803, Samuel and Mary lost all four of their children. Later, they had four more, but only three survived to adulthood: Thomas Smith Richards, another "iron man"; and two daughters, Sarah Ball Richards, who was to marry Stephen Colwell; and Elizabeth Ann, who was to marry Walter Dwight Bell.

Early in the 1800's Samuel and Mary had moved their home to 357 Mulberry (Arch) Street, what seemed then a good distance from the riverfront area. There they lived comfortably with their small family. Less than 20 years later, on May 3, 1820, Mary Smith Richards died in this house. She had reached the age of 50, and despite the loss of so many of her children and the troubles with her father, her 23 years of marriage with Samuel had been congenial and happy.

In his second marriage proposal Samuel Richards was less deliberate than he had been in his first. On October 8, 1822, he married Anna Maria Martin Witherspoon, daughter of Burling Martin of New York and widow of Thomas Witherspoon, Samuel was then 53 and Maria, as she was familiarly called, was 39. This was also a happy marriage. Maria was as remarkable in her way as Samuel was in his. Beautiful, poised, cultured, she possessed great strength of character, affection, and an exceptional depth of kindness and understanding. They made their home in Philadelphia at Ninth and Arch streets. After 1826, however, most of the warmer months were spent in the new mansion Samuel built at Atsion, N. J. overlooking both the ironworks he had acquired in 1819, and the long and pine-shadowed lake.

The ensuing 20 years probably were the happiest and most prosperous of Samuel's entire life. A failure under its previous owner, Atsion proved an instant success under Richards management. His furnaces at Martha and Weymouth were making money, too, producing water and gas pipe for a number of the larger American cities. Speedwell Furnace was less of an asset, but various real estate ventures paid off. Always progressive in outlook, Samuel was quick to adopt new techniques in the iron industry, and Atsion was the first South Jersey furnace to introduce the hot blast in smelting iron. Another experiment, also conducted at Atsion, was the manufacture of silk; but since this took place when he was well on in years it is not likely that he had much of a hand in carrying it on. It was not very successful.[1]

During these years Samuel was more relaxed and contented, and took pleasure in riding with Maria in their handsome carriage even if most of their jaunts consisted of visits to his own and other ironworks. Thomas Sully, the eminent artist, was engaged to do Samuel's portrait. The

Richards entertained a great deal both in Philadelphia and Atsion. No doubt Mrs. Parsons, the housekeeper at Atsion, had many a private chuckle over the master's cooking efforts in the big basement kitchen. And there were many comings and goings through the portico entrance to that mansion as other members of the family arrived for visits, especially when summer heat blanketed Philadelphia.

Samuel was generous to his family. When a friend was touring England he arranged with him to buy three gold watches in Liverpool, for "his girls." They were his two daughters and daughter-in-law, Harriet, wife of Thomas Smith Richards. Two of these watches still survive. One, numbered 2787, was his gift to his youngest girl, Maria Lawrence Richards. This watch is presently owned by a member of the family. Another, No. 2708, left by Harriet to her granddaughter Harriet Robeson, was stolen from a jeweler's when it was left for repairs.

Samuel's Philadelphia residence must have been a busy place. He and Maria had three children, although one died in infancy. In addition to their children scampering about, Samuel's son Thomas also lived there with his family. Thomas, Samuel's child from his first marriage, had four children. Needless to say, Samuel particularly enjoyed the company of his grandchildren. There is one story of Mary, his eldest female grandchild, when she was five years old. It was winter and snow was falling. The thought occurred to Mary that "Grandpa Samuel" should have the sleigh and horses out on such a morning. So she paid a visit to his room. As she entered, Samuel said: "Well, little lady—have you come a-fishing?" She said she had, and the bait was a kiss, perhaps several. And undoubtedly, she got her sleigh ride.

When he was in his twenties, Samuel had greatly feared that he might share the fate of his brothers who had died of tuberculosis. He told his father of a "nasty little cough and . . . a weakness at my brest." Actually he lived to be 73, and of his brothers only one, Thomas, enjoyed a longer life. During his late years, however, Samuel was often confined to his Philadelphia home, and he began turning more and more of his affairs over to his son-in-law Stephen Colwell, after the latter's marriage to Sarah his daughter. Colwell had been a lawyer in Philadelphia, but some members of the family did not share Samuel's confidence in him. Nonetheless, he became Samuel's executor and was highly respected, especially in Philadelphia's literary circles.

Samuel died at his Philadelphia home on January 4, 1842. After providing amply for his widow, Maria, he divided Weymouth between his first two daughters, Sarah and Elizabeth Ann, and Atsion between his two children by Maria, William Henry and Maria Lawrence Richards.[2] Martha Furnace had been sold to its long-time manger, Jesse Evans, but there remained various tracts of real estate and other assets which would be distributed later. There was financial abundance for all, and Samuel undoubtedly died feeling that none of his family would ever want for money. And they did not.

William Henry Richards was the third of Samuel's children to bear the name William. Having done this for his father's memory, Samuel was perhaps fortunate because he did not live to see how unbelievably different the boy was to be from both him and his grandfather. Fourteen when Samuel died, William Henry became what in current parlance would be called an "oddball." He seems to have performed little useful work, probably because he never had to. There was always plenty of money for him.

In family records, William Henry is noted chiefly for the circumstances of his "marriage." The word is put in quotation marks because in the family there was doubt that he ever married at all. In DuPuy's book, William is

noted as "unmarried." Yet the Atsion record books state
that William Henry was "married" on April 29, 1850.

It is certain, however, that he lived for a time with a
woman named Mary Thorne who signed a deed as "his
wife." Mary Thorne Richards also had a daughter named
Anna Maria who from the age of two was raised by Samuel's widow, for whom she had been named. Where was
Mary Thorne Richards then? There is nothing in the records to say. It is known that some years later she was living
in Vincentown, N.J., which is about 15 miles from Atsion.

In his will[3] William Henry calls Mary his "reputed wife"
and Anna Maria his "reputed daughter." And though this
relationship was the talk of the family, he left the income
from one-fourth of his $74,000 estate to his "reputed wife,"
from one-half to his "reputed daughter" and from one-
fourth to his sister (Maria Lawrence). The full principal
was to go, after the deaths of Mary and Maria Lawrence,
to his "reputed daughter."

William Henry Richards died in February 1863, on a
farm he had purchased after ownership of Atsion passed
to others. His daughter married three times: first, her first
cousin, Samuel Richards Colwell (son of Stephen and
Sarah Richards Colwell); second, a Reading attorney,
Robert Cox; and third, another attorney, Robert McGrath.

Even stranger is the story of Maria Lawrence Richards,
sister of William Henry. Seven years after her father's
death she married William Walton Fleming who with his
father and sister had come to Philadelphia from Charleston, S.C. Fleming, 31 years old, was a dashing young
man, full of ambition and big ideas. Already he had established the W. W. Fleming Cobalt & Nickel Works on
Cooper River, in Camden, N.J. Also he owned some property in Philadelphia and passed for a man of means.

Maria, it seems, spent the summer of 1848 at Weymouth.
There she met Fleming. His courtship was fast. When he

gave her an engagement ring, inside was the date December 25, 1848. On June 14, 1849 they were married. There were no clouds on the horizon. Walton, as he was called, was merry, talented, and popular; and Maria was rich, not alone in money, but, like her parents, in character.

Sponsored by the Richards family, Walton was welcomed into all the family enterprises: the management of Atsion, the organization of the Camden & Atlantic Railroad, the development of Atlantic City, and lesser undertakings. All this was in addition to his own business ventures.

Fleming, however, had overstretched his credit, and difficult days came. In September 1854 he assigned all his assets "for the protection of creditors." He lost his interest in a paper mill which had been built at Atsion, his "Cobalt & Nickel Works" in Camden, several dwellings in that city, a farm in Burlington county, a fifth equity in the John Gill farm in Haddonfield, and various other securities and properties. But an even worse blow was to fall: Walton was faced with criminal charges preferred by his own father, who had been one of his major creditors.

Overnight William Walton Fleming disappeared. No one knew where he was, not even his patient and devoted wife who repaid "Old Man Fleming," as her father-in-law thereafter was known, out of her own money to cover her husband's obligations. A year passed before Maria located Walton in Brussels, Belgium. He had fled fearing disgrace. By letter they were reconciled, and soon she went to Brussels to be with him and start a new life together.

With their son Dick the Flemings established a home at 15 Boulevard du Regent, where the rear windows overlooked the Palace Gardens. Shortly, Anna Maria, Samuel Richards' widow, joined them, and there, too, William Henry's daughter was brought up during her childhood years. Fleming's troubles, meanwhile, were at an end. He had no need even to go into business: his wife had plenty of money, and so did her mother.

Fleming was not a confidence man. Perhaps he had no business sense, although many supposed sages have been wiped out in depressions. Looking back over the years it would seem that his was an artistic temperament scarcely conditioned for the rougher aspects of the business world. He was given to writing verses, and some may still be found dimly inscribed on various Cushman watercolors. He collected art in a minor way, exhibiting a sculpture of "Psyche" by Steinhauser at the 1850 annual exhibition of the Philadelphia Academy of the Fine Arts. Evidence of continued regard for him by the Richards family lay first in the presence in his home of Samuel's widow—she remained there until her death—and, second in the frequent visits by members of the family, as well as Bishop Cortlandt Whitehead, of Pittsburgh, and "Old Man Fleming's" sister, Mrs. Burt.

There, in far-off Brussels, Samuel Richards would have seen his money making his family happy. To one of her relatives, Maria wrote cheerfully: "Through the window I see Walton walking in the Boulevard with the dogs."

In the "Cimitière de Bruxelles" is the Fleming family lot, Number 223. Inscribed on the tomb are the following:

Mrs. Ann Maria Richards, Widow of Samuel Richards, Esq., of Philadelphia; Died at Brussels, July 1, 1860.

William Walton Fleming, Born Charleston, S. C., Sept. 1818, Died at Brussels Mai 31, 1879.

Clarissa Walton Fleming, Died at Philadelphia, 1854.

Samuel Richards Fleming, Born at Philadelphia, U.S.A., April 27th, 1850, Died at Brussels September 26th 1886.

Maria Laurence Fleming, Widow William Walton Fleming, Born at Philadelphia Sept. 2, 1826, Died at Brussels Dec. 21, 1899.

Three thousand miles away, Samuel Richards is buried in Laurel Hill Cemetery, Philadelphia. Strongest and wealthiest of William Richards' sons, his line was to leave fewer descendants than most, and so far as can be determined, none carrying the Richards name.

Rebecca: A Governor's Daughter-in-law

More romantic legends have grown up about this daughter of William Richards than any of his other children. But actually Rebecca led an unhappy life. Her gravestone in the Pleasant Mills churchyard bears this inscription:

> In Memory of Rebecca Sevier, wife of John Sevier and Daughter of William & Mary Richards, who departed this life May 10th, 1809, aged 35 years, 9 months and 3 days.

Tradition in some branches of the Richards family was to the effect that the John Sevier mentioned on this grave marker was the handsome, swashbuckling, Indian fighter, first Governor of Tennessee and founder of the short-lived State of Franklin. (The State of Franklin was formed by four counties in what is now eastern Tennessee. It existed for four years, from 1785 to 1788. North Carolina had ceded this land to the federal government which at the time did not take any steps to govern it. This led the inhabitants to form their own State.)

Tending to support the tradition that Rebecca was Governor Sevier's wife are these facts: shortly after Rebecca's marriage in 1794, Governor Sevier became interested in iron and built a furnace in Tennessee (a pure coincidence so far as anyone knows); and also the Governor's personal and family history, which is rather vague during certain periods. Thus arose the notion that Rebecca was possibly a third wife of Sevier, even though that would have made him a bigamist because his second wife was still living on their Tennessee plantation.

Coloring the legend was Sevier's background. Outside Tennessee, where the Governor was popular, he was widely detested. Even the mild-mannered George Washington remarked that Sevier "never was celebrated for anything (that ever came to my knowledge) except the murder of Indians." [1]

Despite the legend, it was not Governor Sevier of Tennessee who married Rebecca Richards, but his son, John Sevier, Jr. Apparently the son had inherited his father's good looks, but not much else of value. Young Sevier had been married before he met Rebecca, and had come to Philadelphia when his father was elected to Congress and served from 1790 to 1792. The son's first wife, Elizabeth Conway, died July 8, 1788, in childbirth along with her offspring. And when a year or so later Rebecca Richards met the dashing young man from Tennessee, it is scarcely surprising that he had little difficulty in sweeping her off her feet. The marriage took place, without any evidence of family enthusiasm, in 1794.

Members of the Richards family certainly disliked Rebecca's husband. Her brother in letters to his father at Batsto makes plain his difficulty in being polite to Sevier and his unwillingness to trust him. In a letter dated June 6, 1805, Samuel observes: "I have sent the articles as ordered by Mr. Sevier with some exceptions which I have invoiced in your name, and leave you to do as you may think proper, only expect you will keep me from a loss. . . . If I had refused complyance it might be injurious to him when there was no danger. I only wish to be safe and do not wish to hurt his feelings." [2]

Rebecca Richards and John Sevier, Jr., had seven children all named after members of the Richards family. Unimpressed by the wholesale naming of the Sevier children after his family, William tried to make the best of his daughter's bad marital bargain. He loaned Sevier money, which he never got back. He apparently provided Rebecca and her family with living quarters although no property is recorded in either of their names. With his influence in Washington Township, William Richards got young Sevier several jobs. He was a freeholder in 1806 and 1807, and again in 1809. In 1818 he was assessor of the township, and later overseer of the highways. Earlier he engaged in some sort of farming as identifying marks for his cattle are listed in the year 1803.[3]

Even though William Richards was willing to obtain employment for Sevier, he took great pains to make sure that none of his money would go to Sevier. His will reads that the share of Rebecca Sevier[4]. . . .

> . . . shall be held by my said executors in trust . . . and they shall pay over into the hands of my said daughter for her own sole and separate use without being in any manner subject or liable to the debts, control or engagements of her said husband, the net rents, interest, dividends and income . . . and in case my said daughter should survive her husband then and immediately on his decease . . . the said

trustees shall yield up and surrender the said part and share
of my estate . . .

On May 10, 1809, just two years after her last child was
born, Rebecca died. She was 35 years old. Bishop Asbury
mentions having visited her on her final sickbed.

After Rebecca's death William added the following codicil:

Whereas my daughter Rebecca having departed this life before me, my will now is that the share of my estate that falls
to her children (after deducting all monies charged to her
account at her marriage . . . together with all that is owing
me from her husband, shall be taken out of said share) be
disposed of by my executors and trustees . . . unto those of
them [the children] as they in their judgment shall think
most deserving.

In the inventory of William Richards' estate, a total of
$19,030.66 in debts were listed as "desperate." Beyond
doubt the debts of John Sevier were included there, but
what they totaled cannot be determined.

After Rebecca's death, the name of John Sevier quickly
disappeared from Washington Township's payroll. But he
had no difficulty in quickly finding a third wife, Sophie
Garoutte, of Pleasant Mills. There is no available record
of the date of their marriage but it must have been shortly
after Rebecca's death since the third child by Sophia was
born early in 1815 (the dates of birth of the first two do not
appear).

Sophia Garoutte was the daughter of Michael Garoutte,
a Frenchman who had come from Marseilles to fight in
the Revolution. Wounded and left for dead near Pleasant
Mills, he was rescued and nursed to health by Sophia
Smith, whom he later married. Garoutte ran a tavern, a stage
route, and at times worked at Batsto. Sevier's third wife

was the Garouttes' third child. Some time not too long
after their marriage the Seviers moved back to Tennessee. There they had, in all, 13 children. It is known that
John Sevier, Jr., held some small political post in Tennessee,
probably procured for him by his father. Thus so far as can
be determined, the chief contribution of John Sevier, Jr., to
Washington Township, N.J., and the U.S.A. was an increase
in the population of both.

With Sevier eager to remarry, he probably was more
than content to leave Rebecca's children under the wing
of the Richards family. Of the seven, two had died in infancy
—Sarah Brown and John Marshall—and the other five
reached adulthood.

A measure of Sevier's interest in his offspring is found
in a pathetic document in which his sixth child, Thomas
Sevier, is bound out as an apprentice for a term of "fifteen
years and twelve days." This indenture takes pains to state
that the act was of the child's "own Free Will and Accord."
Thomas had been six when his mother died, and he was all
of eight when he signed 15 years of his life away, "with his
Father's consent!" How much free will was actually involved may be imagined; most likely the boy did not even
know what was going on.

Superficially, it may have seemed a protective act for
the child, since he was being apprenticed to his own uncle
for whom he had been named, Thomas Richards. However,
the indenture reads "Thomas Richards and Anna Richards
his wife . . . or their assigns." And young Thomas was
assigned to Stacy Atkinson, of Mount Holly.

Eventually, after William Richards' death, his executors
made a measure of amends. On June 18, 1825, they paid
Stacy Atkinson $150 for Thomas Sevier's release—just
about one year ahead of the expiration date on the indenture. The following year those executors filed an opin-
ion "that Thomas R. Sevier should receive an equal

amount with his sister, Mrs. Throckmorton, from his grand-father's estate and do approve of the same being paid to him." The signers were Benjamin W. Richards, Jesse Richards, and Thomas Richards.

Thomas: He Bought Bonaparte's House

One of the least-explored of South Jersey's older stagecoach routes is the road from Long-a-Coming (now, alas, Berlin) to Jackson, Goshen, Atsion, and then on to Tuckerton and the sea. As recently as 50 years ago this road was a tree-embowered wagon track winding leisurely through wilderness once it passed the village of Jackson. A hundred years earlier not even Jackson was there and the whole trip was a jungle jaunt broken only by a little bridge, a sawmill and a few houses at Goshen, and then the ironworks at Atsion. Except for the Goshen section, much of that old road is now black-topped, and while stretches of it have been "improved" with structures of various sorts, it still invites the tourist who prefers byways to parkways.

On this stagecoach route was built Jackson, long known as Jackson Glass Works. It was the creation of Thomas Richards, eighth child of William and Mary Richards. Just why he chose this particular location—about 18 miles from Camden—is not difficult to guess. He knew the old stage-coach road. He knew the woodlands for miles around including those threaded by the Atsion (now the Mullica) River, from Berlin east.

The sandy soil in this area, rich in silica, was particularly suited for glass-making; and the endless woods would provide fuel. It was a similar "find" of superior sand which led the famed Caspar Wister to establish his famous works at Wistarburg almost a century earlier. The best proof of Richards wisdom was the prosperity of the Jackson Works, which lasted about 50 years.

When Thomas decided to purchase three thousand acres there in the pines to establish his glassworks and name it after the president of the United States, he was a man in his middle forties, married and with four children of his own.[1] Thomas had been moderately successful as a merchant in Philadelphia. He also possessed some of the familiar Richards family characteristics: shrewd business sense, a capacity for hard work, and a dynamic temperament.

Thomas was the first in the family, however, to engage in a major undertaking outside the iron trade. Thomas seems to have had little attachment to iron. In his twenties he had made a tentative proposal to purchase an air furnace in Delaware; there was some talk of a partnership with his brother Samuel, and for five years he had a financial interest in the Taunton Iron Works, as will be seen. But Thomas wanted a major field to conquer on his own, and in iron brother Samuel was far ahead of him. Glass-making was then an infant industry. Opportunities in it were fairly plentiful, and whatever competition he might face, none of it at that moment would come from his family.

Most accounts give 1827 as the year Thomas put his Jackson works into operation. A measure of doubt arises, however, from this legend atop a printed invoice of 1868:

The Jackson Works have been in CONSTANT operation since 1829

Establishment of Jackson not long after the settlement of his father's big estate, suggests that Thomas may have inherited the capital to launch the enterprise. He was one of William Richards' executors and attended to many of the post-mortem details for his busier brothers Samuel and Benjamin. (The accounts show him credited $3.62 for "sulky [a two-wheeled carriage for one person] hire to Batsto to attend sale of Sleepy Creek Swamp" and $2.75 for horse and sulky hire to Mount Holly "to make returns of estate.")

One year before the Jackson Works was put in operation a similar venture had been successfully launched about five miles to the east at Waterford, long known as "Waterford Works." How much that encouraged Thomas to go ahead at Jackson is conjecture, but he must have been keenly aware that there had been previously only two window-glass factories in South Jersey—Glassboro and Malaga. Demand for glass was increasing rapidly, and in a field so relatively wide open opportunity was bright—bright enough, it turned out, to make a fortune for Thomas Richards and his family.

A pleasant village grew up around the glassworks. There was a large house—although scarcely a mansion—where Thomas Richards lived when he was at Jackson. In its earlier years he was there fairly often because his sons Samuel and Thomas, Jr., were not yet old enough to play active roles in the business. At least a portion of that old Richards house was standing until recent years. The workmen lived in what the *West Jersey Press* described as a settlement of "neat two-story dwellings with small gardens to each." At its peak the Jackson Works employed about 90 men, plus an additional 60 teamsters and wood choppers. There were three frame structures where the glass-making took place and several adjacent storage buildings. In addition were a store, post office, blacksmith shop, and sawmill. The glassworks tract itself covered about three thousand acres of which about five hundred were farmed, mostly in corn and hay.

Richards recruited his glassworkers in large part from Germany. One of his veterans was Henry G. Hoffman, who went to Jackson when he was 22, and on his 67th birthday estimated that he had blown about eight and one-half million square feet of glass. While the Jackson Works is supposed to have made window glass only, the following from "The American Banner" of April 30, 1853 indicates that some other glass was made, perhaps experimentally:

> Jersey Glass—We were shown a beautiful specimen of blue glass . . . made at Jackson works by Americans. Our informant states that our own countrymen have proved more successful in this than the best imported hands.

As demand for glass continued to increase during the middle years of the 19th century, Jackson Works continued to prosper. It enjoyed particularly brisk trade in window lights for buildings and railroad cars and street lamps. While none of the firm's account books has come to light, it is known from newspaper notices that in 1853 the Jackson factory furnished the glass for the New York Crystal Palace.

If Jackson seemed in later days a "remote" location for a business, it should be remembered that in 1829 it was on a main stage road and there was no shorter or easier way to the Philadelphia markets. Not until 1854 was a railroad built, a little more than a mile to the southeast. Later on, other roads, now heavily traveled, were cut through. Naturally, as backers of the Camden & Atlantic Railroad, Thomas Richards, and his sons, lost no time in shipping their glass in its freight cars, and the rumble of glass-laden wagons along the old stage route ceased entirely.

As he became older, and other interests grew more important, Thomas Richards turned more and more of the Jackson management over to his son Samuel, and after his death the firm name became: "Samuel Richards." *

Not until 1870 did prosperity begin to wither at Jackson. In 1876 the *West Jersey Press* observed that "Mr. Richards has permitted the fire in his glass factory at Jackson to go out, for the purpose of repairs." Only one of the three glass furnaces was in operation then. Fire swept the works the following spring; and they were not rebuilt. In August 1877 there was an assignment of assets for the benefit of creditors.[2] Aside from real estate they were:

6 glass house pots		18.00
About 4000 lbs broken glass		20.00
Abt. 2000 lbs. pot shells		8.00
Abt. 7000 lbs rough glass	35.00	
less cleaning	15.00	
		20.00
Cash		100.00
Batch wagon		1.00
1 Pig		2.00
Lot of books		40.00

Pitiful remnants of a once-great enterprise. The end was noted by the *West Jersey Press* on September 17, 1879:

* To keep the Samuels in the family straight, this Samuel was a nephew of Samuel Richards, ironmaster of Atsion; father of Samuel Bartram Richards of Philadelphia; and cousin of Samuel P. Richards, son of Jesse Richards of Batsto.

"The last of a lot of old machinery, boilers and other old iron which used to be in use at the Jackson Glass Works, was shipped to the city as scrap iron, on Monday last."

Jackson was by no means Thomas Richards' only interest in life. One of his more colorful deals involved "Point Breeze," the famous Bonaparte Mansion and park at Bordentown—what had been the closest thing to a royal establishment in the United States of America.

After Napoleon's defeat at Waterloo, his brother Joseph was quietly smuggled aboard a U.S.-bound ship. He had offered to change places with the fallen emperor, but Napoleon refused to flee. With great forethought Joseph, who had been successively King of Naples and King of Spain, brought a great treasure with him, reputedly a fortune in gold and jewels. It was at Bordentown that he chose the site for his "elegant mansion," built about 1817 and burned in 1820. It was extensively rebuilt, with several so-called secret tunnels lined with brick. Known in New Jersey as the Comte de Survilliers, Joseph lived at Point Breeze for 16 years. Later, after returning to Europe, he died in Florence, Italy, in 1844.

The Bordentown estates were left to his grandson Joseph Lucien Charles Napoleon Prince de Musigrano. He had no interest in them and lost little time in selling the estate. When the mansion and park were put up at auction in 1847, the high bidder was Thomas Richards! [3]

It is possible but unlikely that Thomas ever lived at Point Breeze. He undoubtedly became familiar with his glamorous mansion and made occasional visits there. His interest, however, appears chiefly speculative. He took title to the property on August 11, 1847, and sold it three years after, on October 15, 1850, to Henry Beckett, son of Sir Joseph Beckett of England, and for some years British consul in Philadelphia.[4]

Another of Thomas Richards' ventures, that was shared with his son Samuel, was the establishment, in 1851, of the Lebanon Glass Works. Located near what is now Lebanon State Forest, this factory was also devoted to the manufacture of window glass. It bore a high reputation for the "superior quality of the clear crystal manufactured." [5]

About 150 men were employed at the Lebanon Works. The surrounding village consisted of 60 of the usual frame workmen's houses, a store, sawmill, and probably a blacksmith's shop. For 15 years the factory prospered. In 1866, however, facing the loss of their fuel supply as timber resources of the tract neared exhaustion, the Richards' heirs abandoned the property. What of the workmen? Glassworkers were highly migratory in those days, and they simply took a weary trek to another glassworks to hunt another job.

Thomas Richards was to prove himself different from all of his brothers in one more way: he was to live longer than any of them—80 years. Hale and hearty through his later days, it was in character that Thomas died at an unusual and dramatic moment—on his own golden wedding day, and the day on which the wedding for one of his daughters had been arranged. The date was October 17, 1860.

Thomas Richards had established a village. Two of his sons—Samuel and Thomas, Jr.—were to establish a full-sized town nearby: Atco, N.J.

In the 1850's the great Richards mansion on the hill was built by Thomas, Jr., when the two brothers were taking over most of the Jackson glassworks management from their father. And in 1854 the railroad was built a little more than a mile to the southeast. Down the hill from the mansion was the shipping platform for Jackson glass. A connecting road had been cut from Jackson through the woods and over the hill past the mansion. Wild country it was in those days, and the Richards owned most of it for miles around.

In 1861, shortly after Thomas Richards' death, a new track was being cut through the forests to the north. Only a year before the Raritan and Delaware Bay Railroad had extended its tracks from Port Monmouth (ferry terminal to New York) through the pine barrens as far south as Atsion; now it extended that route from Atsion to the Richards' glassworks station. There it linked up with the Camden & Atlantic Railroad so as to provide direct service from New York to Philadelphia. This work was completed in 1862. The tracks of the two railroads were joined and a terminal was built complete with turntables, sidings, and water tanks. This burgeoning spot was called "Junction," and that name appears on railroad timetables of the period.

One step led to another. The always far-sighted Samuel decided that Junction was a good location for a town, a place with a future. With his brother Thomas, Jr., plans were drawn and in 1866 the town of Atco was laid out and surveyed by George Hancock. Originally the new community comprised 60 acres with 20 streets (a map appears on an adjoining page). The main street—from Junction to Jackson—was named Atco Avenue; and the streets along the two railroads were called Atlantic, for the Camden & Atlantic, and Raritan Avenue for the Raritan and Delaware Bay Railroad.

Much controversy has surrounded the name of Atco. Legend long attributed it to Indian lore, and historian George R. Prowell gives it as an Indian term meaning "place of many deer." Then came a more prosaic explanation: that the name was taken from initials on a freight car —A. T. CO.—meaning Atlantic Transportation Company. Just how the name was chosen cannot positively be determined, but the word "Atco" is far older either than the town of Atco or the Camden & Atlantic Railroad. It was

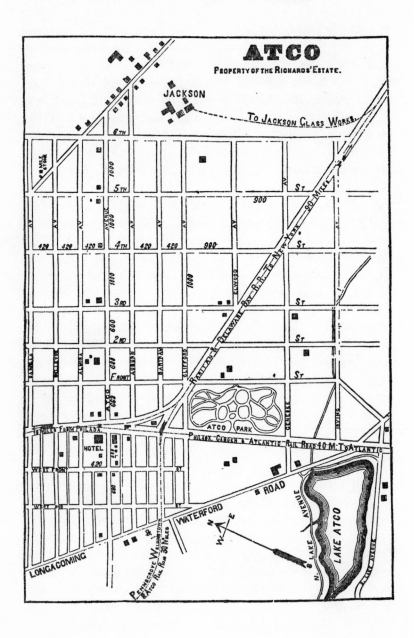

ATCO

PROPERTY OF THE RICHARDS' ESTATE.

an Indian name, and "Atco-Atco" is found on deeds as early as 1765. A newspaper advertisement of 1824 offers "a lot of cedar swamp on Atco-Atco. . . . seven acres more or less." Probably this stream was a tributary of the Atsion river. Originally, it was proposed to name the new community "Richards," but the family would not have it so.

Atco seems to have gotten off to a fast start. Advertised as a health resort, a good place for retirement, and as a desirable location for industry due to its exceptional rail facilities, people began to buy lots in substantial numbers. Most of the early settlers were from New England, and the names of Varnum, Ellsworth, Talcott, MacHarg, Giddings, Ballou, Sloan, Brooks, and Treat go back to those days. Because they were people of character, talent, and industry, the new town grew rapidly.

The first house in Atco was built in the opening year of 1866 by James E. Alton, on the west side of the railroad; the second house was put up by Ira Wakeley; and the first store, at the southeast corner of Atco and Raritan avenues, was established by Wellington Baker, who became the first postmaster also. In the first year a hotel—the Atco House—was also built. Located across the tracks from the Camden & Atlantic Railroad Station, the three-story frame structure accommodated salesmen, travelers, and summer boarders, of whom there were many in those days. The Atco House was built by the Richards family, and served also as a social center. Many parties, weddings, and other festivities took place there. After varying fortunes, it burned to the ground on February 5, 1904.

A measure of Atco's initial growth and cultural interests is found in the organization, on January 21, 1868, of the Atco Library and Museum Association, which later was reorganized as the Atco Natural History Society. Soon churches were being built, a school, more dwellings, and, later, a Hall of Science. From 1878 to 1885 Atco even had its own newspaper, *The Argus,* founded by William D. Siegfried, and later edited by M. J. Skinner.

Scarcely a year after Atco's founding, a third railroad proposed to have a connection there. This was the Pennsgrove, Williamstown and Atco Railroad, which according to an 1867 newspaper article was to "complete a new route from Washington to New York." The account adds:

> Mr. John T. Bodine, the newly elected President, informs us that the Directors have secured some twenty acres of land on the Delaware River at Pennsgrove, with the intention of erecting their wharves and depot.
>
> At the annual meeting . . . resolutions were adopted giving the President authority to commence that portion from Williamstown to Atco Junction, about nine miles. The portion between Williamstown and Glassboro will no doubt be completed at an early date which will give . . . a connection with the Raritan and Delaware Bay Railroad at Atco, where they will both connect with the Camden & Atlantic Railroad, at which place both of the last-mentioned roads have an engine house, depot, turntable, etc.

This project is of interest today in the light of new proposals to link New York and the South by way of Delaware Bay, although not by rail. Despite high hopes, the 1867 program collapsed; the spur from Williamstown was built and existed until recent years,[6] but the link to Pennsgrove and Washington never was completed. Soon the Raritan and Delaware Bay Railroad was bankrupt, and its organizers, the Torrey Brothers, lost control. Later reorganized as the New Jersey Southern, its Atco connection with the Camden & Atlantic was broken by court decree, at the behest of the Camden and Amboy Railroad which had the political power to keep a monopoly of New York-Philadelphia rail traffic.

Despite its setbacks as a rail terminal, Atco's progress

continued. A visitor to the "Atco Fair" of 1879 commented: "The circulation in this village body is remarkably healthy. The secret is that the people are nearly all Yankees, and secondly, that the law of prohibition is the law of the settlement. Temperance and industry, with skill and culture, have made this small garden spot in the Jerseys." [7]

This mention of prohibition may seem to be a curious switch in the Richards family, so many of whose members had tastes in the reverse direction. But Samuel and Thomas, Jr., put into all Atco deeds a ban on sale of liquor over a long period of years. As late as 1882, the *West Jersey Press* reported that "Thomas Richards, who formerly owned the tract where Atco now stands. . . . has taken steps against the parties who are dispensing fire water."

With Brother Samuel's attentions occupied elsewhere, Thomas Richards, Jr., living in the old mansion, ranked for many years as Atco's first citizen. He was active in civic affairs. He donated land for the Presbyterian Church (not on the site of the present church); provided ground for a community cemetery; gave land for building the already-mentioned Science Hall, a building which still stands on Raritan Avenue, although somewhat altered. Thomas, Jr., was also interested in the Atco Chemical Works which was operating in 1879. In September of that year he exhibited specimens of sugar beets "from twelve to eighteen inches long" which he had been cultivating experimentally.

Personally, Thomas Richards, Jr., was what some would describe as a character and others would call eccentric. Tall tales have come down about his activities. On one occasion he somehow put out a sizeable fire "with his bare hands." On another, he felt in an Izaak Walton mood, couldn't find his fishing line, took one of the wire strings from the grand piano, and went fishing with that. One story concerns the day he missed the local train to Atco.

He was in a great hurry as his wife, Deborah, was ill. He then boarded an express and tried to talk the conductor into making a brief halt at Atco to let him off. The conductor refused; the Richards name moved him not at all. So when the train reached Atco—Thomas jumped. He landed in a grassy bank, but broke his leg, got home somehow, and then both he and his wife were laid up in bed.

As the 1900's approached, less and less Atco land remained in Richards hands. A large and active town had grown up; new industries had been started; the Jackson glassworks had been succeeded by a glassworks in Atco, and that too had passed. The Richards mansion had changed hands, and its days of neglect and decay set in. Later it was renovated and today the house still stands, overlooking the community.

Living in Philadelphia in his later years, Thomas Jr. made regular weekly visits to Atco. January 18, 1910 was a nasty and snowy day but it was the day for his trip and he insisted on making it although he was then in his 82nd year. On the steps to the subway at the Fifth Street station he slipped on the slushy treads. Losing his balance, he tumbled to the landing below. He was rushed to a hospital and there died from a fractured skull.

Jesse: Lord of the Manor

Unlike his brothers and his father Jesse Richards spent virtually his entire life in one spot—Batsto, N.J. He was about two years old when his mother, Mary Patrick Richards, took the family there to join her husband, William Richards, who had gone on ahead. This was after William had become part owner and manager of the ironworks, in 1784.

Jesse Richards differed from most of his brothers in several respects: he was more introverted, less aggressive, and imaginative: although he was able and experienced, he was in almost constant business difficulty. In contrast to his father, Jesse was happy living in the pines as Batsto's lonely lord and master. But he was often unhappy over the difficulties inherent in that role.

Rarely did Jesse venture far from his plantation; and even his visits to Philadelphia were infrequent, and usually "by stage." He had watched the smelting process as a child, and iron was his life. He had learned the trade from his father, as had several of his brothers, particularly Samuel. But where Samuel was to virtually transmute iron into gold and become wealthy, Jesse had a hard time. He was often short of funds and in later years spent much of his days juggling drafts, notes, and debts in order to keep the Batsto Iron Works afloat.

When Jesse took over the Batsto management in 1809 he was 27 years old. The works then comprised the furnace, one sawmill, and a small gristmill. The forge had long since been shut down, although some old iron was there in storage. There was, of course, the "stone dwelling house" and barn. Also south of the river lay the workmen's village, then smaller and ruder than it later was to become, with some of the houses log cabins.

William Richards, having retired to Mount Holly, kept his eyes on things at first, but later gave Jesse a fairly free hand in running the Batsto works. Those were profitable years. The time during the War of 1812 was especially lucrative because Batsto as well as Weymouth was furnishing shot, shell, and grenades for the American Army.

This wartime prosperity probably was a large factor in Jesse's decision to establish Washington Furnace in Monmouth County which he founded in 1814. (This story appears in another chapter.) Failure of Washington Furnace, with unrecorded but substantial monetary losses, constituted a business handicap which Jesse never was quite able to overcome. However, so long as his father was alive, Jesse remained boss at Batsto, although on salary.

During his second year as Batsto manager, 1810, Jesse

decided to marry. His bride was Sarah Ennalls Haskins, daughter of Rev. Thomas Haskins by his first wife. Jesse had known Sarah from childhood because Haskins had been a house guest for years at Batsto mansion when he came to preach at nearby Pleasant Mills. Moreover, in 1799, Haskins had married Jesse's sister Elizabeth, so that now she became, in effect, his mother-in-law as well. For the most part, the marriage of Jesse and Sarah was a happy one, and of their seven children, six lived to adulthood. The mansion remained their home throughout their lives.

All went well until the death of William Richards, on August 31, 1823. By the terms of his will, as already noted, his estate was to be divided equally between his children, and that estate was well over $200,000. There was only one difficulty: about $72,000 was owed the estate by some of the children.[1] And one of the largest of these debtors was Jesse. Much of this without doubt represented money advanced to him by his father, and lost at Washington Furnace.

Because of this, when all of William Richards' properties were put up at auction in Philadelphia, on November 25, 1824, Jesse was not able to bid successfully for Batsto.[2] Instead, it was purchased by his 21-year-old nephew Thomas Smith Richards, son of Samuel Richards of Atsion. The price paid was about $60,000, plus a bit over $8,000 for the stock which had been appraised by independent parties.[*] Twenty thousand dollars was paid down in cash (probably financed by Samuel Richards) and the balance was in the form of bonds, callable over a period of years.

Batsto thus remained "in the family," and Jesse stayed on as manager at the works. The finances, however, were controlled by Thomas S. Richards, who was then established in the old Richards office at 111 North Water Street,

---

[*] Included in this appraisal was an "ore boat" which probably is the one now on exhibit at Batsto. It was then valued at $70.

Philadelphia. Before long, however, nephew and uncle arranged a deal: Thomas S. Richards was anxious to join his second cousin John in purchasing Gloucester Furnace, near Egg Harbor, so he offered a half interest in Batsto to Jesse. Now provided with cash from his father's estate, Jesse bought a half interest in Batsto, in 1829,[3] and a year later Thomas S. and John Richards purchased Gloucester Furnace. But even so, the accounts continued to be handled through 111 North Water Street and not through the Batsto office.

During the 1830's Jesse began to take an active interest in politics. The records show that he seems to have kept his employees sufficiently in line to provide regular Whig majorities in Washington Township. When President Andrew Jackson removed government deposits from the United States Bank, Jesse's name topped a list of citizens organizing a protest meeting for Burlington County.[4] That he had enemies in his own party is shown by a letter to the Mount Holly postmaster, in 1838, deploring "the influence of a set of men who care not for the Whig Party when it comes in contact with their private prejudices. . . . If the ticket fails, the party may thank Jesse Richards and some of the Orthodox Friends for it."

The ticket did not fail, in Burlington County, for Jesse, who had been elected to the New Jersey Assembly the year before, was reelected that year. And as a measure of his influence, his Princeton-graduated son, Thomas H. Richards, was himself elected to the Assembly in 1841 and 1842, and to the New Jersey Senate from 1847 to 1849.

Iron, however, remained Jesse's first interest, and before long he was to become complete and undisputed lord of Batsto. Thomas S. Richards died in 1839, and on January 27, 1840, the entire local management was put into Jesse's hands pending settlement of the estate. From that period on Stephen Colwell, who had married Samuel Richards' daughter Sarah (Jesse's niece), was in charge at the Philadelphia office.

Meanwhile Batsto had expanded. From the modest dimensions of 1809, when Jesse first took over, it had grown to a sizeable enterprise. When Jesse became half-owner in 1829, the furnace was rebuilt. A year earlier the sizeable, two-stone gristmill which is still standing had been erected; Batsto mansion had been materially enlarged "in the modern manner"; there were a brickyard, a lime kiln, and a new carriage barn; a second sawmill was in operation. Across the stream the workers' dwellings had gradually been replaced by plain but much-improved houses, some of which still stand today.

Jesse's full control over Batsto was by no means an end to his worries: in a monetary sense they increased. Whether Colwell, in the Philadelphia office, was giving orders to the Martha and Weymouth furnaces which belonged to his father-in-law Samuel, instead of to Batsto, is not clear. It is a matter of record, however, that scarcely a month passed without Jesse pressing Colwell for money collected on Batsto iron shipments. For example Jesse wrote Colwell:

April 6, 1840:	If I have to pay all my debts and receive nothing, I must soon be brought to a standstill.
April 28, 1840:	Money matters get very pressing and you did not answer my last letter in regard to that.
September 11, 1840:	I suppose I need hardly tell you that my necessity gets more and more pressing.
May 28, 1841:	I am sorry your nerves are so easily wrought upon. It must be owing to your having forgot your long-gone-by promise. We have just broke the

	gudgeon to our furnace water wheel. Nothing but trouble in the world.
June 23, 1841:	Money, money, what am I to do for money!
Aug. 2, 1841:	Money, money, money. Good paper money that will pass is all I want.
December 2, 1841:	I wrote to you stating how much I was put to it for want of money, and I did expect an answer.

In the 1840's competition from the Pennsylvania anthracite furnaces was felt increasingly at Batsto and other southern New Jersey charcoal furnaces. In 1843, for example, Batsto Furnace was not put into blast. On October 28, 1842, Jesse wrote that "I have so much iron on hand that I shall decline for the present making any contract for ore next year. Unless I can make sale of some of my iron I shall not blow the furnace . . ."

In 1845—after five years of legal maneuvering—Thomas S. Richards' half share of Batsto was put up for sale, by John L. H. Stratton, Master in Chancery. Notices were posted at Pleasant Mills, Weymouth, Mays Landing, and other places; and on sale day the successful bidder was Jesse. He acquired, for $20,000, the half-share of his late nephew, and thus became, on October 27, 1845, the sole and complete owner of Batsto. To finance that purchase, however, Jesse had been obliged to mortgage the entire Batsto property for $13,425 (and it was foreclosure of this mortgage, 30 years later, which closed the Richards era at Batsto).[5]

Jesse's problems began to increase. Batsto now was his, but his, too, were all of the financial headaches. Faced with the gradual demise of the bog-iron industry, he built in 1845 a glass factory which soon began to thrive. However, Jesse was having personal as well as business troubles. He never resembled a teetotaler, but as the years passed he had taken more and more to drink. He spent one of his "vacations" at a "mansion of health," which helped, but not much. The liquor, plus his great weight—about 300 pounds in his later years—undermined his general resistance. Perhaps it was more than coincidence that in 1847— the last year of lagging furnace operation at Batsto—Jesse was taken seriously ill, and after an extended convalescence took a "tour of the mountains of Pennsylvania for his health."

An old "Letter Book" of Jesse Richards discloses various side aspects of life at Batsto from 1840 on. It has been supposed that Jesse supplied medical care for his community. A letter of April 9, 1840, shows otherwise: Written to Doctor George Barron by Jesse, it reads:

> In order that there may not be any misunderstanding with regard to your medical attendance on the people of Batsto Works at a fixed compensation, this is to assure you that I decline to be accountable for any of it.

One amusing sidelight concerns a piano for his daughter Sarah:

> With regard to the new piano, Sarah has made enough fuss about it and led me to believe that we had the privilege of trying the piano a year before the money would be called for, which I thought was liberal indeed. But I find it is the same principle of the Yankee clock-traders, if it is not liked they will replace it with a worse one, and money down. I enclose you my check for three hundred dollars . . .

Another curious touch was Jesse's use of "thy, thee, and thou" in writing to his Quaker customers.

And in a letter to the president of the Manhattan Gas Company, in July of 1840, he makes the significant statement that "we have made little else but pipe here for twenty-two years."

As years passed, more and more letters were written for him by his son Thomas H. Richards, especially during another bout of illness in 1851. After that Jesse became less and less active, and on June 17, 1854, at eight A.M., he died in Batsto mansion where he had lived his life. There followed a period of genuine mourning in the community over which he so long had presided. To his employees and their families, Jesse typified security. They knew nothing of his financial difficulties, or of the stresses within the family and the pressures from without. Thus there was warmth of feeling when his tombstone, in Pleasant Mills Cemetery, was inscribed: "Beloved, Honored, Mourned."

Supposedly Jesse Richards died a comparatively wealthy man, although his wealth was estimated anywhere from $100,000 down. An inventory of hs properties in 1850 listed a gristmill which had cost $6,750; farm land valued at $15,000; livestock worth $3,500; plus a cupola, sawmill, lath mill, lime kiln, schooner, etc., plus the value of the mansion and the village.[6] All this would seem to have warranted an estimate of at least $100,000, less of course, the mortgage. Despite years of rough going, Jesse Richards had justified his father's faith in him when, back in 1809, he had made him his successor at Batsto.

Luckily for Jesse, he was not to live to see the shambles which his heirs made of his vast plantation estimated at over 50,000 acres, and all the enterprises and structures which stood upon it. He would not see its lands sold off in chunks, its glass business wrecked, and Batsto finances mangled—until the ruins of what was left would be sold, at a master's sale in bankruptcy, for the mere amount of the mortgage—$13,425! Left wholly unpaid were judgments for thousands more; particularly a $20,000 judgment obtained by Jesse's faithful clerk, Robert Stewart, who had loaned him money, given him services, and then still stayed on to see the woodland empire of Batsto swept by fire and left a pathetic prospect.

It has been said that "when a troubled man dies, he is better off." Jesse Richards was.

William III: An Enigma

If obscurity is an essential ingredient of happiness, as Thomas Jefferson suggested, then William Richards III was probably a happy man. Certainly he was obscure; so much so that most later generations of the family never heard of him. Faced with the author's inquiries, many of the latter-day Richards were astonished to learn that he had ever existed.

Fifth son of William Richards of Batsto, and Margaretta Wood, William III was born in Batsto mansion on the hill above the furnace. Louis B. Richards, in his "Sketches" of some members of the family, had this to say of him:

William Richards, born January 16, 1805; died April 19, 1864; married in 1831, Constantia Marie Lamand. He inherited in a striking degree the physical constitution of his father. He was of remarkably large and massive build and possesed the strength of a giant. He had five children.

That is all. Not a suggestion as to what William III ever did with that "strength of a giant"; no indication where he had lived, what he had accomplished, or where he died; no mention of his children's names. Numerous as were the Richards family enterprises, William's name does not turn up in any of them. A William Richards does appear at the Jackson Works, near Atco, but he was yet another William, a son of Thomas Richards. Of the brothers of William III, only George, two years younger, seems to have kept in close personal contact with him. All this adds up to a strange blank spot in an otherwise aggressive and industrious family.

Five years of research on William III has partially filled the blank spot; but gaps remain, and barring some lucky "find" of information the rest of his story may never be told.

It is known that William III lived most of his life in Mount Holly, N.J., the bulk of it in the big brick house which his father had built in the Santo Domingo tract above Pine Street. When William, Sr., moved to Mount Holly from Batsto in 1809, William III was four years old. The first Richards home there was on Mill Street. The family then included William, Sr.; his wife Margaretta; and three sons, Augustus, William III, and George who then was two years old. "Brother Benjamin" was at school in Philadelphia, and the older step-brothers all were engaged in business, and away from home. Most of them lived in Philadelphia.

Since Augustus, two years older, and George, two years younger, both had excellent education, sufficient for them to practice law, the chances are that William III had at least equal opportunity. His elementary schooling took place in Mount Holly, but nothing is known about his secondary studies. His handwriting is legible and uniform, his spelling accurate, and his use of English clear and concise. These are slim indices but they do suggest higher training, perhaps by a tutor. His religious education he received at St. Andrews Protestant Episcopal Church in Mount Holly, where the family attended and his father was a vestryman.[1]

When William Richards II died in 1823, William III was a minor of 18. In consequence, his father's executors—brothers Benjamin, Samuel, and Thomas—became his guardians; and he continued to live with his mother. When his father was 18 he had been a junior grade veteran in the ironworks at Warwick; but there is no indication that William III, then or later, ever had anything to do with the iron business, or any other business.

William III shared equally with his sisters and brothers in William II's large estate. Upon coming of age in 1826, he received a portion of his legacy which the executors had turned over to his brother Benjamin. He wrote:

I hereby acknowledge to have received from Benj. W. Richards, one of my Guardians under the will of my father, four thousand, eight hundred and forty-one dollars 20/100, being the whole amount of monies he received from the Executors for me, with the interest. The whole of the above amt. has been paid me, and for me, in cash, except twenty-three hundred and forty-five dollars, for which amt. I have recd. a certificate of twenty shares of United States Bank Stock at the cost price, which is transferred to me. And I hereby acknowledge myself fully satisfied with the management of said Guardian in the premises aforesaid and with the account he has rendered me.

Philada.   March 29, 1826   Wm. RICHARDS

This by no means represented William's entire inheritance. The estate was not finally settled until 1839, when William, his brothers, and sisters, each was credited with $19,327.92. Since William III had not been given substantial advances during his father's lifetime, he received his full share of the estate. In short, he had become a man of means, and it is not surprising that in deeds and other official papers he signed over the years he is mentioned as "William Richards, Gentleman." Not Ironmaster, Glassmaker, Doctor, Lawyer, Merchant, Chief. Just "Gentleman," a word which in those times meant a man who managed to live without working.[2]

In the *Mount Holly Mirror* of February 24, 1831 the following notice appeared:

MARRIED

On the 6th inst. by George Haywood, Esq., Mr. WILLIAM RICHARDS, of Mount Holly, to Miss CONSTANTIA, eldest daughter of Mr. James Lamand, of Trenton.

This neat formal paragraph concealed more than it told. It did not indicate why there should have been a civil ceremony when William Richards III was an active member of St. Andrew's Protestant Episcopal Church, where the family had worshiped for a long time. There was no mention of festivities: it might as easily have referred to a wake as to a wedding. No explanation was given why George Haywood—lawyer, squire, vestryman of St. Andrew's, and friend of William's father, should have performed the ceremony instead of the rector. Nor was there hint of the family head-shaking, controversy, and comment.

The reason for it all was simple: William III wanted to marry his first cousin. First cousins could not be married in

St. Andrew's under the canons of the Episcopal Church. Therefore, Haywood, as a family friend, helped out.

Margaretta Richards, mother of William III, was a daughter of Isaac Wood, of Moorestown. Margaretta had a sister, Frances, who married James Louis Lamand, who lived outside Trenton on the road to Sandtown. The Lamands had a daughter Constantia. It was not strange that William III and Constantia had known each other during their childhood years; and when they decided to wed Margaretta Richards was probably not even surprised that her niece was to become her daughter-in-law. William, indeed, took his bride to his mother's home and they lived there for about eight years, until the Santo Domingo property was sold. During those eight years, however, the happiness of William and Constantia was overshadowed by the loss of four of their five children.

All the children were baptized at St. Andrew's Church by the rector, the Rev. George Y. Morehouse. Only George Richards lived to adulthood (he was alive in 1880), but no records are available to show where he went from Mount Holly. The other four all died at early ages, of which no record is shown in the church files, although all were buried "before 1850" in St. Andrew's cemetery. There Mary Louisa, Margaretta Francis, William Louis and John Oakman Richards are buried in adjacent graves, close to the marble tomb of William Richards II. One small stone records the names of the first three; there is no stone for the fourth.

In subsequent years William and Constantia lived most of the time in Mount Holly, but for a period they stayed in Philadelphia. That William may have exhausted his inheritance is suggested by the creation, through his brother George, of a trust fund for Constantia. This period of their lives, however, is very hazy. The names of both appear occasionally in legal records as late as 1862, but that is all.

William Richards III died on April 19, 1864. His funeral was from St. Andrew's Church and he was buried in the parish cemetery. There is, however, no stone to mark his grave. When Constantia died, or where she is buried, seems not to be recorded.

Benjamin: Mayor of Philadelphia

---◄◉►---

"Brother Benjamin is well, and goes to school. He is a good boy and not troublesome." So wrote Samuel Richards to his father at Batsto. The letter was dated February 27, 1805. Benjamin was only seven years old, but already he was demonstrating studious nature and amiable disposition. These traits were to make him the "intellectual" of the family and a man with a highly developed social sense plus a capacity for political leadership.

Perhaps Benjamin's father sensed these latent qualities in the child since at that early age he had been sent to live with Samuel in Philadelphia. There he could enjoy those educational opportunities which William Richards, and Samuel too, had been denied. Benjamin was William's 12th child, and the first by his second wife, Margaretta Wood. He was born at Batsto on November 12, 1797, and lived there in his early childhood. An apt pupil during his schooling in the Quaker City, he was then sent to Princeton for his college education. He graduated with honors, seventh in his class, in 1815; and in 1819 he received his master's degree. It was at Princeton, beyond doubt, that he acquired the new directions of thought and wider horizons which were to make him a leader in the public affairs of eastern Pennsylvania.

Handsome was the word for Benjamin as portraits of him attest. Beyond good looks, however, was his gift of presence, a quality more ingratiating than commanding. Endowed with the energy, drive, and virility characteristic of his family, he possessed also personal warmth and a gregariousness which enhanced his natural talents for leadership. More than most of his brothers he had strong political and moral convictions, with a disposition to fight for them, particularly when they concerned social questions and the public good. Although he later became immersed in politics, he remained primarily not a politician but a mildly liberal reformer who sought to use political means to set things right, or at least as he thought they ought to be.

After graduation from Princeton, Benjamin first turned toward commerce and merchandising, in keeping with the family tradition. In 1819 he entered a partnership with Jesse Godley, of 53 Market Street, Philadelphia, and the firm became known as Godley & Richards, Merchants. This association continued for three years.

On January 10, 1821, Benjamin married Sarah Ann Lippincott, daughter of Joshua Lippincott, an auctioneer and commission merchant. He soon joined his brother-in-law,

William Lippincott, as a junior member of the firm, an association which was to last the rest of his life. Father Richards did his part, too. He leased to Benjamin, William Lippincott, and three partners, the site of Pleasant Mills, near Batsto, on which the lessees built a cotton factory. The rent was $250 a year. The lease included an option to buy the land for $4,000, with an additional option to purchase the Batsto Forge Tract, with its valuable water-power, for a like sum. (These options were later taken up.) Even though Benjamin and William Lippincott were able to buy out their partners, the cotton mill was not much of a money-maker. Not long afterward William Lippincott died, and while the whole property later became Benjamin's, he found himself too busy in Philadelphia to oversee it and his hired managers appeared to lack the business ability needed to make the enterprise really thrive.

Benjamin's tepid interest in Pleasant Mills was part of his declining concern for mercantile matters and his fast-developing interest in politics and public affairs. His political start came when he was elected to Philadelphia's City Council. Thereafter his rise was rapid. From 1827 to 1829 he was a member of the Pennsylvania Assembly. A zealous Jacksonian Democrat, his efforts soon were recognized in Washington. In 1829, President Jackson appointed him to two political posts: Director of the United States Bank, and Director of the Philadelphia Mint.

In those days a Mayor of Philadelphia was not chosen by popular vote but by the City Council. When Mayor George Mifflin Dallas resigned in April 1829, Benjamin was named to fill his unexpired term. Undoubtedly Benjamin wanted the mayoralty since, upon accepting it, he resigned both as Director of the United States Bank and as Director of the Mint. In 1830 Richards was re-elected by the city council. As the term of office was one year, he was again re-elected in 1831 and served until October of 1832.

Those were fruitful days for Benjamin Richards. He was an active leader in promoting the public school system, and during his term as Assemblyman in 1827 offered the first resolution to appropriate money for the organization and support of public education. He took seriously his responsibility as Inspector of Prisons; and it was while he was Mayor that the Eastern State Penitentiary—then regarded as a model institution though now obsolete—was completed and put into use. Benjamin was one of the founders of the Asylum for the Blind, an early manager of the Deaf and Dumb Asylum, and also a director of Girard College. A personal friend of Stephen Girard, he was one of the original directors and first president of the bank which became the Girard Trust Company, later the Girard Trust Corn Exchange Bank.

In mid-October of 1831 two young French aristocrats called upon Mayor Richards at City Hall. The acquaintanceship which followed was undoubtedly one of Benjamin's most stimulating and fruitful experiences in public office. At that time the names of these Frenchman meant nothing to the public: even in France they were known only as a couple of commissioners sent to study prison systems in the United States. A few years later one of them was to become famous. His name was Alexis de Tocqueville; and his fame was the fruit of his book based on his travels, one of the foremost books ever written on our government: de Tocqueville's *Democracy in America*.

Benjamin Richards was a substantial although indirect contributor to de Tocqueville's book. For a while his French guests (Tocqueville's companion was Gustave de Beaumont) asked numerous questions about the prisons of Philadelphia and Pennsylvania. The conversation soon centered upon American politics. They asked questions about governmental practices, and particularly the role of intelligent men in politics and the chances for selection of wise and able leaders under universal suffrage. In all, Richards had three meetings with his French friends, at one of which he entertained them officially for dinner. Early in 1832 Richards also wrote them three extensive letters giving further details of the subjects they had discussed and amplifying some of his views on democratic process.[1]

Author of the monumental *Tocqueville and Beaumont in America,* Dr. George Wilson Pierson,* of Yale University, had had this to say concerning Benjamin Richards:

> Mayor Richards interested me because he was, without any doubt, one of the Americans who made themselves most useful to Tocqueville and Beaumont. His name recurs repeatedly in their manuscripts* . . . and Mayor Richards was perhaps one of the five or six who contributed most of all to Tocqueville's famous book (out of the nearly a hundred Americans of prominence whom Tocqueville and Beaumont seem to have made a point of meeting.)

Among those "nearly a hundred Americans" were John Quincy Adams, Daniel Webster, Sam Houston, Charles Carroll, Secretary of State Edward Livingston, Albert Gallatin, Nicholas Biddle and President Andrew Jackson. Benjamin Richards held his own in high company. Indeed Dr. Pierson found in the French archives a number of pamphlets on municipal and county administration which the Mayor had sent to Tocqueville after his return to France.

Most of the Tocqueville-Beaumont interviews in America were taken down in question-and-answer form. It is worthwhile to note a few of those with Richards which are quoted in Dr. Pierson's book,[2] bearing in mind that as an ardent Jacksonian, Benjamin was an enthusiast for univer-

---

* Dr. Pierson, in research for his book, met in France the descendants of Tocqueville and Beaumont, and was given access to their "letters, diaries sketches and other manuscripts."

sal suffrage. In response to one query, the Mayor observed that "in general the people showed great good sense in their choices."

Tocqueville replied: "It has not always been thus in France," and stressed "the ancient enmity in the people against the upper classes which has brought it about that when the people have been master they have often been seen to elect men . . . without education and who presented no social guarantee."

Richards observed in return: "One may say that our Republic is the triumph and the government of the middle classes. In the Middle States and those of New England, for example, there exists no tie between the people and the classes that are altogether superior. The latter betray but little faith in the wisdom of the people, a certain scorn for the passions of the multitude, a certain distaste for its manners; in fact, they isolate themselves. The people on their side, without animosity exactly, but by a sort of instinctive repugnance, seldom name them to office."

"Do you believe that is a good thing?" Tocqueville asked. The Mayor replied:

"The middle classes are the most useful to society, and we find them as apt in public affairs as the rest. What I tell you, however, is not to be found in the South. In the West, also, the march of society is so rapid, there is such a confusion among all the social elements to be encountered there, that it is impossible to make such a remark."

Tocqueville learned from Benjamin (even then) that fathers, as heads of families, had lost their former power. The Frenchman recalled that Richards had told him that in cases of elopement, the sympathy of the public was almost always with the daughter and against the father.

When Tocqueville's *De la Democratie en Amerique* appeared in 1835, first in France, next in England, then in the United States, there probably was no reader more avid than Benjamin Richards. And none more surprised, no doubt, that his friend's book had become internationally famous virtually overnight. Yet even then Benjamin was beginning to drift away from politics as he earlier had drifted away from merchandising. Soon, in high financial position, he might have been regarded less as a champion of the middle class than as one of a burgeoning money elite later to be dubbed "an aristocracy of wealth" and, even later, sneeringly, "economic royalists."

Inspired in part by Tocqueville's visit, and in part by an expanding curiosity concerning the world about him, Benjamin, in 1833, had taken time out to travel in Europe. He was then well-to-do, his final term as Mayor had expired, and his status in the Philadelphia financial world was already assured. With no pressing obligations to stand in the way, he undertook among other journeys to go to Wales to search out some of his kinsmen there. His trip was rewarded. He found the head of the Welsh Richards to be a man of liberal education and worthy attainments, one of whose sons was a Presbyterian minister. Benjamin enjoyed his visits with the various families and after his return to America he continued to correspond with some of them.

Although wholly out of politics, Richards never lost interest in public affairs and public institutions. In 1836 he was made a Trustee of the University of Pennsylvania, a post he held for the rest of his life. Among other interests was the American Philosophical Society; and while his chief activity in later years lay in the banking field, he continued to hold his interest in the family firm, then Lippincott & Richards, and, after 1836 when Lippincott retired, Richards & Bispham, the new partner being Joseph Bispham. Benjamin led in establishing Laurel Hill Cemetery, a substantial undertaking for its day, and most members of his family have been buried there.[3]

Benjamin's business interest in South Jersey had long

since lapsed, but there is record of occasional visits to his old home at Batsto, in those years still a family gathering place presided over by "Brother Jesse." Such meetings, between Jesse and Benjamin, must have had an antipodal quality; for over the years the brothers had grown farther and farther apart. Jesse had remained at Batsto in comparative isolation whereas Benjamin had acquired a world outlook. Save for liquor, Jesse was chiefly interested in iron; Benjamin had become interested in everything. Jesse had led in drafting a petition protesting Jackson's removal of government deposits from the Bank of the United States; Benjamin was one of the President's dedicated followers. Jesse was constantly borrowing from Peter (never Benjamin) to pay Paul to stay solvent; and Benjamin was wealthy and the head of a bank.

It was a wide gulf, but when the brothers met they somehow surmounted it. Good will no doubt made up for the intellectual discomfort. Luckily, too, such reunions were rare, and brief.

Benjamin and Sarah Ann Richards had eight children. They are listed in the genealogical sketch in the appendix. The son named after him, Benjamin Richards, Jr., lived for many years in a house beside Hammonton Lake. Prior to his death he had gathered together a number of items close to Richards family history: a Batsto stove pattern; an old cannon ball; various letters and records; the original plate engraved by St. Memin bearing the portrait of William Richards, Sr.; and also a bronze plaque from Batsto Furnace bearing the three dates of construction: "1766, 1786, 1829." Most of this material has disappeared, long since. There was something of a family scramble to locate the St. Memin plate and the Batsto Furnace plaque. Recently the plaque turned up, and now is in possession of the State of New Jersey. Perhaps the St. Memin will come to light later.

If Benjamin Richards, Sr. was interested in such memorabilia no record of the fact has been found. He was one always to look ahead, always to have a multiplicity of interests. So it was until the day he died, at his home 1601 Walnut Street, on July 12, 1851. The bright young man from Batsto had traveled a long, long way—to become one of Philadelphia's very first citizens. It is right that the fine portrait of him by Henry Inman still hangs in Philadelphia City Hall.

Family Enterprises

The following chapters are primarily stories of enterprises that were carried on during the growing-up days of southern New Jersey. Members of the Richards family had a hand in all of them. The Richards role was predominant in Weymouth, Washington Furnace, Hampton, and the Atlantic City Railroad. But in Taunton and Speedwell, among others, the Richards role was minor.

Readers may be struck by this odd fact: that for a family of ironmasters, in only one instance did they establish an ironworks, and that works, Washington Furnace, was a failure. Most Richards successes lay in acquiring bankrupt or near-bankrupt establishments and building them into money-makers. That was true of William as well as his sons: Batsto was at a low ebb when William gained control. Thomas Richards alone launched an industry and made it pay, and it was not an iron but a glass factory.

Many men had a hand in the following enterprises of the South Jersey wilderness. In addition to again encountering members of the Richards family, the reader will meet the fabulous Charles Read, the ironmaster Thomas Mayberry, Joseph Brick of Bricksburg who shrewdly showed Jesse Richards a trick or two, the Hinchman family whose descendants still live in the area, and particularly the distinguished Benjamin Randolph, who gave up his cabinet-making in Philadelphia to build an iron furnace deep in the Jersey pines.

Weymouth: Iron

Magic often is found in lonely places—Weymouth, for example. It is difficult to explain the special spell which this old iron village has cast upon writers, poets, and the most casual visitors. Indefinable, too, is the faint lingering fragrance one still encounters amid its ruins and the atmosphere surrounding the stream as it splashes under the moss-covered stone arches which once supported a sizeable factory. On dark days the spot is almost spectral; even a slight breeze sparks a curious challenge to the imagination. Magic certainly is there, and the sensitive person quickly becomes aware of it.

Secluded was the word for Weymouth even in its hey-day when the ironworks created a sweaty world apart. The roads of approach were rough and winding, sometimes studded with tree stumps. Two stage lines bounced and bucked over them, and those stages were traveled by iron-masters and workers alike. Weymouth today is still lonely although a fast seashore highway cuts it in two. Millions race back and forth over that concrete ribbon quite un-aware of the old village, for a thickness of forest on either side of the highway screens what little is left.

Two writers in particular have celebrated Weymouth. Henry Van Dyke, essayist and nature lover, explored it many years ago. He told of that adventure in "Between the Lupin and the Laurel," a chapter in his book *Days Off*. Later, George Agnew Chamberlain wrote an exciting novel, *Midnight Boy*, against a Weymouth background, and captured the elusive aura of the place although his tale was wholly fictitious. When *Midnight Boy* was pub-lished in *The Saturday Evening Post*, the entrance to Weymouth mansion was drawn so realistically on the cover of one issue that an elderly member of the Richards family exclaimed: "It looked just like that when I was there as a child!"

Weymouth is worth a journey, and there are several ways to approach it. One is to drive about 40 miles straight down the Black Horse Pike (Route 322) from Camden. This trip involves one interminable corridor of billboards, hot dog stands, custard palaces, bars, and diners. But at least some of the signs will warn when you are approaching "modern Weymouth," which has its own allotment of these depressing structures. Finally, a traffic light and a highway turntable, proclaim that you are "there."

At this point the visitor may turn right or left—either way—and he will find himself in old Weymouth. To the left are the foliage-hidden industrial ruins, the old lake

bed now studded with vacation cabins, the mansion cellar, the gatehouse, and on a lower level, rows of workmen's houses, some collapsed. A right turn on the traffic
turntable discloses the other half of Weymouth, up on a
little hillside. Here is the 1806 church which is still used, the
quiet graveyard with markers of iron cast in the old furnace, and a number of age-seasoned but mostly well-kept
dwellings.

The happiest way to Weymouth long lay by water,
along the winding course of the Great Egg Harbor River.
This was the route taken by Henry Van Dyke. Then the
banks of the river were much as they had been a century or
more earlier when the iron men first came. Much of this
stream still offers a feast to the eye and balm to the soul.
In season one finds not only the lupine and the laurel but
much more: varied shades of green in wild profusion;
trees and grasses and mosses spiced by a richness of holly
and bright patches of wildflowers—all set against the
warm tawny water flowing over beds of white sand.

The best place to start the water trip is a crossroads ham-
let called Pennypot, nearly five miles northwest of Weymouth. Here the Great Egg Harbor River—small in size at
this point—passes under a highway bridge and then
tumbles over a dam as it flows northeast. Surprisingly, this
dam is of teak, expensive lumber salvaged from some old
warships and sent as a gift to the owner of the property.
Marked by the dam is the approximate location of an
early sawmill, and the general area where in later days
Weymouth's charcoal burners made fuel for the furnace.

Just beyond the dam is a sandy stretch of bank, and this
is the traditional take-off point for canoeists. Then, after
paddling only a few hundred feet, a right bend in the river
takes one out of sight of the highway and into a wooded
wonderland through natural green corridors of ever-chang-
ing beauty. Van Dyke's description of the ride is still

fundamentally valid though it was written half a century ago.

Why Van Dyke chose to give Weymouth such an unappetizing pseudonym as "Watermouth" can only be conjectured, yet his story casts a lovely glow. Here is a bit of it, telling of his discovery of the Weymouth mansion.[1]

> The manor-house stood in spacious grounds sloping gently down to the southern shore of the lake, well planted with a variety of shade trees and foreign evergreens, but overgrown with long grass and straggling weeds. Master Thomas and I landed, and strolled through the neglected lawn toward the house, in search of a possible opportunity to buy some fresh eggs. The long-pillared veranda, with its French windows opening to the floor; the wide double-door giving entrance to a central hall; a score of slight indefinable signs told us that the mansion had seen its days of comfort and elegance. But there were other signs—a pillar out of plumb, a bit of railing sagging down, a board loose at the corner— which seemed to speak of the pluperfect tense. In a fragment of garden at one side, where a broken trellis led to an arbor more than half hidden by vines, we saw a lady, clad in black, walking slowly among the bewildered roses and clumps of hemerocallis, stooping now and then to pluck a flower or tenderly to lift and put aside a straggling branch.

The "lady in black" was Laura Colwell, who had married Charles Colwell last of the family which had carried on the Weymouth enterprises after the death of Samuel Richards in 1842. Her father-in-law, Stephen Colwell, had built this mansion (an earlier one once stood nearby). Stephen had been Richards' manager and had married his daughter Sarah, who inherited a half-interest in Weymouth. Mrs. Colwell took Van Dyke and his companion through the mansion. He writes:

> Rest was not an imperative necessity for us then, but we were glad to see the interior of the old mansion. There was

the long drawing-room, with its family portraits running back into the eighteenth century—one of them an admirable painting by Sully—and the library with its tall bookshelves, now empty, and engravings and autographs hanging on the walls. The lady in black was rather sad . . . she was dismantling the house and closing it up, preparatory to going away, perhaps to selling it . . . Here had been a fine estate, a great family, a prosperous industry firmly established, now fading away like smoke . . .

Fading then, Weymouth was soon to crumble. The lake vanished when the dam collapsed. The factory buildings, gaunt and vacant, gradually fell into decay. The mansion itself, dark, hollow, and grim, became a hangout for tramps until the day it burned down. Its ruins now—a partly-blackened foundation embracing a tangled maze of twisted pipes and wild vegetation—are a sort of grave marker for that "fine estate and great family."

Most of the treasures Van Dyke saw in the mansion have found new homes. The Sully portrait of Samuel Richards is today in the Carnegie Institute. Another portrait was of Joseph Ball, long co-owner of Weymouth; it hangs in the board room of the Insurance Company of North America which Ball helped establish. Two others, illustrated in this book, were of William Richards in his later years, and his second wife, Margaretta. Additional portraits and memorabilia from the Weymouth mansion are now in possession of various members of the Richards family; but some, unfortunately, have been lost.

About this time, probably shortly after Van Dyke's visit, a search was made by members of the family for papers of Joseph Ball and Samuel Richards. Both men had lived at the mansion for varying periods and many of their records remained at Weymouth after they passed on. Some documents were found. A number of these are today in the Historical Society of Pennsylvania; some are owned by members of the family; a number by the author, while others are elsewhere in private possession. But a member of that search party, the late Harriet Richards Jeter Robeson, wrote the author: "Uncle Ball's papers were stored in the cellar of the Weymouth house, and when I came along they were so rotted as to be useless . . . all mildewed and falling to pieces at a touch."

Unlike the misty origins of so many enterprises in the Pine Barrens, the beginnings of the Weymouth Iron Works are plainly documented. It is known who cleared the wilderness to build the furnace and the forge and how much was paid for the land. There is a description of the early community written by Samuel Richards himself. The deeds, the business records, and the time books covering a considerable period of Weymouth's history tell the story of an operation which continued after the furnace fires had gone out for good at Batsto, Atsion, Martha, Speedwell, and Taunton.

Legends, so called, cluster about Weymouth as vines cling to the old gate house; one might say, more accurately, misinformation masquerading as legends. The most absurd of these tales has it that Weymouth was built by Samuel Richards in 1756—before he was born. Another legend says cannon and shot were made at Weymouth for Washington's armies during the Revolution—which took place long before Weymouth was built. Munitions were made at Weymouth; but they were for the War of 1812.

The Weymouth Iron Works was built in 1801 and 1802 by five partners: Charles Shoemaker, Morris Robeson, Jr., John Paul, Joseph M. Paul, and George Ashbridge. Earlier, in 1798, these men had purchased Martha Furnace and George Ashbridge became manager of both enterprises.

Negotiations for purchase of the Weymouth lands, from the West Jersey Society, were begun on November 6, 1800, and a down payment was made on January 1,

1801. At that time the famous Robert Morris was agent for the Society; by the time the title had gone to the five partners on December 15, 1802, Phineas Bond had become agent for the Society and signed the deed.[2]

After deductions for bits and pieces previously sold in the area, the Weymouth Company—the partners named their works after Weymouth Township in which much of it was located—acquired about 76,000 acres of land. The price was $28,000 payable over four years. About the same time the partners also purchased "a large bed of ore about two miles from the furnace site" for $1,700, and spent $650 additional for a tract called Ives Meadows. Most important of all, the Weymouth Company acquired control of the Deep Run Sawmill. This key purchase cleared the way for legislative approval of a dam above Deep Run and below the sawmill at Pennypot "for the accommodating of iron works and other waterworks."

Three of the Weymouth partners, Robeson and the two Pauls, conducted a merchandising and importing firm in Philadelphia. In their books, Joseph M. Paul described the main transaction as follows:

The tract purchased by Shoemaker ¼; G. Ashbridge ¼; M. Robeson ⅙, John Paul ⅙, and myself ⅙, from the agent of the West Jersey Society lays in the Townships of Weymouth, Egg Harbour and Galloway, County of Gloucester, New Jersey, on both sides the Great Egg Harbour River about 3½ miles from Blue Anchor to the nearest line . . .[3]

It is difficult today to realize the vastness of this estate which included most of what is now Mays Landing and extended north to the White Horse Pike and east toward the areas of Egg Harbor and Absecon. It's not surprising that in 1805 the Weymouth Company could sell 5,000 acres to William Richards and never miss it.

Joseph Paul's records are meticulous in certain details:

he even includes entry of his "Marriage Certificate," for three dollars, which was charged to "Profit and Loss." Unfortunately his records give no information on costs of erecting the furnace and forge. They do indicate that furnace operations began during the latter part of 1801 or early in 1802, and that the forge was built and in operation in 1802. In May 1802, George Ashbridge, as manager, published the following advertisement in several newspapers:

FORGE-MEN WANTED

Wanted, immediately, a full set of FORGE-MEN to work a new Forge now erected and in complete order, with four fires and two Hammers, on the Great Egg Harbour River; the stream is powerful and can never want water in the dryest season. Good encouragement will be given for workmen. Apply to Robeson and Pauls, merchants, No. 53 North Water Street, Philadelphia, or to the subscriber at the Works, Gloucester County, New Jersey.

Products of Weymouth under the Ashbridge management included the usual stoves, firebacks, pots, skillets, and other hollow ware, as well as special items on commission. One of the latter was the "cambosse"—probably a cooking pot for use in ships' galleys—which was manufactured to order for an ironmonger George Youle. Pig iron was shipped out frequently, and there was a steady call for wrought iron.

Since cast-iron pipe was to be the principal Weymouth product from 1819 on, there is interest in a story that the first water pipe laid in Philadelphia was made at Weymouth. This is based on the fact that Morris Robeson and John and Joseph Paul (the name of their company was Robeson and Pauls) furnished that city with an experimental supply of cast-iron pipe in 1801. It was a small order: only 14 lengths of six-inch diameter. Wooden pipe then in use in Philadelphia had proved unable to withstand the increasing water pressure and tests indicated that iron pipe would be the answer. In 1804 Robeson and Pauls were given a much larger order: for 56 tons of three-inch pipe, which were laid chiefly in Philadelphia's Water Street.[4]

That Robeson and Pauls supplied cast-iron pipe to the Quaker City is certain: that the pipe was manufactured at Weymouth is less certain. Weymouth was not put into operation until late fall of 1801 or the spring of 1802. Title to the property did not pass until 1802. Yet the first order of cast-iron pipe was delivered prior to October 12, 1801.

Where did the pipe come from, if not from Weymouth? Robeson and the Pauls were partners in Martha Furnace at that time, but all available evidence refutes the idea that pipe was being made there. There is another, and more likely, possibility. Robeson and Pauls were primarily importers and merchants, so that the 1801 supply of pipe for Philadelphia—and perhaps the supply in 1804—may well have come from England, or from some other American ironworks. Pipe-casting and core-making techniques were not simple: ten years later Weymouth was having trouble in pipe-making experiments. Thus to suggest that Weymouth made satisfactory pipe at its very first operation is like suggesting that a student could do calculus before gaining a knowledge of arithmetic.

In June of 1807, the situation at both Weymouth and Martha Furnace changed, because George Ashbridge died. He had been the manager of both enterprises. Shoemaker, Robeson, and the Pauls were merchants and investors; they lacked the skill to operate an ironworks. Since no qualified manager appeared to whom they could turn quickly, Weymouth was shut down. Then the partners decided to offer it for sale, along with Martha.

Weymouth had become a valuable property. According to Joseph Paul's accounts, the total profit from the begin-

ning to the time of Ashbridge's death was over $20,000.
This compared with an estimated profit for Martha of
$24,000 for a year-longer period, and Martha was an old
and established furnace. Also, in 1806, the partners appear
to have been paid some interest on their Weymouth investment.[5] Both ventures were doing well enough to attract
any purchaser who had enough financial backing to buy
and the ability to run an ironworks. Two such purchasers
soon appeared—Samuel Richards and his wealthy cousin
Joseph Ball.

Samuel, oldest surviving son of William Richards of
Batsto, had been managing the family store at 111 North
Water Street, Philadelphia. He knew the iron market thoroughly, in England as well as in America and he knew
from his training at Batsto the ins and outs of iron manufacture. Joseph Ball himself had managed Batsto during
the Revolution, and since had amassed quite a fortune.
Thus between them, Ball and Richards had both money
and know-how. Ball took a three-eighths share of Weymouth and Martha; Samuel took a similar three-eights
share, which was financed by his father; and the Ashbridge
family chose to retain their one-quarter share as an investment. That completed the new ownership picture.

Weymouth was not idle long. On March 31, 1808, according to the first entry in the Martha Diary, Charles
Shoemaker, Samuel Richards, and George Garrit Ashbridge "finished taking an inventory of the personal property at Martha" and accompanied by Jesse Evans, Martha's
manager, went on to Weymouth "to take an inventory and
appraisement of the property there." Just a week later,
the three-fourths interest—and control—was deeded to
Richards and Ball. The sale price was $34,500. Allowing
proportionately for the one-quarter Ashbridge interest the
value of the Weymouth works in 1808 was about $46,000.
A few years earlier $28,000 had been paid for the land; but

how much of the other valuation was offset by the cost of the furnace, forge, gristmill, etc., is impossible to say. But in 1808 Weymouth's most prosperous days lay ahead.

Pinpointing the start of the Richards and Ball management at Weymouth is an old and worn record book which covers the period from April 4, 1808 to mid-September of 1810. Here, it appears that the new owners quickly put the ironworks back into operation. The book lists the names of many of the employes of those days and gives important facts about events at Weymouth.

On April 9, only ten days after title passed, the forge was back in operation. Preparing the furnace for a blast was time-consuming but by May 12, smelting was under way, and continued as late as December 6 of that year. In March 1809 some furnace improvements were made, and the stack was partly if not wholly rebuilt. Robert McCartney spent eleven days on masonry; and Michael Mick worked over a week building a new "in-wall" (lining of the furnace) and putting in a hearth, helped for a time by Edward Rutter.

Weymouth's sawmills continued in operation through the period of management change. Two were then running: one at Pennypot, the other on Hospitality Greek. Both were under lease to one Evan Ewan who paid his rent to the Weymouth Company in barter. On May 25, 1808, for example, Ewan delivered "15,000 feet of square-edged boards on a/c rent for Hospitality Saw Mill." Later he shipped 20,000 feet of boards to pay the rent on the Pennypot mill.

The best description of Weymouth at this period was written by Samuel Richards himself. It appears in an advertisement written when Richards was in financial trouble but never published because the trouble was otherwise overcome. In this advertisement the following description of Weymouth appears:

On the Great Egg Harbour River, thirty-five miles from Philadelphia. There are upwards of fifty thousand acres of land. The works consist of a Furnace now in blast; a Forge with four fires; a Grist Mill and a Saw Mill all on one dam for all of which there is plenty of water in the driest season, and a good boatable navigation to Mays Landing which is six miles, from which Vessels are constantly sailing to New York and Philadelphia.

There is at said works a good dwelling house and barn, a store and twenty tenements to accommodate workmen. There is also a Saw Mill four miles from said works called Penepot [Pennypot], at which there is a good dwelling house and barn, and three small tenements to accommodate workmen. There are also several other houses and improvements on said tract of land. There is a canal from the Furnace to the Ore Beds so that ore is brought to the Furnace at small expense. The Iron made at said works is of excellent quality. The Furnace went Eleven Months last year during which time she made eleven hundred and fifty tons of Iron.

Weymouth became the center of a life for the people clustered nearby. All-pervading was its influence, from the ironmasters' house to the humblest cottage. Operation of the furnace was, to a degree, a sort of entertainment as well as a livelihood. To modern eyes it would be spectacular. Crowning the stone stack was the bright glow of a clear flame, sometimes rising, sometimes falling, with the pulse of the blast. For accompaniment there was the deep roar of the furious fire, fed by a stream of air pumped from the bellows; and the thunder of heavy forge hammers and the stamping mill. Then the molten iron spilled into gutters of sand. To feed the furnace there was a constant march of men back and forth across the ramp to dump fresh charges of ore, limestone, and charcoal into the top of the stack. Keyed low, yet a vital part of it all, was the fitful splashing from the great waterwheel, the music of power.

Iron-smelting was man's work. Old-time furnaces demanded great strength of muscle and will; endurance amid soot, grime, and almost-searing heat; skill in preparing the charge, or mixture of ore-flux-charcoal, and in managing the blast so the iron would be of good quality, fit for casting and fit for the forge. Skilled iron founders were said to possess a touch of genius. Theirs was a craft which commanded respect; and it commanded employment also unless the iron industry as a whole was in the doldrums.

In such a world of Vulcans there was little room for women. Their role lay outside: cooking meals, tending children and bearing more, sewing, knitting, keeping as much "house" as was possible in rude workers' tenements. There were part-time jobs at the Big House, and, for some, work in the fields at harvest season.

The fair sex sometimes was honored in the naming of furnaces—Martha, Elizabeth, Mary Ann, Joanna. And at certain works women played a brief ceremonial role when the furnace was put into blast for a new season after winter's lull. It was usually the wife of the ironmaster, or perhaps his daughter, who "drew the gate" which set off the smelting process. Such brief rites took place at Weymouth, especially in its middle years. In 1825, Mrs. John Richards, wife of the manager, "drew the gate." The books mention her again in 1826. In 1827 the honor was given to "Miss Rebecca Pugh."

If a furnace made incessant demands upon men, so did it thirst unceasingly for raw materials. The search for bog ore went on continuously. Unusual with Weymouth was a long canal to the principal ore beds, which lay to the north. Another large bed was in the Pennypot area, but ore from that location was boated down the river and across the pond. The old canal is still visible as it runs alongside the Weymouth-Elwood road for about half a mile on the west side. Less easily seen are the remains of the lateral diggings (trenches at right angles to the main canal) which ran parallel through the bogs to the west. Ore from this area was loaded on scows and poled down the canal to the furnace. This system of canals was built under the Ashbridge regime.

Never did there seem to be enough bog ore. The Weymouth Diary frequently mentions Lewis B. Walker, John Richards, and others going out to search for untapped deposits. Rewards sometimes were paid to employes who found such deposits. In later years, as at Batsto, ore was brought by ship to Mays Landing and then hauled to Weymouth. Sources of this imported ore were Albany, Poughkeepsie, Staten Island, Smyrna, Del., and surprisingly close by, Timber Creek in Gloucester County. Timber Creek ore, dug in the upper reaches of that stream, was floated to Chews Landing and there reshipped by schooner to Mays Landing, and then hauled to Weymouth—a long way round indeed.

Most old charcoal furnaces were built into a small hillside adjacent to waterpower, so as to provide two levels of activity. The upper level was called the "bank." There the team loads of ore were deposited; the limestone was stored; and the charcoal house built so that this fuel could be kept dry until it was needed. From the "bank" the "fillermen" would wheel their loads of ore, limestone flux, and charcoal over a trestle which led to the top of the furnace stack. Into the opening there they would dump these materials, in alternate layers, until the furnace chamber was full. At Weymouth this trestle was an inclined ramp, because the level of the "bank" was somewhat below the top of the furnace stack.

Weymouth's stack was built of native sandstone, in the usual shape of a pyramid with the top cut off. It was about 30 feet square at the base, from 25 to 30 feet high, and about 15 feet square at the top. Tradition has it that the circular opening at the top was eight feet in diameter. The iron was smelted below in the central chamber, which was lined with a refractory material, supposedly slate at Weymouth. Between this lining, or "in-wall," and the sandstone exterior was an insulating space. This was filled with clay, brick, mortar, or other materials used to protect the outside sandstone wall from the intense heat within.

Toward the bottom of the central chamber, buttress walls were slanted at an angle to support the great weight of the charge of ore, limestone, and charcoal. These buttress walls were called boshes. The size and angle of the boshes varied from year to year as new ones were installed, often along with the building of a new hearth at the beginning of a season's blast. This hearth lay below the boshes, and at its bottom was a small circular receptacle called the crucible. It was in the crucible that the molten iron collected, and adjoining it were tap holes through which the metal was released.

Starting a cold furnace—putting it "in blast"—was a considerable bit of business. First a fire was built in the central chamber, and when the stack was judged ready, usually a day later, the "burthen"—i.e. the first filling of ore, limestone, and charcoal*—was put in. Meanwhile the air blast was applied, and soon the smelting process was under way. The air blast machinery at Weymouth consisted of tub-bellows: pairs of cylindrical tubs, each with a slightly smaller tub moving up and down inside it like a

---

* The proportions of ore, flux, and charcoal were trade "secrets" of the old-time founders, apparently decided by rule of thumb like grandmother's method of making a cake with a bit of this, a pinch of that, and a sprinkle of something else. Actually, experience was the key factor and results were surprisingly good. Later, the proportions were determined by weight, and production was more uniform.

piston, which forced a stream of air through a long pipe into the furnace. The nozzle through which the air entered the chamber was called a *tuyere,* usually pronounced "twear." It was this air blast which fanned the furnace flames to the high temperatures required to melt the iron. These tub-bellows were, of course, operated by the water-wheel. At Weymouth, when one of the tubs was discarded —it was put to use for storing pork!

On the lower level, built out from the hearth and the arch above it, was the casting and moulding shed. Soon after the furnace was running smoothly, the molten iron would be tapped—several times a day—and run into a bed of gutters to form "pigs," bars of cast iron in sizes convenient for sale or for refining in a forge. Here, too, some of the fluid iron was poured into moulds for casting the hollow ware—pots, kettles, skillets, etc.—and also firebacks and special orders made from particular patterns. Meanwhile, drawn off from the furnace through another "tap hole" was the residue from smelting, the slag. This is to be found in rough chunks at almost any old furnace site. The casting house, as may be imagined, was a steaming place and its close proximity to the stack, with its oft-belching flames, resulted in frequent fires there.

Second most important unit in Weymouth's ironworks was the forge—a refinery forge in which cast iron from the furnace was reheated to a molten state and then pounded into wrought iron by great hammers weighing from three hundred pounds up. At some ironworks the forge was distant from the furnace; at Batsto it was half a mile away, with separate waterpower from another stream. At Weymouth, as at most plantations, it was close by the furnace and its machinery was run from the same waterpower.

Weymouth's forge had four fires and two hammers. In it an observer would have seen a group of powerful, sweating, half-clothed men moving a bit like actors silhouetted on a strangely lighted stage. One would be seen taking a pig of iron, pushing it into the forge fire, gradually, until it was entirely within the cauldron, a white-hot and pasty mass. At the proper moment wide-jawed tongs would grip this pasty mass and swing it onto a nearby anvil. There the huge hammers would rise and fall, rise and fall, literally battering the impurities out of the iron, which the forge man would shape into bars, usually an ancony, or bar with wide knobs at the ends. These bars would then be sold for reworking into tools and implements requiring great strength.

Not far from the furnace and forge was another noisy unit: the Weymouth stamping mill. The charcoal iron process was so relatively inefficient that the slag residue from the furnace still contained enough iron to make it worthwhile to crush the slag, under the hammers of the stamping mill, and run it through the furnace again, usually in a mixture with fresh ore.

The vicissitudes of maintaining furnace and forge were varied and often complex. Weymouth's records show that an entirely new furnace was built in 1817. Here are the entries:

March 15: Samuel Pettit went to Mount Holly for masons.
March 17: S. Pettit returned from Holly with masons.
March 18: Began foundation this afternoon.
March 20: Store caught fire this morning. Masons could not work.
April 10: Began pointing stack and putting in in-walls.
April 11: Finished stack.
April 12: Masons left this afternoon.
April 28: Put ore on furnace at 9 A.M.

Many things could happen to a furnace, some halting operation and some not. At Weymouth there were many interruptions for repair of the bellows. Other notes: "Bearing on furnace wheel loose"; "Flume busted"; "Sent for new Furnace shaft"; "Flood gates give way"; "All hands fighting fire near the coaling." Care of the bellows was particularly important and on one occasion was attended to by Samuel Richards himself. More serious was variation in the quality of iron produced. Iron quality was influenced by several factors: the mixture of ore, limestone, and charcoal; the speed of the furnace waterwheel, which required careful regulation; and the weather, the wind, and the rain.

The fall of 1819 was a troublesome time at Weymouth. The furnace itself was halted on two occasions, making for three separate blasts. The season began on April 4, but in June the iron was so bad that on the 21st the furnace was "blown out." It was put in blast again on July 15; "blown out" on September 6, and started up the third time on September 17. And during October of that year there was "Bad Iron" seven days of the month.

In 1825 there were major repairs to the waterwheel. On February 14, "Messrs. Samuel Richards and Thomas Richards came for the purpose of altering Furnace wheel." Ten days later "Mr. S. Richards, Mr. Dotterer and two workmen came for W. Wheel." The work was finished on April 2, and the furnace back in operation on the 14th. But by April 20 it was necessary to obtain a new furnace shaft, and a week later new springs were required for the bellows.

Problems at the forge could be even worse. In July and August of 1819 an entire new forge was built after the workmen "throwd the Old Forge down." On August 9 they began the frame; raised the frame on August 16, and whitewashed the forge on October 4. Time and again the forge was shut down by the breaking of an anvil or a hammer. In 1820 an anvil broke on February 16 and the forge was not started again until May 1 (with but two fires). In addition to the time occupied in getting a new anvil, three weeks were spent by "Wentling" in building a new forge chimney. On July 17 another anvil broke; on July 26 the hammer broke; on August 17 the new anvil went the way of the old; and before the end of the year another anvil and yet another hammer were lost. Another bad year at the forge was 1825. On March 11 the anvil broke and on the 22nd "C. Shinn returned from Atsion with new anvil and was some tipsy." A day later the forge resumed, but in July it was shut down for two weeks, and in August another hammer went. Much the same troubles beset the forge in 1826, and to celebrate the coming of 1827, the entry for January 4 was "Forge hammer broke."

Production during the first year of management by Richards and Ball was, in character, much as it had been under Ashbridge. Business in bar iron was particularly brisk. Soon, however, came the first significant change. On April 19, 1809, Charles Shinn was paid $3.85 for "Cleaning Bombs." This is the first of numerous entries which show Weymouth's role in the munitions business. Tension was high on the eve of the war with Great Britain. And secluded as Weymouth seems today, how much more remote it must have seemed a century and a half ago. Yet there in the wilderness, cannon, shot, and shell were made before and during the war in behalf of the American cause.

Earliest record of munitions manufacture is an entry dated June 2, 1809:[6]

32 Pound Shot and Grape Shott patterns and gauges $34.70.

Thereafter munitions production mounted steadily. On October 6 of 1809 there is a note concerning "Grape Shott" charged to the account of Henry Foxall, who operated the

Eagle Iron Works in Philadelphia, in which Samuel Richards and his father had an interest. Again, on January 22, 1810, Edward Rutter, a veteran ironworker was credited $21 for making:

182   32-inch shells; 268   24-inch shells; 212 of 18-inch; 65 nine-inch, and 41 four-inch.

Two days later Frederick Hart was given a credit of $150.66 for moulding among other items "2697 Grape Shott," 186 Bombs, and half time on an additional 160 Bombs. A further credit covered labor on 80 Bombs, 1,125 "Grape Shott," as well as ten large stoves, ten small stoves and 30 steam pipes." For cleaning the bombs John Ackley, William Kears, Mark Adams, and Jacob Pettit were paid respectively "$14.30, $2.31, 33 cents, $2.31."

On February 1, 1810, Pettit, Kears, and Adams moulded 585 Bombs, and on the following day Michael Mick, another Weymouth veteran, was credited with moulding 506, 32-pound "shott," 103 Bombs, 1,643 "Grape Shott," as well as non-military items. On February 22, 1811, Michael Halley is noted as having moulded 4,189 "Grape Shott" and worked on 251 Bombs.

The latter is the last entry dealing with munitions in the first Richards-Ball account book. The volumes covering immediately succeeding years have not been found and may have been destroyed. There is no doubt, however, that later on, and especially during the War of 1812 itself, increased supplies of ammunition were produced at Weymouth. Included were a considerable number of cannon. Many of these apparently became surplus and after the war quite a few were placed along Delaware Avenue in Philadelphia for use as hitching posts. Their Weymouth origin was evident in the initial "W" cast on the butt.

Shortly after the war Weymouth shared in another unusual contract: manufacture of castings for a steam engine for the Fairmount Waterworks in Philadelphia.[7] This was the first engine installed in the Fairmount plant, which was then new. The cylinder was 44 inches bore and 72 inches stroke, with a cast iron beam. Boilers were of cast iron, and made in sections which were bolted together. This engine began operation on September 7, 1815. While Samuel Richards held the contract, not all of the work was done at Weymouth; some, particularly the cylinder, was cast at his Eagle Works in Philadelphia. It has been stated that the castings for this cylinder "took all the metal that the Eagle Works would hold, vis.—35 hundredweight." Total cost of this engine was $54,341.

Brick-making was another side enterprise at Weymouth. The brick works was built in 1810, and first mention of it in the records is as follows:

October 23: To John Keeler:
For making 57,000 Bricks @ 8/p 1000	60.70
7 days work @ 50¢	3.50
4 setting kiln by his Father	4.00
4 Days & Nights burning	5.96

Keeler had been hired in the fall of 1810 presumably to get the brick works started. In November 1810 he spent two more days working there, and on December 24 Solomon Reeves was paid four dollars for "working in the Brick Yard" and $57 for "tempering clay for 57,000 bricks." The brick works did not last long for there is no mention of it in the book for 1813 nor does it appear in later volumes.

Cast-iron pipe, as noted earlier, was to become the chief product of Weymouth as well as Richards' other ironworks. Initial mention of pipe in the Weymouth books was on January 23, 1810:

To Frederick Hart for Moulding:

6 steam pipes without flanges	1.50 ea.
20 steam pipes with flanges	2.00 ea.
4 steam pipes with Elbows	2.50 ea.

This seems to have been an isolated order as there is no further mention of pipe that year. The next pipe item is dated November 19, 1813 (the books for part of 1811 and 1812, as well as those for most of 1814 to 1816 are missing). On this date "Robert Miskelly's team carted 2 large pipes to the Landing." However, pipe does not again appear in this book up to March 1814, where the record stops; or in the book for 1817.

The year 1818 marks the transition from sporadic production of smaller-sized pipe to the more or less steady output of larger sizes. On May 3, 1818, the Weymouth foundry "cast a bell." This is recorded as though it were an "event." Another bell was cast the following day, and two more, on the 19th and the 20th. Since there is no other record of bells cast at Weymouth it would be good to know the sizes of these and where they were sent; but the books do not say.

On July 16 this note appears, "Began to ram up side pipe" and that pipe was cast the following evening. But the significant news came on December 11, when arrival of a "Big Pipe pattern" took place. Not until February 9, 1819, however, do we find that "C. Shinn started for Phila. with the big pipe."

Experiments—trial and error aplenty—went on, and 1819 brought steps toward full-scale pipe production. It was a year of troubles, too, as these entries show:

April	7	Laded a pipe this evening.
	25	Made 1 pipe today.
May	2	Made one pipe and lost another.
	5	Mr. Richards and others came to try pipes.

July	21	Made 2 pipes.
Aug.	8	Made 2 pipes.
Sept.	22	Made no pipe on a/c rain.
	26	Made no pipes today.
	27	No pipes on a/c of bad iron.
Oct.	3	Iron bad. Lost the pipe.
	4	No pipes. Bad iron.
	14	Iron good. Made 2 pipes.
	22	Made no pipes good. Iron bad.
	23	Made no pipes. Iron bad.
	27	Made 2 pipes.

At this period the limit of pipe production at Weymouth seems to have been two per day, with many days showing none. By 1825, however, pipe-moulding was so well organized as to be taken for granted and only one instance appears in that year of "moulders losing several pipes." There were many entries like this: "Boats took pipes and pig iron," "teams took pipes," "no pipes on the Landing now." On July 19, 1826 there is mention of another important product: "Teams took pipes and *lamp posts*." So it went over the years in Weymouth's foundry, and the products were carried far and wide. An order from J. Raffignac, Mayor of New Orleans, dated 1823, provides that while some patterns will be lent, "Mr. Richards is called upon to make patterns for most of the pipes ordered."

Many of Weymouth's pipe contracts were with the Philadelphia Waterworks. In the Richards' papers are found notes of contracts in 1822, and again in 1824. In September of the latter year Richards wrote the City of Philadelphia:

My Weymouth Furnace has been exclusively employed all the forepart of the present year making castings for you and the contract is now completed (and I hope to your satisfaction). It would be some advantage to me to have an additional order to make out the years work.

Richards' contract was renewed, and ran through 1826 and 1827. He also had a contract with the Union Canal Company in 1826, and a bit later in this period he was shipping large quantities of stoves to Albany, Troy, Boston, and New York. Weymouth was making a number of types and styles:

Wm. T. Jones Coal Stoves, Franklin, new pattern; Oven boiler stoves; box stoves; Canada stoves, Mr. Richards' small round stoves; Lehigh coal stoves.

Most of the Weymouth pipe production was inspected at the works, and teams of pipe-provers made regular trips to all the Richards furnaces with special testing machines. Occasionally, but not often, there were rejections, sometimes for quality, sometimes for deviation from specifications; but cast-iron pipe had become Weymouth's big business.

Shipbuilding was another Weymouth industry, although the shipyard was six miles away at Mays Landing. The "Landing" as it is called in the company's books was Weymouth's port. Since before the Revolution, ships had been docking and departing there. Later many of the outgoing vessels bore Weymouth products, and vessels arriving were laden with goods needed by the furnace community. Still later, many incoming schooners carried iron ore to supplement the diggings from the bog-ore beds which were becoming increasingly depleted.

This profitable maritime trade led to establishment of Weymouth's own shipbuilding industry, about 1830. Over the subsequent 50 years more than a hundred vessels were built there at the head of tidewater on the Great Egg

Harbor River. Appropriately, one of the first ships launched at the new yard was named *Weymouth*. Her skipper for some years was Morris Pilgrim, and the records show that most of her outward cargoes consisted of wrought iron, iron pipe, fireplugs and lamp posts. A second *Weymouth* was built in 1870, and it is said that her remains still lie on the river bottom a few miles downstream from Mays Landing. Other vessels regularly engaged in serving Weymouth were the *Dispatch, Express, Gouverneur, Betsey Taylor, Tropic, Lydia Godfrey, Jane, Amelia,* and *William Henry*. This last one probably was named for Samuel Richards' sole surviving son.

Boom times came to Mays Landing in the wake of this growing river commerce. The big year was 1837. Atlantic County was then created from the eastern portion of old Gloucester County, and Mays Landing became the county seat. The still-handsome public buildings were erected in that period; newcomers flocked to town; and business was so brisk that Samuel Richards built the "Mays Landing Hotel," a three-story structure near the site of the old Richard Wescoat tavern and "within a few steps of the Court-House and Offices." An advertisement states that it:

> affords great facilities for the transaction of business. Gentlemen, with or without families, traveling on business, for health, or pleasure, will find this a very desirable and healthy resting place.

The advertisement was signed by the lessee, William Westcott.

Expansion and progress marked the tempo of those days. In 1840 the iron business at Weymouth was brisk, and the main sawmill was "running double time," partly on a contract to make wooden paving blocks. The contractor, Thomas M. Moody, of New York, agreed to pay Samuel

Richards seven dollars per thousand feet of logs which were to be "cut of an Hexagon shape" and in various sizes. The "said paving blocks" were to be shipped from Mays Landing.[8]

During this period, too, plans were launched for a "railway" through the woods from Weymouth to Mays Landing. In 1840, Walter Dwight Bell, one of Samuel Richards' sons-in-law, wrote William Moore, the new manager at Weymouth: "I was pleased to learn . . . that you had fully got into the spirit of business and especially of my hobby, the railroad. With you I believe it will be a valuable improvement and one that we ought to have made long since." [9] Not until 1846, however, were obstacles overcome and the railway—actually a mule-powered tramway—constructed. Three six-mule teams pulled the freight formerly trucked or poled on scows, and there was also a horse-drawn passenger car. Remnants of the tracks of this railway could be seen deep in the woods for many years after it was abandoned.

Weymouth continued to prosper in spite of absentee ownership. For some time prior to his death in 1842, Samuel Richards had become increasingly inactive at Weymouth, and actual control was largely in the hands of Stephen Colwell, who had married Samuel's daughter Sarah, and Walter Dwight Bell, husband of another daughter, Elizabeth. After Richards' death, Colwell and Bell built an ironworks in 1845 in Conshohocken, which occupied much of their attention. They were fortunate, however, in their Weymouth manager, William Moore who was extremely capable.

It will be recalled that early in 1820, John Richards, Samuel's cousin, had succeeded Lewis M. Walker as manager.* In 1830 John joined Thomas S. Richards (Samuel's

---

* Walker then established his own forge near Mays Landing, long known as Walker's Forge or Monroe Forge. He remained in close association with the Richards family.

eldest son) in purchasing Gloucester Furnace, on the Mullica River not far from Egg Harbor, and from 1830 Weymouth's manager was John C. Briggs, a former clerk there.

In 1840 Briggs seems to have been difficult, understandably perhaps when he was superseded as manager by William Moore but retained in a vague capacity with duties which included signing checks. Under such a setup, Moore's lot was not an easy one. Bad enough to have Briggs on the premises to watch and criticize his every move; but in addition, Briggs' friends were spying and reporting behind his back to Colwell and Bell in Philadelphia. Those gentlemen, in turn, were also restricting Moore's authority.

A letter of April 3, 1846 from Colwell must have stretched Moore's patience to the snapping point. Six years after having become "manager" he was being told to "take great pains to keep on good terms with Mr. Briggs . . . he is easily offended and therefore you must be on the watch." [10] Then Colwell disclosed that one John Venable, from Weymouth, had been to see him and had criticized Moore for, among other things, giving his brother a job. Not only did Colwell order him to fire his brother, he also scolded him for "employing a clerk without consulting us." He added that "we will not make any sudden change . . . but as soon as we can find a person to suit the place" Moore's employe would have to be discharged.

Somehow, Moore managed to run Weymouth efficiently and profitably in spite of such handcuffs and double-crossings. It is perhaps a monument to his endurance that he kept the job more than twenty years. During his management a new sawmill was built, experiments were made in farming—Bell proposed to cultivate artichokes; and in 1846 there were discussions about returning to the old system of day-and-night operation of the furnace, to increase production. This last came at a time when most South Jersey furnaces had closed or were about to close due to lack of orders. That year, too, Colwell sent out a new "stamp for the iron—it ought to be put only on good iron." This was to replace the "W" brand which had been used in earlier years.

Weymouth's exceptional durability in the iron business testified that it had something special, although not identified. Skilled management, perhaps; a particularly efficient furnace, possibly; or maybe just good fortune.

Weymouth: Paper

In 1836, Stephen Colwell came to Weymouth and married into the Richards family, into wealth, prominence, and eventually control of Weymouth during its last period of prosperity.

Born in Brooke County, West Virginia, on March 25, 1800, he graduated from Jefferson College, Canonsburgh, Washington County, Pennsylvania, in 1819. He studied law, was admitted to the Ohio bar in 1821, practiced seven years in St. Clarirsville, Ohio, and eight years in Pittsburgh, Pa.[1]

Colwell was a widower with two children when he met

Sarah Richards and soon after—on October 25, 1836—
they were married. That Samuel was a satisfied father-in-
law is evident for after the marriage, he began turning
more and more of his business affairs over to Colwell to
manage. And three years later when he made his will, Colwell was named one of the three executors.* Meanwhile,
Sarah was doing a bit of managing on her own account.
There were, first, Stephen's two children by his first wife,
and soon enough, three of her own.

Colwell was more a merchant than a lawyer. An active
member of the American Iron and Steel Association, he
was a director of three railroads, the Pennslyvania, the
Reading, and the Camden & Atlantic. He was a trustee of
the Princeton Theological Seminary and the University of
Pennsylvania, an energetic member of the Presbyterian
General Assembly, a member of numerous charitable or-
ganizations, and one of the founders of the Union League
in Philadelphia. In his later years he was much given to
writing pamphlets on such a wide range of subjects as law,
religion, economics, slavery, taxation, iron, steel, and even
wool manufacture.[2]

Colwell's wealth came from several major sources: Weymouth; management of the Richards estate (in a manner
which brought challenge from some members of the family); his mercantile agency in Philadelphia, where he represented Batsto among other concerns as a selling agent;
his ironworks in Conshohocken; and his vast dealings in
real estate during the latter years of his life.

The Weymouth Mansion, often called "The Manor" was
built by Colwell in the early 1840's. A much older house
stood a bit to the rear of the newer one, and examination
of its woodwork, particularly around the fireplaces, indi-

---

* The other two executors were Samuel's wife, Anna Maria, and his "trust-
worthy clerk" James McClure. After Samuel's death his widow and McClure
withdrew, and Colwell was sole executor.

cated construction about 1800, with a wing added later. This undoubtedly was the house built when the Weymouth Works was established. It was there that Samuel Richards, Joseph Ball, and their sisters and their cousins and their aunts were put up on their many visits to Weymouth. Long since gone, it is not possible to give here an accurate description of it. Luckily, however, a distinguished restoration architect, Mr. Munroe W. Copper, Jr., years ago acquired two mantels from the house and made a careful examination of what was left of it. He has written the author as follows:

The roof of the old house was completely caved in. The floor joists and beams had rotted and had fallen through to the basement. The three chimneys were standing. The chimney breasts and mantels were intact, plus some of the cupboards and doors near the chimney wall. The large kitchen fireplace, as I remember, had an opening about ten feet in width with a large beam and shelf running across the top. This was not worth saving. Two other mantel pieces, together with the chimney breasts were also in bad condition, but fortunately had enough paint on the woodwork to protect them from the weather.

Judging by the two fireplaces [which Mr. Cooper rescued and acquired] one is presumably forty or fifty years older than the other. This would indicate that a later wing was built on to the older building.

Mr. Copper has furnished the picture of one of these mantels which appears in this book. And the house from which it came is the "Big House" mentioned in Samuel Richards' own description of Weymouth, and in the extracts from the Weymouth Furnace books which appear in the next chapter.

A picturesque feature of the Colwell Mansion—the second "Big House"—is its tower, shown clearly in the illustrations. There have been legends about that tower room, a romantic place certainly, overlooking as it did the shimmering Weymouth pond. From its east window one could see the Weymouth Gate House, portal of the imposing property. Beyond that lay the furnace stack and the sheds; and still farther on the waters and the woods.

On the first floor of this mansion was the already-mentioned gallery of portraits, documents, antiques, and mementoes. In the hall also were hung oil paintings of members of the Richards family, while beside the staircase were small watercolors in medallion-shaped frames. Among the paintings, incidentally, is a partly finished portrait of Thomas S. Richards, Samuel's oldest son, who died shortly before his father.

Impressive to the visitor was Colwell's study. Here was housed only a fraction of his vast library. The rest was in his Philadelphia home. Colwell owned thousands of volumes including one large specialized section on political economy, a subject close to his heart, as his writings show. Colwell deeded his entire library to the University of Pennsylvania, with a plea that a chair of Social Science be established there.[3] It was a wise gift, for so many Weymouth treasures have gone beyond trace and recall. Gone, too, is that once gracious home of a cultured family, together with its broad, inviting verandas, colorful gardens, winding walkways, and even the lake which once must have seemed as permanent as anything in the world which the Richards family knew.

Due no doubt to Colwell's merchandising skill, Weymouth kept on smelting, casting, and forging long after all the other Richards' iron enterprises had closed down; and cast-iron pipe continued to be its principal product. Not until 1862 did the Weymouth Iron Works finally come to an end; and then it was the result of a fire which leveled the forge and the moulding sheds. Two years later another fire destroyed the furnace, whose stack remnants were soon pulled down.

Iron had been king a long time at Weymouth. It had brought wealth first to Samuel Richards, then to the Colwells. In 1834, for example, the furnace was turning out 900 tons of castings, the forge 200 tons of bar iron; and while production was tapering off in later days it was still profitable for Colwell to carry on until the disaster by fire.

After iron, paper. Hardly had the furnace ruins been cleared away when Colwell put the Weymouth waterpower to a new use: he built a paper mill on the site of the ironworks. That was early in 1866. This mill he leased to McNeil, Irving, and Rich for ten years. These men had been connected with the Pleasant Mills Paper Factory for a short time, and enjoyed sufficient success at Weymouth to warrant them exhibiting waterproof-building paper among other products at the great 1876 Centennial Exhibition in Philadelphia.

A business directory for 1866—the first year of the paper factory—gives this picture of Weymouth: [4]

* Agent, Real Estate	E. Wright
Blacksmith	F. Minger
Butcher	B. Mick
Carpenters	Jacob Campbell
	James McKay
Charcoal Burners	Hugh Rodman
	Archibald Scott
Country Store	S. R. Colwell
Engineer, Civil	E. Wright
Flour & Grist Mill	S. R. Colwell
Lumber Mill	S. R. Colwell
Paper Mill	McNeil, Irving & Rich

* Elias Wright, who had been a Brigadier General in the Civil War, was here actually representing Stephen Colwell. Later he was to become general land agent for Joseph Wharton.

Success of the leased mill led Colwell to erect a second paper factory at Weymouth in 1869, and for some years both enterprises prospered, side by side. Their chief products at that time were manila paper and waterproof-roofing paper similar to that displayed at the Centennial Exhibition.

Stephen Colwell died in 1871. He left behind him both wealth and problems. After bequests to several sisters and to the Theological Seminary at Princeton, the bulk of the estate was left to his wife Sarah. This included the Weymouth Works, the mansion, and some 50,000 acres of land. That same year, however, Sarah Colwell deeded a third interest in Weymouth to each of her sons, Samuel R. and Charles R. Colwell, retaining a third for herself. However, Samuel, the eldest son, survived his father by only two years so that by 1873 the weight of Weymouth responsibilities fell upon the youngest son Charles, who was neither prepared to shoulder them, nor sufficiently hard-headed to meet the challenges of the business world.

There is momentum in every successful business which carries it safely through the first tides of trouble. So it was at Weymouth. For some years after Stephen Colwell's death the paper mills prospered. But when the lease of McNeil, Irving, and Rich expired in 1876 it was not renewed, and young Colwell decided to operate both mills himself. One was called the Weymouth Mill, the other the Atlantic Mill. On August 6, 1879, the *West Jersey Press* reported: "The Atlantic Mill, at Weymouth . . . makes one ton and the Weymouth Mill two tons of manila and roofing paper per day."

Not until 1886 did real trouble appear—when one of the mills, apparently the Weymouth, was destroyed by fire. When the mill was rebuilt, it was put to a new use—the manufacture of wood pulp by a chemical process. Such a venture had been discussed as early as 1881 and it was at about that time that Charles Colwell entered into a partnership with Robert and Samuel Fulton, of New York. Thus was created a new firm: the Weymouth Paper Mills Company, with a head office at 46 South Street, New York, and a Philadelphia office.

This partnership established a sulphite pulp mill in the reconstructed factory. A large 12-ton boiler, ordered from England, was made from special plans, and delivered late in April of 1886. It arrived by rail at Elwood—once called Weymouth Station—and hauled to the site by mule teams, over the old Weymouth road past the long-abandoned ore beds. The *Camden Daily Courier* of April 28, 1886, reported: "The boiler is designed for making wood pulp from Jersey pine by the sulphite process. Fifty thousand acres of timber will provide the material for the mill to work on. This will be the only paper factory of the kind in the United States."

Meanwhile, the Atlantic Mill was still making "manila paper exclusively," and in June 1886 was reported "running night and day to fill orders." And a few weeks later the new pulp mill was completed and ready for operation.

Stationery of the "Weymouth Manufacturing Company" lists the following products: "Sulphite pulp, Manila Paper, Cedar and Pine Lumber." This listing suggests that Colwell's partners had moved in on the entire Weymouth enterprise, enjoying a measure of control not only over the new pulp plant but also over the previously successful Atlantic Mill and its manila paper output, as well as the sawmills and lumber trade. Worst of all, Colwell handed the entire management over to the Fultons while his own attention was occupied elsewhere.

The pulp scheme collapsed, and in less than a year the entire Weymouth Works was insolvent. Colwell was "financially ruined." The story was told on April 9, 1887, by the *Camden Daily Courier:*

THE WEYMOUTH MILLS FAILURE

Mr. Colwell Confident That He Can
Liquidate All Liabilities

The Weymouth Paper Mills Company, of Weymouth, Atlantic County, is insolvent. It has been known for several days that the affairs of the firm were involved, and two weeks ago there appeared in the COURIER a notice of dissolution of partnership existing between Charles Colwell and Robert Fulton, who constitute the firm.

Mr. Colwell called a meeting of his creditors on Thursday last and informed them that the liabilities of the firm amounted to $123,000. Fulton declared that they did not amount to more than $58,000. Mr. Colwell said this morning that he has been financially ruined by his partner, but that, if time is given him, and he has every reason to believe it will, he can pay every cent of indebtedness. Mr. Colwell trusted entirely to Mr. Fulton's management and never discovered until too late that the company's name had been used in commercial transactions which involved it to the amount of many thousands of dollars. In one case notes were given to a man named Ragy and taken up by New York banks to figures reaching over $40,000. The paper mills are in good condition and are, when properly run, remunerative. Mr. Colwell is confident he will recover his loss in a few years.

Efforts were made to recoup the losses. Even during the crisis, manila paper production had been carried on. The pulp mill itself having proved a failure, there were plans to make heavy wrapping paper from old rope, jute, salt grass, and other materials. But now the momentum from Stephen Colwell's day was almost gone; and the pulse of the surviving machinery grew increasingly feeble. Soon afterward all production halted. And for the first time in almost 90 years Weymouth was in the grip of industrial paralysis.

During these difficult days Sarah Colwell, Samuel's widow,

passed on. After her death in 1888 her will disclosed that her share of Weymouth had been left not to her son Charles, but to her daughter-in-law, Laura Ritz Colwell. This fact may explain a sheriff's sale on May 19, 1890. On that day Smith E. Johnson, Sheriff of Atlantic County, granted Elias Wright (then of Atlantic City) "certain lands" which Wright held in trust as follows: One-half for the American Sulphite Pulp Company, one fourth for August Stephany of Egg Harbor, one fourth in his own right.[5] Presumably this was the "new company" which that year made one last effort to reopen the mills. The paper-making machinery was started up again, but in vain. Before long the old factories were silent again.

On February 13, 1893, the American Sulphite Pulp Company deeded, for one dollar, its interest to the Weymouth Manufacturing Company, which that same day assigned the Weymouth property to Laura R. Colwell.[6] The latter document was signed by Samuel Fulton, as president of the Weymouth Manufacturing Company, and E. M. Fulton as secretary.

One later effort to reorganize paper production met no success, and soon Weymouth's factories were not only silent but empty. Equipment was moved out; the once-busy workrooms were left bare; the great chimney stood—and still does—as a lonely sentinel over the grave of a once-prosperous enterprise.

Charles Colwell died in 1901 and his devoted wife, Laura, was left alone in "The Manor," alone with only memories of bold and exciting days. True, the buildings and the village remained. The Gate House was still there. But more and more of the people moved away to find employment elsewhere. Time passed and the old company store closed, the same store where it had not been unusual over a weekend to weigh out four or five barrels of pork, a ton of flour, and a hogshead of molasses. The post office closed, too, and eventually even Andrew G. Stewart, postmaster for many years, moved away. The buildings began to crumble, and once the windows were gone decay was rapid. Some of the little houses literally fell apart. Then the dam broke, and Weymouth Pond was no more.

All this time Laura Colwell was trying to cope with the increasing problems of the mansion: repairs, tending the garden, keeping down the grass and holding back the encroaching march of wild vegetation. As the reader learned early in this chapter, these cares were proving too much for even so redoubtable a soul. Soon Laura Colwell was to leave the home she loved, and only an empty house remained. Squatters and derelicts were to move in later, until fire destroyed the mansion completely. Now, not far from the blackened foundations, a partly fallen tree stands on guard over the desolation.

Today Weymouth has only the memories which may be evoked when vagrant breezes rustle the trees and underbrush; and a few relics of things past to mark the place for future generations. Fortunately, some four acres, including the ruins of the paper mills and the site of the furnace, has been deeded to the Atlantic County Historical Society. Now it will be maintained as a memorial to a colorful and historic community and the men who helped make American industrial history when they cut into the wilderness at Weymouth.

The Weymouth Diary

Here is the detailed human side of the picture at Weymouth: the humble joys and personal tragedies of the workers; the story of Hosea Anderson, the schoolmaster who was sent to jail, probably for debt; of Benjamin Barnes, who with his family was taken to the poorhouse, where they stayed four months; of the heavy drinking; of the hunting in which a fabulous "Bare" was captured; of the little church and its Sunday "go-to-meetings."

This diary of the Weymouth Iron Works was kept in the company's time books. It covers the following periods: March 1813 to the end of March 1814; February 1817 to the end of February 1821; and February 1825 to the end of January of 1827. Save for very brief excerpts none of this "diary" has been published before.

The following account of operations at the Weymouth Works and of life, loves, births, and deaths in the surrounding community was put down by various hands. Ellwood E. Smith was clerk when the "diary" opens. Samuel B. Finch, later active at Atsion, took over this post on December 22, 1817. There is no identification of another clerk. However, in both periods the "diary" shows numerous differences in handwriting, spelling, and style, as well as personal judgment in recording what was considered important, interesting, or amusing.

Comparison with "The Martha Diary," published in *Iron in the Pines*, (Samuel Richards also owned Martha Furnace) reflects a number of contrasts between the two furnace communities and their enterprises, although both were then under the same management. Weymouth was a larger establishment than Martha. While the output of their furnaces was comparable, Weymouth in those years had a forge, more extensive moulding facilities for water pipe, side industries, and a generally larger roster of employees. The Weymouth Diary shows more numerous comings and goings, especially of members of the Richards family nearly all of whom made visits at one time or another, including William, Sr., and his wife Margaretta. Weymouth's management, too, maintained fairly close liaison with other furnaces, particularly Cumberland, Wading River Forge, Speedwell, and Aetna Furnace at Tuckahoe.

Two other contrasts may be mentioned. The odd words and phrases which made up the vernacular of the Martha Community, due perhaps to its ingrown way of life, are little found in the Weymouth records. Again, there is the strange fact that Weymouth's mortality rate was considerably greater: in the first years of the diary illness reached epidemic proportions. It may be significant that there is a considerable graveyard adjoining the Weymouth church; nothing comparable is to be seen at Martha.

The following extracts from the Weymouth Diary have been chosen and edited with the object of providing a running story of the operation of the ironworks and the changing tides of its community life. Where necessary the author has tried to render the spelling of names consistent, and to provide sufficient punctuation to clarify otherwise confusing phraseology. As recently as 30 years ago a number of other Weymouth books were known to exist. Since then they seem to have vanished beyond trace. It is too bad.

GLOSSARY

Burthen (modern "burden"):	Putting the ore, flux and charcoal into the furnace prior to starting operation.
Coaling:	Making charcoal.
Boating Ore:	Moving it by ore boats from the bogs and ponds.
In Blast:	The Furnace in operation.
Blowed Out:	Taking the furnace out of operation.
Puff:	An interruption in the smelting process.
Work in the Kitchen:	Cooking at the Ironmaster's house.
Training:	Supposed military instruction, usually held at taverns.
Stamping Mill:	Machinery to crush slag so as to reclaim unsmelted iron ore.
Draw'd the Gate:	Releasing the water supply to start the air blast machinery.
Proving Machine:	Devices for testing the quality of iron pipe.

Bar Iron: Wrought Iron; iron resmelted
                                       at a forge, to create metal of
                                       great strength.
Pigs: Bars of cast iron, formed by
                                       running molten iron into sand
                                       gutters.
Shells: Oyster or clam shells; *not* mu-
                                       nitions.

THE WEYMOUTH DIARY

1 8 1 3

March

30 Filled furnace. Put fire in at 9 o'clock this morning.
31 Blowed at ten o'clock this evening.

April

1 Died this morning very suddenly John Pettit. Peter Cox began to fill the furnace.
3 Jacob Wentling went to Martha this morning.
4 Jacob Pettit taken sick this day. Light rain.
5 Alexander McDonald drunk. Joseph Grant [master ore-raiser]
did not go to ore beds. Drinking last night. Sick today.
6 Joseph Ackley died yesterday morning. Buried at the Landing [Mays Landing] today. Mark Adams, Jr., taken sick.
7 Lewis Walker went to Philadelphia. Mr. Samuel Richards
came here. Doctor came to visit Jacob Pettit.
8 Samuel Wright's family moved here from Atsion.
9 Mr. Lewis Walker and wife with Mrs. Ashbridge came from
Philadelphia to meeting. Mr. Fugery here.
11 Mr. Samuel Richards and Mr. Fugery departed for Phila.
12 Jacob Pettit separated this life about 10 o'clock this morning.
Died this evening at 6 o'clock Jacob Pettit's wife after a short
illness.
13 Jacob Pettit and wife was buried this afternoon. Sam Pettit
was taken sick last night.
15 Perrine and Elijah Applegate began to work this morning.

Abel Smith's boy began to stock the Forge. Forgemen began to do the Forge carpenter work at Five Dolls. per Fire per month.

18 Joseph Grant drunk at Davises. Doctor went to visit Robt. Davison's and wife in the woods.

20 Discharged John Brown for setting the woods on fire. Very warm.

22 Cool and like to rain. Mr. Evans team came here this evening from Monmouth for tea.

24 Stopped the Furnace this afternoon to repair the bellows.

25 Robt. W. Keen went to Speedwell Furnace. Stopt repairing the bellows shaft.

26 Put the Furnace in blast at 2 P.M. Mrs. Elwell died this morning at Pennypot.

27 Jacob Wentling moved his family here this morning. Mrs. Elwell buried at new Meeting House.

28 Caleb Keeler left with load of Iron for Phila.

May

 1 Budd's team came and got one hearthstone. (Budd's Furnace).

 2 Sam Pettit's wife taken sick this morning.

 7 Constables came and took Wm. Cross house for debt.

12 Sam Pettit began to put in ore. Perrine Applegate sick after drinking.

13 Mr. Walker, Robt. Davis, Jos. Grant went to search for ore. J. Kindle's child died. Ox team carting wood.

19 Hugh Conly and Thomas Estell worked at the Locks of the Canal.

23 Abel Smith and Ben Crane went to the Landing yesterday and got very drunk. Discharged Ben Crane. Joseph Champion takes his place.

25 Mr. William Richards and wife, Mr. Jesse Richards and wife and Henry Abbot came here at noon. Went away in afternoon.

26 Mr. Joseph Ball and lady came here this evening. Perrine Applegate was taken dangerous ill in Mt. Holly. Guessed typhus fever, man came to inform his wife.

27 Elijah Applegate and Perrine's wife and Thomas Estell's wife went to see Perrine Applegate at Mt. Holly. Rained all day.
28 Perrine Applegate departed this life this morning. Team went to the Landing with Iron and brought back flour.
30 Elijah Applegate and Perrine's wife came from Mt. Holly. Mr. and Mrs. Ball went to the Landing. Dan Beaty drunk, laying at the side of the Swamp.
31 James McCracken nearly drunk all day.

June

2 Martha Furnace burned down this day.
4 Departed this life at 3 o'clock P.M. Edward McGrary. Mr. and Mrs. Ball left the Landing for Martha Furnace.
7 Teams went this afternoon with Iron to Phila. James Mc-Curdy drinking. Mr. and Mrs. Ball and Mr. and Mrs. Richards came at 11 o'clock forenoon from Martha Furnace.
9 James McCurdy very drunk at the Training. Mr. Smith came from Pennsylvania for mould boards.
10 Rain. Furnace made small puff this evening.
18 Wm. Miskelly fishing, idle ½ day.
20 Mr. Walker, Mr. Richards went from here to Tuckahoe. Robert W. Keen went to W. R. Forge (Wading River Forge).
25 Mr. Walker sick. Nicholas Scull worked at Casting House. Mrs. Ashbridge came here on the Stage, with daughter.
26 Dan Beaty drunk. Mr. Joseph Ball came here.
28 Team went to Phila. with Iron. Two teams came from Mr. Youle's (Stafford Forge) for iron.
30 Will Moore ran his wagon against a tree by the barn. Broke his axletree by neglect.

July

1 John Kindle did not work, was at Budd's Furnace. Team came from Phila. with patterns.
2 Joseph Champion went to Hampton Forge with his team. Abel Smith went for molasses. Warm this day.
11 Michael Mick, Jr. came this day from Martha Furnace. Grant and R. Johnson drinking at Steelman's, fell in creek.
19 Sent 4 teams to Phila. this evening with Iron.

August

1 James McCurdy and William Boner drinking at Steelmans and Davises. Will fight when drunk.

6 McCurdy and Boner drinking all week.

8 Miss Woolfield beat Dan Beaty with the broomstick as he has taken to hard drinking.

11 Martha Furnace put in blast this day. Watson team came for bar iron. Philip Emmell shot and killed his calf.

13 Mr. Ashters came from Phila. to get stoves made. Two teams came from W. R. [Wading River] Forge for scrap iron.

14 Thomas Estell nearly drunk. W. J. McCurdy, Dan Tremble, Dan Beaty all went to drink down the town. Richard Dempsey laying very drunk by the roadside below Deep Run.

15 Beaty and Trimble fight.

18 Richard Johnston drunk all day. Abel Smith boy at work with the oxen.

22 Furnace puffed at 10 o'clock P.M., like to burn carpenter shop and buildings.

27 Departed this earthly prison at 10 o'clock forenoon Sam Pettit's child, age about one year.

31 Mr. McKeen left early for Speedwell.

September

10 Mr. Large left this A.M. for Atsion.

15 Mr. Conover came here to see his vessel. Got very drunk.

October

6 Wentling, Mark Adams, John Kindle went to Atsion. Mr. Walker at the Landing loading sloop.

7 Team went to Phila. with Iron.

12 Persons that lost time this day was at Election. Barns and Estell drunk and fighting at Election. Richard Dempsey departed this life at 4 P.M.

14 Robt. Davison left the woods for Squankum Furnace. Mr. Richards, Mr. Ball here this evening. Archy Pifer sick after drinking.

19 Robt. Miskelly's team carted 2 large pipes to the Landing. Jacob Wentling drunk.

November

1 Mr. Joseph Ball departed this place in Stage for Phila. Master Clerk drinking.
2 John Kindle making a pit in casting house.
3 Three Indians passed here today.
6 Sloop JUDITH came to Landing.
15 Snowed. Forge stopped work.
24 Mr. & Mrs. Walker, Mrs. Kenedy went to Batsto.
30 Sloop arrived at the Landing.

December

5 Peter Cox cut Connolly's boy in head with stone.
6 Hugh Connolly drunk. Alex. McDonald came here from Davises after drinking 9 days.
10 Went to Landing to attend Law Suits.
13 Joseph Grant drinking this and eight days before.
15 Discharged Joseph Grant.
18 Mr. Walker went to Budd's Furnace.
25 Christmas. James Richards and wife came this evening. Wm. Miskelly did not work but $\frac{1}{2}$ day.
26 Married John Scull to Miss Hanna Pettit last evening by Revd. John Daily.
27 Gloomy and like for storm.
31 Furnace blowed out at 12 noon. Some disputes but of small magnitude.

1 8 1 4

January

3 Last of coal came in. Colliers drinking.
4 Jacob Wentling began to work in Smith Shop.
5 Mr. Hall came with Pork. Began to snow.
6 Mark Adams, Jr., had son born this evening.
9 Snowed heavy.
11 Robert Tyler and Susan Adams was married this evening by Mr. Dailey.

18 William Moore left for Phila. Stormed so he had to return.

19 Nicholas Scull began to work at Hammer Wheel shop.

22 Coldest day this winter. Nicholas Scull quit.

24 Filled the ice house this day.

30 Snow squall this evening. Very cold and high wind. Jacob Wentling drunk. Went to Davises tavern with Joseph Champion.

February

2 Robt. Davis 2-horse team carted ore. Mr. McKeen went to Speedwell.

16 Uriah Steelman framing the Moulding Room.

21 John Steelman came to survey the road to Wm. Brittens. [tavern].

22 Michael Mick began to take out the Hearth.

28 Discharged Joseph Champion.

March

1 Mrs. Michael Mick departed this life about 4 P.M. Extremely cold.

3 Buried M. Mick's wife at Batsto. Raised Moulding Room.

6 Mr. Ireland came to preach.

14 First loads ore in Boats came in this day. Team came from Martha Furnace for Iron.

18 Mr. Walker had son born about 4 o'clock this morning.

23 Began to snow. Sam Pettit moved to Mark Adams house.

25 Joseph Champion [He's hired again—Ed] left for Phila. with load of Iron.

31 Filled the Furnace this day and fired at Noon. Rained excessive heavy.

1 8 1 7

February

12 Samuel Adams married this evening. Very cold. Capt. Pennington and Sq. Watson came with Mrs. Hunt—all drunk.

14 Thos. Elwell could not loosen the sawmill. Abel Smith got run over.

21 A. Pricket got run over coming from Landing.

March

1 Mr. Walker went to Turky-hoe and Budd's, returned in evening.

7 Set fire in lime kiln this morning.

12 Snowed all day. Town meeting. Burcham Tyler came home from meeting sober.

15 Samuel Pettit went to Mount Holly for masons [To build new furnace stack—Ed.] U. Steelman cut himself very bad.

17 S. Pettit returned from Holly with masons. J. Wentling and J. Adams found drunk in the road coming from Millville.

18 Began foundation this afternoon.

20 Store caught fire this morning. Masons could not work.

31 Snow this morning. Masons began work in afternoon.

April

1 Mr. Richards left for Batsto and Martha. Chas. Major began to drive ox team.

3 Burned lime kiln last evening.

8 J. Wentling, J. Keen dressing bellows. Henry Thomas died last evening.

10 Began pointing stack and putting in walls.

11 Finished stack.

12 Masons left this afternoon. A. Prickett fell in grist mill stream. Jesse Keen drunk.

21 C. Major began to stock forge.

28 Put ore on furnace at 9 A.M. Put fire in 7 P.M. [This is the new furnace].

May

2 Mr. Walker went to Indian Cabbin.

6 Began to flux with limestone today.

9 Furnace flume busted about 12 o'clock. Drawed pond off.

12 Training this day.

14 Charles Major drunk.

27 Mr. Walker went to Washington. [Washington Furnace—Ed.]

June

2 Catherine Phifer began to work in kitchen.

4 Training at Mays Landing.

12 Mr. and Mrs. Ball came.

18 Mr. Powell left this morning for Batsto. [Mayhem Powell, a close friend of the Richards, ran a store in Philadelphia].

30 Charlotte Pricket began to work in the kitchen.

July

6 Burcham Tyler's child got drowned this afternoon. Pleasant.

15 Charles Shinn had a fit, got run over. Sam Pettit driving Shinn team.

23 Bearing on furnace wheel got loose last evening. Jesse Keen got drunk.

August

5 Mr. Walker went to unload sloop.

13 Mr. Walker's pocketbook stole.

28 John Richards came here about 4 P.M.

30 Molly Applegate came to work in kitchen.

September

1 J. Wentling, Wm. Miskelly, Jeff Keen, U. Steelman, John Adams, T. Estell, T. Elwell, C. Bartlett, B. Tyler and Job Evans went hunting. Furnace working BAD.

2 Molly Applegate left yesterday.

4 Thos. Estell got drunk on cider. Threatened to fine Sqr. Ackley for selling it.

8 Elisha Smith began to cart ore with oxen.

29 Wm. Miskelly went cranberring [sic]. B. Tyler drunk at Davises.

October

5 C. Pricket began to work in kitchen.

7 Samuel Pettit & B. Taylor working on canal. Rain heavy.

25 Anna Downs went home. U. Steelman lost 7 meals this week.

31 Molly Foster came to work in kitchen.

November

1 Charles Major began to stock Forge.
8 U. Steelman lost 6 meals this week.
12 Thos. Estell boating alone down canal.
15 Uriah Steelman lost 16 meals this week.
26 U. Steelman moved this day.

December

10 A. Pricket died this evening.
11 Blowed out Furnace at 9 o'clock & 40 P.M. A. Pricket buried this afternoon. Wm. Miskelly went hunting.
16 M. Pettit working on canal.
22 Ellwood E. Smith gave up the clerkship this day and Samuel B. Finch commenced.
24 A Frolic at Thomas Estell's today. Considerable shooting this evening, it being Christmas Eve.
25 All the coal came in today. Merry time at the Landing this evening with some of our head men.
27 Mr. Finch went to unload vessel.
31 Teams hauling hearth stone. Pork came this afternoon.

1 8 1 8

January

1 Several deer killed today. Pork came this evening.
3 Benjamin Barnes told quite a lengthy story about himself.
7 S. Pettit hauling wood for School House.
12 Hosea Anderson began teaching school.
14 C. Bartlet put boiling water on a barrel of shad.
16 Messrs. Jesse, John and Benjamin Richards here today.
19 D. Beaty drunk and fell down by the Grist Mill and bumped his nose.
26 Stage had no passengers today.
27 Plenty of lawyers here today. Mrs. Bashti Wescoat died last night.
31 Snowed all day. About 12 inches. Very cold.

February

2 Very windy and stormy. Killed 3 deer.

10 Forge froze up. Lent Mays Landing store I Hhd Molasses.

19 Snow about 9 inch deep. Hauling dung.

25 Beef pedlar here today. Teams hauling cedar logs.

27 Jacob Wentling returned pr. Stage.

March

2 Two boys here after stove patterns. J. McCoy to be Master Collier. Began to take out the furnace hearth.

3 A man from Leesburg & Philip Emmell came early this morning and took Hosea Anderson [the schoolteacher—Ed.] to put him away in Woodbury jail. Hosea Anderson returned this evening.

4 Hosea Anderson keeping school again.

11 B. Barns finished taking out the hearth. Town meeting today.

14 Launched the ore boats this evening.

17 Enos Coil began to clear the canal yesterday. The pond drawn off.

18 Finished the canal about noon. A frolic at Jacob Adams last night.

19 Let the water in the flooms this morning. Started the Grist Mill. Started ore boat about 10 o'clock.

23 Elizabeth Green began working in the kitchen.

24 Ox team moved a man from Batsto coaling. Began dressing the hearthstone yesterday morning.

25 Aetna Furnace teams past here this evening with load of goods from Martha Furnace.

April

1 Two men from Washington began to raise ore.

2 Hetty Smallwood began to work in kitchen.

8 Launched the ore boat. Rain this evening.

15 Mr. Walker went to Gloucester Furnace.

17 Put fire in Furnace at 6 H 40 M P.M.

19 Drawed gate this morning 25 minutes past 8 o'clock (Sunday). David Daily preached here at 10 o'clock A.M.

20 Let out the first bed of pigs at 11 A.M. Mr. George Richards came this evening.

23 Moulders ladled for the first about 8 o'clock this evening.

May

1 Put the new stove up about 2 o'clock.

2 John Adams married this afternoon. C. Shinn took a load to the wedding.

3 Cast the bell. J. Wentling a little battered.

4 C. Shinn started with B. Barns & family to the poorhouse this morning. Snowed. Cast another bell.

8 Jacob Wentling started for Cumberland to put in furnace hearth.

9 Training at Mays Landing today.

10 Some of the moulders and ore raisers are keeping up training yet. Forgemen not working. W. S. Downs here.

14 Furnace gave a very heavy puff this morning about one o'clock. Throwd out 5 half charges.

16 Rain. No pork today. Weather continues cold.

17 Water broke across the causeway.

19 Made a bell this evening.

20 Fixed up another bell.

June

3 Training at Mays Landing. Nearly all came home sober.

11 Philip Emmell sold Hosea Anderson's goods.

13 Cast the side pipe but did not come good.

15 Philip Emmell took Hosea Anderson to Jail.

July

2 Mr. and Mrs. Ball came this evening.

16 Began to ram up side pipe.

17 Cast side pipe this evening. Stage well loaded with passengers.

18 Simeon Brown started with side pipe to Phila. Hauling in oats.

20 Charlotte Wescoat began to work in kitchen.

24 U. Steelman repairing forge bellows.

31 Hosea Anderson returned from jail today.

August

4 Mr. Ball taken sick this forenoon.

6 B. Barns and family returned this evening. [From poor house —Ed.]

9 Mr. Ball very poorly. Mrs. Ball went to Landing and Returned.

10 B. Barns began to work.

16 Mr. Samuel Richards & family came this evening.

18 Mr. S. Richards and family started for Cape May.

27 Mr. S. Richards & family and Mr. & Mrs. Ball started for Phila. The Sheriff here today. Wentling keeping.

September

1 Nearly all hands hunting.

6 Mrs. Lottons had a fine son last evening. B. Tyler drunk.

9 All hands after a bare this morning but it got away.

10 Charles Bartlet broke his thigh. Set by Amos Ireland.

17 Mr. Walker went to Clark's Landing. Quite windy. Rain.

22 Began boating ore again.

28 Mr. Lock came with sweet potatoes. Stage 3 passengers.

30 Mr. Finch went to B. Anchor to serve Supinies.

October

1 Mr. Walker & Mr. Abbett went Ore beds.

8 Furnace made a heavy puff this evening.

14 Election at Mays Landing. B. Tyler and Th. Stewart fought.

15 J. Grant and others drunk.

17 Wm. Meskelley shot the Big Bull yesterday.

20 Jacob Wentling went to Etna to put in Hearth.

25 Mr. Long preach'd in Meeting House. Capt. John Williams brought home very sick.

26 John Williams buried between 3 & 4 P.M.

November

8 Mr. Van Nest preached in Meeting House.

23 Mr. Sharp here with corn. Stage no Passengers.

25 Mr. Jesse Richards here.

27 Rained all day. Stage one Passenger.
30 Mr. Lotton commenced Staging.

December

2 John Estell & Co., vessel launched.
6 Quarterly meeting at Bargaintown.
7 Mr. Lotton had five passengers. Mrs. Winner one passenger.
10 Richard Estell departed this life about noon.
11 Richard Estell buried about 3 P.M. Big pipe pattern came.
12 Snow last night. Wentling fixing for the pipe.
14 Doctor Baker commenced with the Stage.
22 Took burthen off [Furnace] at 2 P.M. Pleasant.
23 Blow'd out the Furnace about 2 o'clock this morning. Messrs. Jesse and John Richards here.
24 Charles Scull married this evening at Th. Lottens. [Tavern] Shooting this evening.
25 Very warm for Christmas. No Passengers in the Stage.
29 Several of the furnace men started for Phila.

1 8 1 9

January

1 Furnace men returned from Phila.
2 Jacob Huffman hung himself twice, but did not hang long enough.
3 Snowed nearly all day. Mr. Van Nest preach'd at 10 o'clock. R. Ware drunk.
4 Snow nearly 12 inches deep. Both Stages had passengers.
6 Jacob Huffman moved to Aetna Furnace.
7 Mr. Lotten arrived with new Stage.
21 Began to repair the Stamping Mill.
24 David Matten and Ann Wheaton married last evening.

February

1 Mr. Lotten 3 Passengers. Mr. Baker's Stage has new driver.
3 Job Evans drank too much cold water.
7 Constable started with J. Barlow to Jail.
9 C. Shinn started for Phila. with the Big Pipe.

13 Mary Walker taken very sick.

19 Nine men killed 44 rabbits.

20 Mary Walker departed this life about 1 A.M. & was intered about 3 P.M.

22 Began to take out the Furnace Hearth.

March

3 Cold weather. Began to dress Hearth Stone.

7 This day commenced a Sunday School at Mays Landing.

9 Atsion team here after Hearth Stone.

10 Town meeting at Mays Landing.

15 Atsion teams after H. Stone. Cool.

28 Mr. Fougery arrived with 2 boxes Stove Patterns.

29 Mr. Fougery left for Phila. pr. Stage. Rain.

April

2 Filled the Furnace this afternoon. Put fire in 20 M before 8 o'clock. Mr. Graves died this morning.

4 Mr. Graves buried at Landing about 1 P.M. Furnace gate drawn 11 A.M.

7 Mr. Walker went Coaling. Laded a pipe this evening. Iron bad.

10 Four men came from Atsion.

11 Samuel Richards, Esq. came P.M. Rain. Windy.

12 Furnace puffed this morning. Mr. Richards left for Batsto and Martha.

25 Made 1 Pipe today. Pleasant.

May

1 Mr. Parker started for Martha with Stove Patterns.

2 Made one Pipe and lost another. Killed 2 R. Snakes.

5 Mr. Richards & others came to try Pipes.

8 Mark Adams, Jr. & N. Wentling went Atsion. 2 Loads clams came.

10 Training at Mays Landing. Several fought. N. Wentling got hurt.

15 No Molasses, Coffee nor Sugar today for people.

31 Some rain. Mail Stage 4 passengers. Lotton 1 passenger.

June

3 Proving pipes, Messrs. Richards & Fougery left for Batsto.
4 Pipe men left for Batsto. Fillers & keepers charged Furnace.
8 All hands fighting fire near the Coaling.
9 Training at Mays Landing. All hands came home sober.
15 Michael Mick, Jr. left for Batsto.
21 Took off the Burthen half past 5 o'clock A.M. Blow'd out half past 5 P.M.
26 Began to take out Furnace Hearth.

July

5 Stages one passenger each. Hearth Stone in.
6 A comet appeared last evening. Teams all after Hearth Stone.
9 Frolic at Sam Pettit's this evening. Women. Quite warm.
10 A Portugee here yesterday.
12 Put fire in Furnace at 8 P.M.
15 Draw'd the gate [of furnace] at 7 P.M.
21 Made 2 Pipes Mr. Quinn came pr. Stage.
23 Mr. Walker surveying. Mr. Fougerys 2 sons came.
29 Teams hauling lumber for Forge. Quite warm.

August

6 Throw'd the old Forge down. Jacob Adams left for Beach.
8 Carpenters came. Made 2 Pipes.
9 Began to frame the Forge.
12 Mad dogs about. Edward Brown's child buried P.M.
16 Raised the Forge frame A.M.
21 Molasses came. Mr. Keen left for Atsion.
28 Capt. Pennington here. Archibald Phifer Founder. Iron better.
29 Capt. Pennington started for Bermuda.

September

5 Mr. Saml. Richards came. Took Burthen off Furnace at 6 P.M. Carpenters went Pennypot.
6 Furnace blowed out at 9 A.M. J. S. & M. Adams fixing for Atsion.

William Richards in his later years.
Portrait by Rembrandt Peale.

LEFT: *Mary Patrick Richards, first wife of William;*
portrait stated to be by St. Memin although not listed in his catalogue.

MIDDLE: *Margaretta Wood Richards,*
second wife of William; portrait by Rembrandt Peale.

RIGHT: *Thomas Richards*

Samuel Richards of Atsion.
Miniature by G. H. Cushman.

Anna Maria Richards, wife of Samuel.
Miniature by G. H. Cushman.

Batsto Mansion and outbuildings,
now restored by the State of New Jersey.

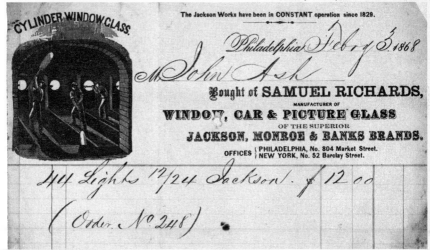

The Jackson Works have been in CONSTANT operation since 1829.

Philadelphia Feb'y 3 1868

M *John Ash*

Bought of **SAMUEL RICHARDS,**

MANUFACTURER OF

WINDOW, CAR & PICTURE GLASS

OF THE SUPERIOR

JACKSON, MONROE & BANKS BRANDS.

OFFICES { PHILADELPHIA, No. 804 Market Street.
{ NEW YORK, No. 52 Barclay Street.

444 Lights 12/24 Jackson . $ 12 00

(Order. No. 248)

T O P : *Batsto Glass Works buildings.*
Last surviving structures, long since gone;
photograph taken about 1910.

A B O V E : *An invoice from the*
Jackson Glass Works of Samuel Richards,
nephew of Samuel of Atsion.

L E F T : *Washington's Batsto cypher.*
Iron casting used at Batsto in 1787
to mold firebacks for George Washington.
The casting is about six by nine inches.
Two of the firebacks are still at Mount Vernon.

Courtesy of the late Nathaniel R. Ewa

Courtesy of the late Nathaniel R. Ev

TOP: *Weymouth "Manor," west-end view, showing the four-story tower.*

ABOVE: *Weymouth paper mill, interior view in the days of disintegration; only a few foundations now remain.*

*Fireplace from Weymouth Mansion, the first "big house" built
by Samuel Richards. The closet turned at right was originally flush
with the chimney breast. Preserved and now installed in
the "Jersey Room" of Mr. and Mrs. Munroe Copper.*

An 1823 order to the Weymouth foundry for
water pipe, signed by J. Raffignac, mayor of New Orleans.

Mr. Richards is requested to add to the quantities of Iron works, commanded by Mr. Ogden, the following quantities of Branches and Pipes — to wit

— Five branches, thus —— 16 ⊐)16
— one d.to —— 16 ⊐)16
— Seventeen d.to —————— 12 ⊐)12 .
— Nine hundred fifty four feet (running measure) of pipes, sixteen inches Diameter in the clear
— Seventeen hundred & ten feet pipes, twelve inches Diameter in the clear
— Eleven hundred twenty five feet pipes, ten inches diameter in the clear.

When a pipe of either Diameter is not sound at either end, or at one end, if it is trimed to whatever length, that is sound, it will be very acceptable.

Likewise, the piece of pipe the drawing of which has been forwarded by Mr Ogden, since his return to Orleans, is wanted immediately

J. Raffignac

TOP: *Taunton. The early mansion, torn down about 1951.
Taunton's second and present mansion can be seen at the right rear.*

ABOVE: *The "salamander" or crucible ingot,
actual size about two feet high, found at Taunton
long after the furnace operations had ceased.*

A B O V E : *Benjamin Randolph's ornate business card during his famous days as a cabinetmaker in Philadelphia. Original card was 7 1/2 by 9 3/8 inches.*

R I G H T : *Benjamin Randolph chair. One of six "sample chairs" attributed to Randolph and now in the Stampler-Blackwell Parlor at Winterthur Museum.*

7 S. Pettit & C. Shinn went with moulders to Atsion.

13 The gentlemen pipe provers came this evening.

14 Pipe men left for Phila. Finished proving pipes.

15 Filled the Furnace at 6 P.M. and put fire in. Wentling drunk.

16 Put ore in furnace at 6 A.M. Put Branch Pipes in Boat.

17 Drawed the gate 15 minutes before 7 A.M. Thomas Estell drunk.

19 Saml. & M. Adams went Atsion after their tools.

22 Made no pipe on a/c rain.

23 Deep Run water gates blowed.

26 Made no Pipes today. Mr. Bartine came and preached at 10 A.M.

27 No Pipes on a/c of bad iron.

30 Saml. Pettit went to Atsion to take the proving machine.

October

3 Went to Atsion with Mother. Iron bad. Lost the Pipe.

4 Whitewashing Forge. No Pipes. Bad iron.

10 Mr. Jesse Richards here. Iron bad.

13 B. Fox's Cabbin burnt up with all his goods. Simon Dailey died last evening. Iron better.

14 Iron good. Made 2 Pipes. Simon Dailey buried at 1 P.M.

15 Capt. Pennington & Capt. Rape arrived from Bermuda.

17 Made 2 Pipes.

18 James Adams, Sr. died this morning. Pipe moulders done nothing.

19 Started with corpse to Atsion. Made 1 Pipe.

28 S. Brown started to Phila. with load of castings.

November

9 Pipe provers and machine came this evening.

15 M. Mick came A.M. well grogg'd. Mr. Estell here.

22 Tin pedler here. Made no Pipes good. Iron bad.

23 Made no pipes. Iron bad. Doctors here.

27 Made 2 Pipes.

29 Snow this morning. Mr. Walker went to Landing. Boatmen settled.

December

3 A load of flour and a load of beef came.

6 Vessel arrived with Hearth Stone.

14 Proved all the Pipes. Mr. John Richards came.

15 Messrs. Pipe Provers left for Batsto. M. Pettit left for Batsto with Proving Machine. Mr. J. Richards left for Atsion.

19 Rain. Love Feast & Sacrament A.M. Mr. Bartine preach'd at 11 A.M.

21 Several after a bear.

22 Mr. Riley came this evening with Pork. Took the last of the Pipes to the Landing.

23 Took a/c of Castings on Bank.

24 Took Burthen off Furnace half past 4 o'clock A.M. Furnace blow'd out about 5 P.M. Mr. Richards left for Atsion.

25 Snow. Mr. Walker went to Landing. Several hunting. [No note of Christmas].

28 Pipe men settled. Mr. Abbett killed a deer.

30 Snowed all day. Cutting up Pork. Shoeing mules.

1 8 2 0

January

1 Very cold. 9 men went hunting and killed 44 rabbits.

2 Furnace men killed 114 rabbits this day.

13 This day Mr. Walker moved his Family to Mays Landing. Cold.

Note: This marks a change in management from Lewis Walker to John Richards, a second cousin of Samuel, Jesse, etc. Walker established his own forge near Mays Landing, and became quite active in politics.

15 Filled ice house today. John Babington went to Atsion.

20 Turned the Furnace Wheel P.M. Cloudy.

27 Two teams hauling ore down canal.

February

1 Took an inventory of Stock.

6 Samuel Adams went to Atsion yesterday.

9 Mrs. Walker had a fine son this morning.

10 Snow P.M. Mr. Richards moved from Atsion to Weymouth.

11 Teams returned to Atsion. Mr. Walker and Mr. Richards went to Coaling.

14 Making preparations for gardening

16 Anvil in forge broke this afternoon.

17 Shinn left for Atsion A.M. Forge not going. Hail today. I. Penn drunk. Leroy groggy.

18 Shinn retd. with Anvil. Forge not going.

23 Team brot bellows shaft. Mr. Richards went to Landing.

24 Mr. Richards left for Atsion. Champion after timber for Forge.

28 Mr. Richards left for Washington Furnace.

March

1 Danl. Frazure repairing bridge.

6 S. Prickett took 30c Bar Iron to Landing, Beef came.

9 School commenced this morning. Teams went Landing and brot last of the Mountain Ore.

14 Mules team went to Landing after brick.

16 Took 3 tons Bar Iron to Landing.

17 Mr. Richards trimming and putting up Grape Vines.

19 Mrs. Babington had a fine daughter P.M.

23 Began boating ore from Pennypot.

29 Three teams left for Atsion. Planting potatoes.

April

6 Wentling began Forge chimney. Doct. Fisler here. Mrs. Richards was bled. Cold.

13 Carpenters working at the Bridge.

15 All hands raising ore up the Pond.

16 People at Meeting House but had no Preacher. Doct. Fisler left for Port Elizabeth.

19 Woods on fire. 2 Pedlars here.

23 Mrs. Babington departed this life about 11 A.M. All hands fighting fire. James Adams, Jr., left for Speedwell.

24 Mrs. Babington buried about 2 P.M.

25 All hands fighting fire. Mrs. Champion came with herring.

26 Wentling finished the Forge chimney. Mr. Richards & Mr. Walker left for Phila. P.M. and took the Atsion books.

27 Making preparations to start forge again.

May

1 Forge started again. 2 Fires.

4 Mr. Richards & others hunting ore.

8 Training at Mays Landing. Aunt Rosy went with Cake and Beans to Training. Some little fighting.

17 Saml. Pettit took blind woman to Atsion.

24 Two fish waggons here.

June

2 Mr. Richards painting sulkey. Mr. Brewer here from Washington Furnace.

7 Training at Mays Landing. One battle fought. All ret'd this evening except the Schoolmaster.

8 Schoolmaster ret'd this morning.

12 Mr. Samuel & Mr. Jesse Richards here & Mr. White.

13 Mr. Richards put Henry to the Sulkey last evening.

14 Thomas Estelle's wife had a daughter A.M. One of the coal teams left for Martha Furnace.

20 Esq. Watson & Uncle Mark [Adams] left for Woodbury pr. Stage.

21 Coal stack caught fire this morning. Wm. Meskelley not well.

23 Ploughing in meadow. Burning brush. Man here from Hanover. Women in swimming, P.M.

July

6 Fire in swamp and crossed the Canal. Both Stages loaded with passengers.

15 Mrs. Wentling had twins last evening, a son and daughter.

16 Old Mrs. Wentling [mother-in-law of above—Ed.] departed this life about 3 P.M. Mr. Barting preach'd at 10 A.M.

17 Two waggons started to Atsion with Corpse at 9 A.M. Anvil broke in Forge.

26 Babington drawing spindles. Forge hammer broke.

August

2 Cleaned the Store A.M. Mrs. Richards and Aunt Rosy whortleberrying.

5 Mr. Richards killed a pig this evening. Mr. Walker and family came.

7 Mr. Richards went to Etna Furnace. Team from Batsto after Stove Patterns.

17 Anvil broke in Forge. Mail Stage came this way.

18 Mr. Richards and John Adams hunting ore but found none.

19 John Babington and Priscilla Huffman married last night.

25 Mr. Haskins, Mrs. Richards & Mr. Sevier came this afternoon.

29 Killed a Rattlesnake at the Blacksmith Shop.

30 Mrs. Wentling here with her twins.

September

4 Mr. Richards shooting crows. But one fire in Forge going.

7 The Sun eclipsed this morning. Shinn, Pettit hauling rails.

21 Cleaning out Moulding Room to put coal in.

22 Began to cut the buckwheat and husking corn. Capt. Rape here.

27 Drawing Iron for Capt. Rape.

October

3 Finished cutting buckwheat. Ox team done nothing.

5 Camp Meeting began near Port Elizabeth.

6 James Adams, Jr. & Wife had a fine daughter last night.

7 John Adams had a Husking Frolic this evening.

8 None went to Camp Meeting from here.

19 Uriah Steelman fixing bellows for Forge.

23 Mrs. Wells commenced with her School this morning. Teams came from Millville for Iron.

26 Forge Hammer broke.

27 C. Shinn went to Batsto for Forge Hammer.

November

1 Making apple butter last night. Making Sour Crout this evening.

2 Made Peach Butter last night. Boiling Pickle for beef.

7 Mrs. Barns & Mrs. Sherry had each a fine daughter last night.

9 B. Barns began work again this morning.

10 S. B. Finch in love with a young lady. He has some notion of making a grab. Nights rather cold to sleep alone. Heavy snow this morning.

13 Mrs. Green had a fine daughter last night.

15 Adams carting wood with Oxen.

16 James Adams brought the anvil block.

21 Wentling at work at anvil block.

24 Mr. Walker, Mr. Richards, Miss Ludwig left for Phila. about 3 A.M.

December

4 Expected a company of hunters but they did not come. S. Bartlett stocking Forge.

7 Company of hunters came from Phila.

8 All the hunters went out in the woods (except Mr. S. Richards) but killed nothing. Happy times this evening.

9 All hands up before daylight. Hunters left for Batsto early this morning. Mr. Richards left for Atsion.

12 Fixing Forge today. Snowed some little.

15 Vessel in with potatoes.

20 Mrs. Richards had 12 chickens hatched last night. Anvil broke in Forge. Began taking out anvil block.

21 Putting in new anvil block. Pettit getting frame for Pork House.

24 Mr. Criskinch came last night and frightened some almost into fits.

25 Mr. Walker's mother came. Several went hunting and killed 1 Bear, 1 Deer, 1 Pheasant and 35 Rabbits. Shot 40 Christmas Guns this evening.

28 Forge started again this A.M.

1 8 2 1

January

1 All hands shooting. Eslow tipsy, B. Barns ditto. Killed 25 Rabbits.

2 A load of Coal burned up on the road. Two loads of pork &
two loads of Rye came this evening.

6 Moved the Pork Tubs. 2 Loads of Shell came.

7 Snow. Nearly 12 inches deep.

11 A sleigh here this morning.

17 Snowed last night and this forenoon. Quite deep.

18 Very good sleighing.

19 Four sleds with Rye came this evening.

21 S. Prickett, Th. Adams, E. Downs & Mr. Prickett went sleighing to the Glass House. Mrs. Eslow had fine son last night.

22 Four sleds with Rye and Corn came P.M.

24 Sleigh broke near here. Very cold. Forge froze fast.

28 Mr. & Mrs. Richards, Mrs. Wells, Miss Ludwig and myself
went sleighing to Mrs. Meskelleys P.M.

1 8 2 5

February

3 Repairing Stomping Mill. Very cold.

8 Mr. Richards at Election at Cammels Inn.

9 Election at J. Adams Inn. Mr. Richards and his force went.

14 Messrs. Samuel & Thomas Richards came for purpose of
altering Furnace Wheel.

17 Lumber came for W. Wheel.

23 Mr. Jesse Richards & his Founder here.

26 Proving pipes today.

March

8 Putting in Hearth. Teams went to Batsto for brick.

10 Col. (Richard) Wescoat decd. 9 o'clock last evening.

11 Anvil broke today. Mr. & Mrs. Richards went to the burial.
P.M. Etna Furnace sent after iron.

14 Dr. Fisler & son here. R. Meskelley operated on by them.
Pleasant.

17 Pulling down F. Gearing. (Probably Forge),

21 Sent to Atsion for anvil.

22 Shinn returned with anvil & was some tipsy.

23 Forge started today at noon. Gear pedler here.

24 Mr. S. Richards, Mr. Dotterer & two workmen came A.M. Dotterers men began to work P.M. (fixing Furnace Wheel).

April

2 Mr. Dotterer left for Atsion. Finished and started wheel.
8 Hoisted Flood Gates P.M.
9 Raised the Saw Mill P.M.
12 Put fire in the Furnace this evening at 8 o'clock.
14 Started Furnace 20 minutes before six P.M. G. Shinn & C. Shinn tipsy.
15 Let out the mettle at the same hour as they started.
19 Four vessels in with ore.
20 Mr. Lane sent for Furnace shaft.
28 Mr. Richards painting bellows.

May

16 Pipe prover came from York. The pipes would not do for him.
23 Salt came today. Teams took pipe.
30 Started the Sawmill today.
31 Wm. Taylor killed. [Taylor was a Forge stocker—Ed.]

June

4 Let the mettle into Pigs this evening.
6 Four Misionaries here. Proved some pipes.
11 Flood gates give way A.M. All hands at them P.M.
13 J. Richards returned A.M. from Union Furnace. Proving pipes.
16 Furnace blowed at 12 o'clock.
28 Put in new springs to bellows. Clay boated down the river.

July

1 Finished cutting grain. David Seaman working at store.
7 Mr. Frambus here after Iron. Forge Hammer broke.
9 Forge men tearing down Forge.
11 Started young mule team today. Repairing Forge.
12 One of the young mules choked to death.
16 Trying the pipes. Teams brought shells. Very busy in store.
22 One Forge fire got in operation.

25 All but Mr. Richards on a Huckleberry Party.
26 Boat took pipes and pig iron.
29 Water low in Pond today.
30 S. Pettit went to Absecon. W. Rubart to Atsion.

August

2 Repairing piers at the house.
3 Teams took Pipes. No Pipes on the Landing now.
9 Opened the Crockery. Teams took pipe.
10 Sold considerable Crockery today.
11 Mrs. Richards spun 3 3/32 # wool & Mary Pool 2¼ # wool.*
    * Note: Mrs. Richards spun on a little wheel, Mrs. Pool on
     a large one.
12 Constable took David Seaman with a warrant.
26 Forge man putting in Hammer.

September

12 David Seaman left here this noon. Proving pipes.
14 Mr. Richards took D. Seaman at the Landing and searched
    his goods and found his tools.
16 Millville sent for Iron. Beef came this evening.
22 Killed a Bare this evening.
    Note: The Mount Holly Mirror reported this event as
    follows: "A hunting party composed of Messrs. William
    Meskelley, David Sherry, John Phifer and Thomas Adams,
    Jr. went out after deer . . . and perceived a large Bear
    advancing toward them. He was first noticed by Mr.
    Adams, who fired, his comrades following in immediate
    succession. This salutation proved too warm for Mr. Bruin.
    . . . He measured seven feet in length [another paper said
    7′ 3″] and five feet in circumference, and weighed three
    hundred and sixty pounds. Upon dressing him, a large
    quantity of buckshot was found in his body, entirely healed
    over."
24 J. Penn went to Atsion. Iron bad today.
30 Husking corn. Beef came. Clay boated down river by R. Tyler.

October

6 Teams took bar iron. Stage came this way.

7 D. Champion carted 4 pipes in place of five.

25 Quilting at B. Lafferty's. Proving pipes.

26 Mr. Rape here. Shells came. Made Sour Crout this evening.

November

5 Rape & Bowen launched a Sloop today.

21 School began today.

24 Mending Flood Gates.

25 Beef came. Thos. B. Sood here.

December

3 Finished proving pipes. Oysters came P.M. Wm. Meskelley hunting.

16 Teams carting ore down canal.

18 Prayer meeting A.M. Dr. Pitney came P.M.

20 Pork came. One of the Locks broken.

22 Took the Burthen off Furnace at 10 P.M. Cutting up pork.

23 Blowed out the Furnace at 8 A.M. McLaughlin tipsy.

1 8 2 6

January

9 Coaled 8576 cords last year. Quite warm.

20 Repairing Stamping Mill. Shells came today.

26 Dressing Hearthstone. Hooping big pork tub. Getting cedar logs.

27 Filling the ice house.

February

3 Teams went to Pennypot after lumber. Atsion came after Iron.

6 Putting bottoms in old Bellows.

11 Carpenters getting the Bellows tub into Store for Pork Tub. Finished the Hearth.

15 Forgemen hunting. Amos Ireland decd. A.M. Oysters came.

17 Laying the floor in the Bridge House. A. Ireland buried.
21 Forge broke the hammer. Began to boat sand for moulding.
23 Mr. James Richards from Pennsylvania came.
24 Batsto sent after Iron.
25 Bot 3 doz. straw hats today. Filled large pork tub with pickle.
28 Put fire in Furnace after 5 P.M.

March

1 Put burthen on Furnace 10 o'clock.
2 Furnace started after 1 P.M. Mrs. Richards drew the Gate ½ past one P.M.
4 Teams took tank plates. Mr. Richards & son went to Atsion.
8 Town meeting at the Landing. Mr. R. bot a horse and gig.
20 Gaskill making Mill Gears today.
22 Making gears today.

April

3 Samuel Richards came P.M. Some goods came up from the Sloop.
14 Sawmill crank broken.
18 Several fish waggons here. Quite warm & high winds.
22 Finished proving pipes.

May

6 Patrick Dougherty fell from the Coal Box.
7 Prayer Meeting. Mr. & Mrs. Richards went to P. Dougherty's in the coaling.
11 Planted W. Melons today.
18 Proving pipes. Mr. Irick here. All hands went to fight fire.
24 Washing wool today. L. Woodlan working at the house.
30 Forge going. Mr. & Mrs. Richards left for Phila.

June

1 Mr. Richards ret. with an assortment of Dry Goods.
13 Making a new Moulding Room. Stage went this way.
14 Moulders lost several pipes.
16 Proving pipes all day. Samuel Richards left for Batsto.
20 The Pennypot gates blowed A.M.
28 Cradling rye. Forge started today.

July

4 Plowing corn. Jesse Richards sent after Bar Iron.
5 Musquetoes plenty.
7 Martha Matthews began to cook at the house.
14 Repairing Furnace Bellows.
18 Building an addition to the Moulding Room. Proving pipes.
19 Teams took pipes and Lamp Posts.
31 Jacob Wentling's house and all his goods burned up today.

August

2 Mark Richards, Mr. Lane & Co. here.
4 M. Lock brot mellons. Casterated 4 mules today. Warm.
9 Forge Hammer broke. Prayer Meeting this evening.
17 Sloop Hamilton came in.
18 Five ore sloops in the River.
21 The other Forge fire started A.M. Drawing coal in W. Coaling.

September

11 Jesse Richards & wife here. Mr. Heritage here from P. Mills.
13 Trimming oaks at the Mansion House.
18 John Pettit quit the Furnace. Robart began keeping.
23 Wm. Bartlet and R. Adams married.

October

4 Proved some pipes. Martha teams here.
5 Mr. Winters here with clothing. Weighing pipes.
9 Forge Hammer broke P.M.
11 Election at Jacob Adams Inn.
21 Setting anvil block.

November

6 Framing Casting House.
14 Mr. Richards went to the appeal of taxation.
18 Mr. Dilks [Teacher] came.
20 School began.

December

3 Prayer Meeting A.M. E. Champion began to work at the house.

7 Forge started today.

18 Some snow fell. Mr. Roberts sent corn.

22 Forge Hammer broke.

23 Watch Night meeting. Mr. West here.

25 Christmas. H. Shinn tipsy. Mr. & Mrs. Richards went to Lewis M. Walker's.

1 8 2 7

January

4 Forge Hammer broke.

9 Some rain A.M. S. Richards came and surveyed today.

11 Wm. Hazelton brot pork. Drizelly weather.

18 Took Burthen off Furnace 3 P.M.

19 Blowed out 3 o'clock A.M. Benj. Barns & M. Pettit tipsy.

Jesse's Folly: Washington Furnace

Experience, it is said, is the name we give to our mistakes. The most unfortunate mistake in the career of Jesse Richards was Washington Furnace. No records survive to show the size of his financial loss there, a loss which haunted many of his later days. But the crowning indignity of all was when one of his own employes acquired Washington Furnace and made a success of it.

By yet another paradoxical twist of events, Washington Furnace village which Jesse abandoned became a thriving, prosperous community—one of New Jersey's better resorts which today is called Lakewood. In contrast, many of the towns which once surrounded big ironworks are now heaps of rubble and cellar holes hidden deep in the forests.

Lakewood is located on the south branch of the Metedeconk. Its lower reaches, below Laurelton, are lined with colorful cottages, often in pleasantly wooded settings. Come spring and innumerable pleasure boats pass in gay parade. Many follow the river as it widens to empty into the upper part of Barnegat Bay; and there the yachts, cabin cruisers, and outboards navigating the Intercoastal Waterway mingle in bewildering maritime traffic. Throughout the area, the accent is on pleasure.

This was not so a century and a half ago. The Metedeconk then, as now, was a gracious stream. But what little traffic it bore consisted of schooners and scows bearing cut timber from sawmills well inland, and, later, cargoes of iron destined for New York. The stream itself was chiefly a corridor through wilderness as settlers were sparse in that part of Monmouth County. A rough road led from Toms River to Freehold; a rougher one found its way northeast to Squankum; and little more than a wagon track ran through the woods along the south branch of the river to the Three Partners Sawmill. Timber was abundant. Waterpower to run the mill was handy and the river itself would float the wood to market. But business seems not to have been very brisk in 1814 for the two partners who owned it were happy to sell the mill, plus 70 acres of land, for only $850.

The purchaser was Jesse Richards, then running Batsto for his father. Eager to start out on his own, Jesse learned that much bog ore was to be found in that part of Monmouth County and decided it would be a good spot to erect a furnace. While the location was a bit outside the area usually considered piney country, he knew that 18 miles farther north the Tinton Falls Iron Works had smelted bog iron well over a hundred years earlier. In his eagerness

Jesse apparently neglected to test the composition of the ore very thoroughly, or so he indicated later. He just moved in swiftly so that the Three Partners Sawmill soon was dwarfed by a sizeable furnace town.

Jesse Richards had purchased a half-interest in eight tracts—a total of 71 acres—from James Skidmore, on June 13, 1814, including a half-interest in the Three Partners Sawmill.[1] Those lands were on the south side of the Metedeconk River, and the price was $425. Three days later Jesse bought the other half-interest in the lands and sawmill from Henry Waggoner (or Wagener), also for $425,[2] making the cost for that main property $850. That same day Skidmore sold him an additional 30 acres in the area for $650.[3] Tradition has it that the sawmill was built in 1800 and that the "Three Partners" were three Skidmore brothers. The date is probably correct, but deed records show that James Skidmore did not acquire his half-interest until May 3, 1804, and then from Henry Perrine; Waggoner purchased his half from John Bray on June 15, 1814.

That same month Jesse Richards negotiated agreements for rights to dig ore for 50 years on various other tracts totaling more than 150 acres. The lessors were Joseph Goodenough, Solomon Ketcham, Daniel Emmons, Thomas Riddle, and Peter Cook. The cost of these rights varied from $40 to $60 depending on the size of each tract.

Little time was lost in erecting what Jesse decided to call Washington Furnace. He put diggers to work, and soon mule teams were hauling ore. The work began, of all days, on the Fourth of July. Brick for the furnace was made on the site and in August two men, John Ayres and James Cotterall, were hired "to raise clay for the brickmakers." One Joseph Shamard was engaged to dig for stone; John White was paid at the rate of $25 a month to get timber; and Henry Chary was hired in November "to take care of the riding horses and six mules, to cut firewood, and to do all work required about the [ironmaster's] house." In July of

1814 the laborers' payroll had included 20 men; by August the total was 30; by September 46.

From the start Jesse's right-hand man appears to have been M. Woolston. He was hired in May 1814; he kept most of the surviving account books.[4] He supervised the extensive surveying done that summer by James H. Newell, who had David Estell, Nehemiah Francis, and David Ytle as chain-bearers. Interesting is the fact that Henry Waggoner, from whom Jesse had purchased half the land, was working as ax-man on the surveying team.

Those were days of great activity. Carpenters were brought in; workers' houses were built; on October 18 a barn was completed; construction of the casting house began on November 15; and on the 17th the carpenters were so fired by enthusiasm—or were so hungry—that they "gave a day gratis to build a kitchen." The "scales and lever" were put in place; and by December 15 the casting house had been completed. During this period a gristmill was erected, and later a school house, with wooden benches.

All the while, the old Three Partners Sawmill was providing the lumber with Joseph Britton "hewing timber" and James Cox working at the "Butting Saw." Work on the furnace itself was going forward. Late in October "hearthstone was being carted from Red Bank." The stack was well under way; and since winter was just ahead there would be plenty of time to build the "in-walls" and install the blast machinery. By March of 1815 a lime kiln had been built, work on the bellows had started, the bridge house was raised, and in April "C. Willis and Elias Emmett were working on the Boshes."

Not until May of 1815, however, could the furnace be put into blast. These notes from the record tell the story:

May 4   Put fire in the Furnace.
May 10   Furnace blowed this evening at 11 o'clock.

June 18   Furnace stopped at 11 o'clock to dress the bellows.

June 21   Samuel Richards, Jesse Richards and Jesse Evans [from Martha] came here today.

June 26   Furnace blowed at 4 o'clock this afternoon.

There was a particular reason for the visit of Samuel and Jesse Richards on that 21st day of June. Even before the furnace had been constructed "Brother Jesse" found himself in financial difficulty and by February of 1815 had sent a hurry call for help from "Brother Samuel" who then was the richest of the Richardses.

Result of this appeal was an agreement, on February 20, 1815, in which Samuel was given "one-third part of and in the new Furnace erected in Monmouth County . . . called Washington Furnace." The price to "Brother Samuel" was "seven hundred and fifty dollars . . . plus one full third part of the actual cost and charges of the said Furnace, Lands, Stock and Premises." It was further agreed that "the said Furnace, works and Estate shall be carried on in Partnership between them . . ." In a codicil Jesse acknowledged receiving the $750. How much he received against the third part of his costs is not recorded.

More than $750; more than the great skill of "Brother Samuel"; more even than the advice of "Father William" Richards, who was called in later, was necessary to help Washington Furnace.

In September of 1815 the Furnace was halted on the 4th, for undisclosed reasons, and put back in blast on the 19th. On the 27th of that month there is a note: "Began to make Kentlage." This is iron ballast for ships. By October 25 "fifty tons were finished," and on December 28, at "six o'clock in the evening," the Furnace was blown out. It had been a brief and scarcely fruitful working season.

Eighteen Sixteen has long been known as "the year without a summer." It was a particularly rough year at Washington Furnace. Smelting began on April 6 and continued through a chilly Spring. On June 7 and 8 there was severe frost; on the 10th it is noted "Froze Ice last night. Killed the garden." On June 25 "Captain John Rogers got drowned scowing Iron" near Toms River.

Waterpower became a problem and in September of 1816 a dam was built over Watering Place Brook, a small nearby tributary of the Metedeconk. The flume of the gristmill collapsed on September 17. Even snow came early, on December 2. But somehow, through it all, the Furnace had been kept going much of the time. It was blown out on December 12, "making 8 months and 2 days of a Blast.— 509 tons of iron exclusive of scraps." This total, however, was only a little more than half the average annual production of other Richards family furnaces.

Two unprofitable years had passed. What was Jesse to do? There seems to have been no disposition then to blame the poor quality of the ore. Sources of trouble were sought in other directions, and in 1817 some drastic changes were made. On February 28, Woolston, the manager, was called to Batsto to see his boss, Jesse Richards, "on business." Two weeks later Woolston "resigned," and on April 3 it is noted that "John Richards moved here this day." John Richards, who was to become manager of Weymouth a few years later, was Jesse's second cousin. He had been working at Atsion for Samuel Richards, who probably hoped that his prótegé could salvage his one-third investment in Washington Furnace.

John Richards, however, had no better luck than his predecessor. The year 1817 proved even more unprofitable than 1816. An effort was made, however. Michael Mick was brought in from Martha Furnace to "help Tom Baxter put in the hearth." The furnace was fired on the afternoon of April 29 and put into blast on May 1. Jesse Richards himself traveled from Batsto to be on hand for the "blowing" which took place at 9 o'clock that evening. And for a time, all seemed well.

In September—at one A.M. on the 22nd—the furnace stopped for reasons unrecorded. It was back in blast six days later. On November 16 it was "stopped up," with production halted again. Four days later it was running and was not halted until New Year's Eve when "ice stopped the water wheel."

The Furnace was blown out at midnight of January 1, 1818. It was not to be started again by Jesse Richards. No production figures for 1817 are available but almost certainly the iron output was smaller than ever.

Judging by the account books not even an effort was made to resume operations in 1818. The scanty entries for that year tell the story:

January	Only 9 men working.
February	Eight men working.
May	Four men working; planting corn.
June	Four men working.
July	Three men working.
October	William Richards, Esq., here this afternoon. [At the age of eighty, the elder Richards had traveled from Mount Holly to see what hope there was to salvage Washington Furnace. The following entries indicate that he advised against throwing more good money after bad.]
November	Four men working.
December	Two men working.

And there the record book ends. The Richards era at Washington Furnace was over.

"Jesse's Folly" was the first ironworks failure in the Richards family. How much money was lost does not appear, but it is indicated that the sum was substantial. Not only were Jesse and Samuel losers but their father as well. Little was salvaged from the works. Some lumber was cut over the years, but there is no indication how much. A few bits and pieces of the outlying tracts were sold. But Washington Furnace itself stood gaunt and idle for about 15 years.

It was then that one of Jesse Richards' own employees at Batsto managed to acquire the furnace—and make it pay.

Joseph W. Brick first appears in the Batsto books in May of 1826, as a hired hand. He may have been there earlier in some capacity. Later Brick was put to work in the Batsto store, and there his quick-thinking, administrative ability, and skill with figures so impressed his superiors that by July of 1826 he was made clerk of the works. This post he held until about 1830. Judging by the neatness and clarity of his bookkeeping entries during that period, Joseph Brick was careful, clever, and shrewd. More shrewd, certainly, than his employer Jesse Richards suspected; and also gifted with sharp powers of observation.

Brick learned much at Batsto. He learned the technique of iron-making, and what was probably more important, the accounting details which often made the difference between success and failure in that highly competitive field. He learned management methods and undoubtedly noted the weaknesses in those at Batsto, which so long kept it close to the edge of bankruptcy. As clerk, Brick also was in a position to learn the identity of Batsto customers. Above all, he knew the inside story of the failure at Washington Furnace; and he knew also that while Jesse Richards claimed that the ore was no good, he was having it dug and hauled for use at Batsto. Jesse Richards himself went to Washington Furnace as late as May of 1827 to help hunt additional ore; and the Batsto books show that Washington ore was arriving there as late as 1830.

When Joseph W. Brick purchased the Washington Furnace property in 1833, he knew quite well what he was getting. He knew that: the ore was far from worthless, with more careful management there was a chance of success; and the old furnace stack was still worth rehabilitating. His inside knowledge may also have told him how to avoid some of the mistakes which made Washington Furnace fail in the first place.

Whether Jesse Richards was aware of Brick's ambitions, it is difficult to say. Probably not. More than three years elapsed between the date Jesse conveyed the "tract commonly called Washington Furnace" to William Remsen, of Dover Township[5]—April 12, 1830—and the date Remsen sold the property to Brick, September 30, 1833.[6] More than likely Jesse's thoughts about Brick's purchase were tinged with contempt or even pity for a fool barging in where the Richards had trod in vain.

Brick was a man of action. He restored the furnace and changed its name, to Bergen Iron Works. The surviving village was named Bricksburg, after himself: he was less modest than Jesse Richards. A plank road was built to a landing near Butcher's Forge, on the lower Metedeconk from which schooners sailed regularly to New York. Most important of all, Brick began combining his local bog ore with imported Scotch pig iron and smelted the mixture in a cupola near his furnace. This same mixture was used by Jesse Richards but it is impossible to say who used it first.

By 1844 the population of Bricksburg had grown to over 200. The Bergen Iron Works had its own store and its own post office. The post office was opened on June 22, 1848, although Jesse Richards is credited with having started the first mail service in 1815, by means of mounted messengers to Freehold where connection was made with mail stages stopping there. The Bergen Iron Works even had its own currency, issued during the national suspension of gold payments between 1837 and 1842.[7] Bergen Iron Works "money" was accepted not only at the company store but by most shopkeepers in the surrounding country.

Somehow, Joseph W. Brick had succeeded where Jesse Richards had failed. Bergen Iron Works had prospered on the very spot where Washington Furnace had lost a lot of money. That Jesse Richards viewed all this with something less than pleasure is scarcely surprising, especially when Brick began underbidding him for his old customers.

On July 29, 1844, Jesse wrote one of those customers, John C. Hains, as follows:

Mr. Brick cannot make good iron from the ore he uses, and cannot obtain good ore on terms that will answer to make good iron. His furnace being landlocked, he has to use the ore from the neighborhood of the Furnace which is . . . the worst kind of iron. I built the Furnace he now owns and abandoned her on account of the quality of the iron.

Unmentioned was the fact that up to 1830, Jesse had been having that very Washington ore carted to Batsto for use there.

As Jesse Richards was to outlive Joseph Brick, so was Batsto to outlive the Bergen Iron Works. After Brick's death, the property went to his five children; before long, according to Boyer, it was sold to "Campbell & Pharo" who in 1854 moved the plant to Perth Amboy. Subsequently the waterpower was used to run a new gristmill, and still later a silk mill.

Far greater changes, however, were in store for the still-wooded region of the Three Partners Sawmill. As the years passed, roads had been improved; not paved, of course, but still improved. Then word spread that the area was particularly healthy and soon bog ore and iron were forgotten. In the wake of the Civil War people became increasingly resort-conscious; and while Bricksburg was not on the ocean, there was rest and beauty amid its surrounding woods and waters.

In 1866 the Bricksburg Land Company was organized and began buying large tracts in the area. A town was laid out threaded by a broad and tree-lined avenue. Lots were sold. Eventually the old silk mill was used for a community house, the river was dammed not for water power but to form one of the attractive lakes which now grace the community. Still more lots were sold; hotels began to go up, and soon vacations in Bricksburg became "the thing to do."

On March 20, 1880, it was decided to change the name to Lakewood as befitted a high-grade resort. Some felt that Bricksburg sounded like an industrial town where bricks were made. By then Joseph Brick had been largely forgotten so that few if any objected to abolishing whatever memorial the ironmaster may have had in mind when he gave his name to the community. From that moment on, progress from wilderness to a fine city was uninterrupted. The lakes still gleam; the parks are green and inviting; and the wagon tracks of old are broad modern highways making Lakewood cheerfully accessible from all points of the compass.

Explorers of southern New Jersey may ask where in Lakewood is the spot upon which Washington Furnace once stood? The question can be answered. The site is on the easterly side of the main street (New Jersey Route 9) almost directly across from the principal lake. There they will see the borough waterworks: and that is it. Portions of the walls of its sizeable building are very old, as close examination of the brickwork will show. Moreover, it is the logical location. Splashing past, in a spillway running beneath the street from the lake dam, are the waters of the Metedeconk; the waters which powered the ironworks.

Further downstream, although not easy to find, are some bits of ruins which once may have been the cupola, or perhaps the Metedeconk Forge which had a brief existence around 1825. Nearby, but unlocated as to site, once stood the Three Partners Sawmill.

All this was wilderness then. And most of it—once— Jesse Richards' folly! But folly no more; the portly lord of Batsto little knew what he had started.

Three at Hampton

There are, or were, three Hamptons: Hampton Furnace, Hampton Gate, and Hampton Lower Forge. None was ever easy to find, and even when the sites can be located today there is little to see. Yet to find the locations is challenging to explorers of South Jersey forests, if only to imagine the furnaces and forges that existed then and the nearby hamlets where the ironworkers and their families lived.

The best way to Hampton Furnace lies through a narrow roadway in the pines. (Since this is private property and not State land, one should arrange in advance for permission to make the trip.) These have often been called whispering pines, although there is much disagreement as to their alleged whisperings. For some there is a quick sense of foreboding upon entering these woods; for most it becomes easier to believe in ghosts here. And if there still is, or ever was, a "Jersey Devil," it surely would be seen in this shadowy setting.

The path in the pines veers off east from U.S. Route 206 a short distance north of Atsion. Before long the gravel road emerges from the tree shadows into the bright open land of the cranberry bogs. Iron was the industry here a century and a half ago, but the growing of cranberries has been its successor enterprise for well over fifty years. The stretches of bogs—still rich in iron as well as berries—are broken by stretches of forest. One passes over a succession of cranberry dams as the road continues to an area still flecked with chunks of iron slag. These are no longer obvious; it is simpler if a native points them out. Here, in any case, is the general location of old Hampton Furnace.

A pond at this spot was once called Hampton Furnace Pond, and not far away a second small lake was known as the Forge Pond. The latter was the more important since Hampton Forge continued operation long after the furnace was shut down. It reached one of its most prosperous periods after the tract was acquired by Samuel Richards and integrated with his ironworks at Atsion. Both these ponds lie in the headwaters of the Batsto River, at the junction of Robbins Run. It is good to pause here and survey the receding woodlands. One quickly feels a pervading sense of isolation; and it becomes easy to imagine how infinitely remote this region must have seemed in Hampton's heyday.

Hampton Furnace was built in 1795, by two men: Clayton Earl and Richard Stockton. They had purchased the Hampton lands on April 10, 1795, from Restore and Mary Shinn. On the property at that time was the Unknown Mill, a curious name for what appears to have been a sawmill. Earl and Stockton also acquired a half-interest in another sawmill "called Mount Skit Mill," including its "mill, houses, outhouses, gears, dam and millpond."

In deeds, Clayton Earl is described as an "ironmaster." Three years earlier he had been one of the builders of Hanover Furnace, on the Rancocas Creek a few miles east of what is now Brown's Mills. One year later Earl was to buy a half-interest in Pleasant Mills and its wool-working plant. This latter deal—in which iron was nowhere concerned—invites the assumption that Earl was primarily a speculator. He kept his share of Hanover Furnace only two years, and his interest in Hampton—legally, at least—lasted only a month, for he sold his share in that during May 1795. But somehow during his brief tenure the furnace was built: his deed of purchase mentions only sawmills; his deed of sale specifies "that certain furnace called Hampton Furnace."

The buyers of Earl's half share of Hampton were William Lane and John Godfrey, merchants of Philadelphia.[1] They, too, were speculators, but if the buying and selling prices in the deeds are correct, they got their fingers burned. They paid Clayton Earl 4,000 pounds for his interest; they sold it for 2,562 pounds, 10 shillings. But the purchasers this time were serious iron operators: George Garrit Ashbridge and his brother William Ashbridge.[2]

Meanwhile, Richard Stockton, original partner of Earl, had died, and on January 2, 1797 his heirs—Mary, his widow, and William and Benjamin Stockton—sold their half interest to the Ashbridges.[3] Thus when they acquired Earl's half, they owned all of Hampton Furnace. They operated it jointly until 1810, but in that year George Ashbridge sold his interest to his brother so that thereafter William Ashbridge owned the Hampton Furnace outright.

About 1810 the furnace had been supplemented with a forge nearby, and a second forge several miles below on the Batsto River. During their joint ownership the brothers had acquired several thousand additional acres of land. An interesting record of this period is the statement from the Philadelphia Society for the Promotion of Agriculture that castings for a mould board, the invention of David Peacock, were made at Hampton Furnace.[4] Other products were wagon axles, flat and round bar iron, sledge hammers, kettles, skillets, and hollow ware of various kinds.

Not actually a furnace operator himself, William Ashbridge often rented or leased Hampton to others. In 1812, for example, Joseph Doran was assessed for 4,900 acres and a six-fire forge. Probably the furnace was not then in operation. Some years later, according to Charles Boyer, historian, a Joseph Austin ran the forge.

After William Ashbridge's death, an advertisement for sale of Hampton mentions "two forges." That advertisement gives the following description of the Hampton establishment: [5]

This property contains about 20,000 acres of land . . . adjoining the lands of Batsto and Atsion. There has been erected on the premises a large Mansion House, a Furnace, two Forges, a Grist and Sawmill, also stabling sufficient to accommodate 4 teams of horses, and a number of dwelling houses for workmen. There are large tracts of fine timber, numerous deposits of iron ore, and a large body of sand of the quality best suited for making the finest kind of glass.

The water power at the lower forge is allowed to be amply sufficient for a Rolling and Slitting Mill or Cotton Factory.

Possession will be given on the 1st of March, except the Upper Forge, and two or three of the Dwelling Houses . . . which are let till the 1st of July next.

A sale was made "pursuant to an Act of Assembly of the State of New Jersey" naming trustee—Jonas Preston, et al.—for the heirs, minor children named Mary, Jane, and Richard Ashbridge. An auction was conducted at the Merchants Coffee House in Philadelphia, on February 3, 1825, by J. & W. Lippincott & Co. The purchaser was Samuel Richards.

That the actual condition of Hampton was less happy than the advertisement indicated is confirmed by this recitation in the deed from the trustees to Richards: [6]

> . . . the furnace had been burned down, the forge dam broken, the buildings in a state of decay, the real estate unproductive and depreciating in value.

It was this state of affairs which led to the note on Gordon's 1828 "Map of New Jersey" that both Hampton furnace and forge were "in ruins." That was repeated in Gordon's 1834 *Gazeteer*. Consequently it has generally been assumed that Samuel Richards, busy elsewhere, just abandoned Hampton. Records now show this was not so. Gordon certainly can be forgiven for not having made the long trek to Hampton to check the facts for his *Gazetteer*, but well before that time Samuel Richards had rebuilt the forge and operated it until his death. After that his successors kept it going until after 1850. From all accounts it was busier during that period than it had been earlier. But whether Hampton Furnace was in blast during those years is doubtful.

Rebuilding of Hampton Forge took place in 1829, and records show that the work was done by James Colkit for $325. Colkit also built a coal house for $75, and was joined by his sons and Clayton Haines in erecting "a dwelling house and iron house." His bill for the latter work shows:[7]

42 days work himself and Clayton Haines	36.75
His son 24 days at 621/2 [cents. Ed.]	15.00
13 days himself and son	10.00
10# nails . . . and 3 pair hinges	1.10
5 doz screws and handles	.65
5 Gallons Wiskey paid for by himself	2.25

Sketchy yet fairly graphic is the picture of Hampton under Richards ownership as given in some of the Atsion Furnace books. Only the forge is mentioned and the records indicate it was operated as a part of the Atsion establishment. Following are some of the more interesting entries:

June 6, 1836:	Furnace Accts Dr. to Moses Wills for 1 mo 1 day Stocking Forge @ 20	20.77
Aug. 23, 1838:	For Hammer shaft & expenses	40.00
June 27, 1839:	Pd. Jon. P. Taylor for Carpenter work at Hampton	4.82
Oct. 8, 1839:	Furnace acct. for 2 bellows for forge; to Isaac Bozarth for cutting frame for Hampton	
Nov. 30, 1839:	Pd. Jon. P. Taylor for repairing Hampton Forge	13.00
Feb. 1, 1840:	Dr. to Weymouth Furnace for Castings for Forge; two Wrought Iron Twears [tuyeres]	
Mar. 13, 1841:	To Wesley Taylor, timber for anvil block	12.27
May 25, 1841:	Joseph Austin, Dr. to Furnace	
	For old forge hammer	10.00
	For old forge plate	2.03
	For new forge plate	12.02

[Note: Joseph Austin is the man who supposedly moved Hampton Forge equipment to Dover prior to 1830. This purchase suggests that he also bought the old forge on hand from Richards when the latter acquired Hampton]

Although Samuel Richards died in 1842, the forge continued at Hampton as did the works at Atsion. On May 20, 1845, William Bareford was paid $17.25 for repairing the forge, and Thomas Bareford was paid $34.12 1/2 for previous repairs in February. Other entries of this period:

July 1, 1845:   Samuel Hilliard, Dr. to Cash for amt. sent him
                   by Francis Mingin/ bill for hammer shaft of
                   forge   22.51
July 14, 1845:   To Edward B. Thomas of Lumberton for the fol-
                   lowing to go tomorrow to Lumberton by Mingin
                   and Chas. Taylor in 24-mule team to bring iron ore
                   to Hampton Forge
Jan. 23, 1846:   Samuel Richards (Est.) not charged by request of
                   W. Richards for drawing over and altering Iron
                   seat to Forge, including $1 each for labor to Bare-
                   ford, Holloway, Chamberlain and Ashley.
March 12, 1846:   Working Forge by Thomas Bareford, at 20 pr. ton
                   —30 days at Forge Wheel
April 24, 1846:   Timber for Hampton Forge Water Wheel

On August 17, 1846 a general rebuilding program was started at Hampton, and operations continued much as usual.

On June 14, 1848 the books show that Joshua Hilliard delivered some scrap iron at Hampton, and on July 3 of that year Absalom H. Smith was hired to "cart iron from Hampton to Mount Holly."

During 1848 Israel Chew is listed as blacksmith; a new 680-pound hammer was purchased from Weymouth; Thomas Bareford was still working the forge, and in 1850 Philip Souders was helping. Last two entries are:

October 10, 1850: Hampton Mill, Dr. for $150 paid Mark Moore
                   for Iron Wheels
January 1851:   Hampton Forge, Dr. to Mathias Carter for re-
                   pairing wheels, $130.

Washington Township birth records make available some of the names of the laborers at Hampton in those days: Nathan Cheeseman, whose wife, Margaret, had a daughter

Rebecca Ann on June 18, 1849; Jason and Susanna Shinn, who had a son, Charles Henry, born June 22; George and Mary Wells, a son John born July 1; George and Elizabeth Chamberlain, a son George, Jr., born July 27; Samuel and Sarah Wells, a son Samuel, Jr., born November 7; John and Elizabeth Sutt, a daughter Levisa, November 25. Listed as living at Hampton Gate was George Mackey, whose wife had a daughter, Ann Elizabeth, at an unspecified date.

Both the forge records and birth records of Hampton terminate simultaneously, and almost precisely at midcentury. That was the period when competition from Pennsylvania's more efficient anthracite smelters was gradually driving New Jersey charcoal-burning furnaces out of business. In turn, the economic pressure drove the ironworkers from their homes, to seek other jobs. There were no other jobs in their iron trade since most furnaces elsewhere were shut down, too; and unless they could find jobs in some Pennsylvania works—and most could not—there was tough readjustment to some new and unfamiliar field. Some workmen made it; many did not.

What of the other two Hamptons? One of them, Hampton Gate, can be located on many maps; the other, Hampton Lower Forge, cannot. So it is best to consider Hampton Gate first.

The approach is quite simple: follow U.S. Route 206 south from Red Lion for nearly a mile; then bear left on a road whose signposts point to Tabernacle. Beyond Tabernacle the road bends a bit but there is no point in pausing until one has passed the junction of a road from Flyat and Oriental, which comes in at an angle from the right. A thousand feet or so farther on is the place where Hampton Gate once was. It is marked, approximately, by a small bridge, over a branch of the Batsto Creek, and a sign stating that one is entering "The Wharton Tract."

Once there, the journeyer will endeavor in vain to see Hampton Gate. There is no gate; not even a ghost of a creaking hinge. There is no town such as some maps suggest. There is not even a sign which says, frankly: "Hampton Gate." In view of these difficulties Hampton Gate soon seems to move into the realm of the imagination—unless one encounters a kindly native who will point out where he thinks the gate once stood.

There was a gate, once; over a century ago. It was the more or less formal entrance to the Hampton tract, already described. A long lane connected the gate with the furnace community which lay over half a mile to the south. The main road which passed the gate was used by stages and other traffic as well as by Hampton's own teams and drays. At the gate Hampton's traffic would turn down that long lane to carry supplies to the town; and on the way out it was not unusual to see great 12-horse teams dragging Hampton ironware to the stage road and then to Lumberton or Mount Holly for shipment to market, by water.

Even if that old lane can be spotted, tramping down it today is not advised. For one thing, it is private property; for another, so little is left visible that the way would be hard to follow. As a road it recalls the comment about certain old stage routes: "the road isn't passable, not even jackassable."

In early days there was a tavern by the "gate," and it was called, oddly enough, The Gate Tavern. In the beginning it was run by David Cavileer (or Cavilear).[8] Here the Hampton workmen would refresh themselves for the long journeys to town; and upon returning, probably stop again, to celebrate homecoming. After 1824 Cavileer was succeeded by his widow, and in later years the place was known as "J. Smith's Hotel."

More exciting and romantic, though more difficult, is a trip to the third Hampton: or Hampton Lower Forge. Many years ago the author was informed that on Batsto River, about two miles above Quaker Bridge, were remains of "the oldest and most mysterious ironworks in South Jersey." Actually, the "remains" were chiefly pilings of an old dam, still in place, while clearings along the side of the stream indicated where buildings had stood long ago.

What enterprise was really located in that forsaken spot? It was a forge built about 1809 by the owners of the Hampton Iron Works, George Garrit Ashbridge and his brother William. By agreement with William Richards of Batsto,[9] who owned the land, the Ashbridges were authorized "to build a dam or pond on Batsto Creek below its junction with Springer's Creek for the purpose of working a forge or such other works as they may think proper."

The construction was undertaken and the Lower Forge as it often was called was given the official name of Washington Forge (not to be confused with Washington Furnace at Lakewood). Conducted as part of the Hampton works, Washington Forge continued in operation into the 1850's. None of the old account books has been located, but there is record of two families living at Washington Forge in 1855, and most likely there were more.

The two families were those of Loveman P. Jackson, whose wife was named Mary, and Contine Chew, whose wife was named Alice. Both men were "laborers." The reason it is known that they were there at the forge is that Washington Township records show that on July 9, 1855, the Jacksons had a son named Andrew; and on December 13 of that year Alice Chew gave birth to a son named Alben. These records, incidentally, go almost five years beyond those known for Hampton itself. In its later period, of course, Samuel Richards owned the Washington Forge, having acquired it when he bought the entire Hampton estate.

Best approach to this old forge site is by water: via canoe from Quaker Bridge up the Batsto River. This is a refreshing ride along a slowly-winding stream banked chiefly by thick cedars and pines, but with sufficient other vegetation to persuade the botanically-minded to pause frequently and investigate. As the canoe glides on, green vistas succeed each other at every turn of the river. True, only a few stumps of rough pilings are to be found at the end of the ride. But getting there is the best part of the fun; and the hushed loveliness of sky, water and woods offers balm in a hurried, worried world.

No account of Hampton is complete without at least a brief bit about its "murder mystery." It was "murder most foul," a bloody business which took place long after Hampton's furnaces, forges, mills, and cottages crumbled in ruins. Vast acres of cranberries commanded the terrain instead of iron.

Owner of those acres in 1916 was Andrew J. Rider, since deceased. The story begins at the close of the cranberry-picking season that year. Since most cranberry pickers lived far from the bogs where they worked, many journeying from Philadelphia in trucks, it was customary to pay off in cash, at the bogs. It was an old and well-known system. Too well known in this instance.

On October 5, 1916, Andrew Rider went to his bank in Hammonton, 12 miles to the south. There he got cash— four thousand dollars—to meet his payroll. Driving his car was a daughter, Mrs. Elsie Smathers. Also in the car were Rider's brother, Henry D. Rider, of Howell, Michigan, and John Rigby, of Roxborough, Pa. Rigby was to repair some of the cranberry-processing machinery.

Passing Atsion on their return trip, no one in the group took notice of a car parked there, with a girl and two youths beside it, laughing and joking. They seemed to be waiting for someone. Luckily, an alert Atsion resident did take notice. Slightly suspicious, he jotted down the Pennsylvania license number of the car, on the side of his house.

While the merriment continued at Atsion, the Rider car turned off the main highway into a narrow road through the woods. It was the old road to Hampton already mentioned. Soon the way led over several cranberry dams, then through a thicket. Upon approaching yet another cranberry dam the Rider party caught sight of a group of people crowding the road ahead. There seemed to be five men and three women. Later the "women" turned out to be men in women's clothing.

With the highway thus blocked, Rider's car slowed to a crawl. As it came close to the group there was a slight and furtive movement among the eight figures; then they turned. Suddenly, revolvers were pointed from every angle at Rider and his companions.

The leader of the gang barked an order to halt; and when his demand was not met instantly, his men began firing. What followed was a wild, harrowing, and scrambled scene. Having a gun of his own, Rider returned the fire. His daughter, with great presence of mind, stepped on the gas and drove straight into the gang. The men scattered, shooting all the while. Before the fusillade was over, all four occupants of the car had been hit. Mrs. Smathers, though wounded, got the car to safety at the cranberry headquarters. In the meantime the bandits fled across the fields. The shooting was over. The four thousand dollar payroll had been saved. But Henry Rider was dead.

The usual routine followed. Doctors were summoned and emergency treatment given the survivors. Police sent out a general alarm for the killers; nearby bogs and farms were alerted; a watch was kept on highways and at railroad stations; and efforts were made to check passengers at the Philadelphia ferry terminals. But all this took time; and by nightfall the eight fugitives had made good their escape.

Ellis Parker was Chief of Burlington County Detectives in those days. Criminals had learned that his was a name to remember, and that his methods were something to worry about. He was to solve this mysterious crime—which developed international ramifications—as he solved so many others.

One solid clue was found: the Pennsylvania automobile license number which William Cavileer of Atsion had marked on the side of his house. This quickly led to apprehension of the girl and two youths who had been having such a jolly time while the murder ambush was being laid. It developed that the one youth had been hired to drive "three men"—three of the gang—to Atsion; the girl and the other youth had gone along for the ride. All insisted they were unaware that their passengers were thugs. Next it was learned that the other five men involved had gone to Atsion by train the night before and had spent "the witching time of night" in the woods near the murder scene.

Each discovery led to another. Soon most of the gang members had been identified, including the ringleader. The latter, it developed, had once worked at the Rider bogs and was familiar with the payroll arrangements there.

First member of the gang to be arrested was charged with murder and locked up in the Mount Holly jail. He managed to escape, was quickly recaptured, convicted, and electrocuted. Another key member of the gang took passage on a boat for Italy; the Italian government was notified and he was seized when the boat docked, tried in an Italian court, convicted, and given life imprisonment. A third member of the group was killed in a Newark, N.J. gang fight before police had caught up with him; a fourth was tracked down in a small town in Pennsylvania where he was living under an assumed name; a fifth fled first to South America, then to Spain, next to Italy, and—15 years later—was located in a California prison, doing time.

The search for the Hampton criminals went on relentlessly over the years, and the fact that the mystery was solved and the key bandits captured shows the tenacity of the police in general and Ellis Parker in particular. Most important of all, a substantial measure of justice was done.

Since 1916 much water has passed over the cranberry dams of the once-sprawling Hampton tract. The amber tributaries of the Batsto River still swirl past the site of the old Skit Mill, the Hampton ponds, and the remnant pilings of the Washington Forge dam, to flow silently on beyond Quaker Bridge. It is understandable that few persons explore these areas since so little is left in them of man's handiwork. Beside the waters and beyond the bogs are the still-shadowy forests, soft fragrance in the air, and a restful sense of private communion with nature. This last may be due to the majesty of the pines themselves, although some say it is due to the absence of people.

Breakneck Road to Taunton

"Breakneck Road" is a quiet trail today. Whoever gave it that unofficial name did so in long-gone times when sparking youths whipped their horses and buggies to galloping speeds. "Breakneck Road" is worth one's acquaintance if only for the rich natural beauty which unfolds as it passes Taunton Lakes, once Taunton Furnace.

The main lake at Taunton nestles in the woods like a gem in its setting. Two hundred years ago the prospect must have appeared much the same, without, of course, the houses which unobtrusively dot the banks. In addition to what later became "Breakneck Road" there were several other trails, rough sand tracks and not much more. There was the winding path which connected with the old route to Tuckerton; another found its way three miles to the northeast going to what now is Medford, and then on to Mount Holly.

Woodsmen had long been active nearby. Pricket's saw-mill was a mile-and-a-half away; and a bit farther to the south whined the Goshen sawmill of John Inskeep. Two miles distant on the Medford road was the gristmill of David Oliphant, venerable even then. But Taunton itself was lonely, lovely country.

Charles Read, who speculated in real estate before he gambled in iron, had for some years been buying land in the Taunton vicinity.[1] His first purchase was 80 acres from John Pricket, on November 1, 1750. From the Proprietors of New Jersey there were four surveys to Read: one of 23 acres; another of 15 acres and 38 perches; a third of 26 acres, and a fourth of 216 acres. Finally, Read bought a tract of 298 acres which had been surveyed to John Wilkins, Benjamin Thomas, and Absalom Thomas. This gave him "Taunton lands" totaling a bit more than 658 acres—but then his iron-works ambitions crystallized.

For an iron furnace Read needed much more than this: more land for digging bog ore, and more land for "coaling," i.e., the making of charcoal. On April 3, 1765 Read acquired from Benjamin Haines, Jonathan Haines, Michael Branin, and Emanuel Stratton the right "to enter into the lands belonging to any of them . . . to take stone or iron ore and to cut and Coal a certain piece of maple swamp near Kettle Run and to make roads and to take timber for the building and repairing of collier's huts." [2]

One of Read's neighbors, David Oliphant, also had some ideas about iron. Since a dam for Read's ironworks and a dam for the site which Oliphant proposed to use for a forge (the author finds no record that it was ever built) would both be on the same stream, the two men made an agreement. Dated July 1, 1765, it read in part:

> In order to accommodate two Forges or Iron Works proposed to be erected by them separately . . . which they cannot conscientiously do but by making mutual concessions, therefore . . . the said David Oliphant shall and may erect a dam for such Iron Works at a place taken up and surveyed by him and is to be below a bridge known by the name of Braddock's Bridge . . . and the said Charles Read may at any time forever hereafter erect a dam above Meadow Run on the survey made by John Pricket and extend the same over Kettle Run . . . or Oliphiants Mill Creek . . .

This pact was signed both by David Oliphant and Charles Read.[3]

Later that year, or early in 1766, Read built a forge at Taunton, and constructed the dam agreed upon to provide waterpower. This forge was of three fires, and with his Etna Furnace only about three miles distant he could count on a steady supply of pig iron for refining.

Labor was Read's principal difficulty at Taunton, as it was at his three other ironworks: Etna, Atsion Forge, and Batsto Furnace. On August 25, 1768, the following advertisement appeared in *The Pennsylvania Journal:*

TWENTY-EIGHT DOLLARS Reward
Run away from Taunton Forge, Burlington county, the following indentured servants.

Zebulon Hoge, country born, about six feet high, and slim, black or dark brown hair, slow spoken; he left the forge in September last, and it was expected he would return, but is now in or about Augusta county, Virginia, where his father lives.

Joseph Vanote, born in Monmouth county, New Jersey, aged about 30 years, well known in his present walks, which are about Monahockin and Little Egg Harbour; went off this spring.

Randle M'Donald, by trade a finer, and has worked a little at blooming, aged near forty years, was born in Ireland, about four feet ten inches high, black hair and large black beard, slow spoken (if not in liquor) hard of hearing and smoaked much; left the forge the 21st instant: he wore oznabrigs shirt and trowsers, blue lapelled jacket with metal buttons, a narrow brimmed hat which has been painted, and has with him oznabrigs shirt or frocks which reach to his ankles & a new pair of shoes tied with strings.

Whoever takes up said servants, and secures them in any of the goals of Pennsylvania or New Jersey, shall have FIVE POUNDS for the first; THREE POUNDS for the second; and FIFTY SHILLINGS for the last, paid by

CHARLES READ

Labor was still short the following year when Read, on February 9, advertised that "Good Colliers and Forge Men, bringing recommendations, and a good KEEPER will meet with encouragement at Etna Furnace and Taunton Forge, in Burlington County, sixteen miles from Philadelphia. The Colliers should be there by the 10th of March."

Even before any of Read's iron enterprises were built, he had advertised, on July 26, 1765, the sale of all four of his tracts, offering also "to enter into partnership with any persons of good dispositions, fortune and integrity." Read was facing financial difficulties; and while he acquired no less than four partners at Batsto, that did not help much, so he sold his own share of that furnace shortly after it began operation. In 1768 he sold a 449/1000 interest in Atsion, and in 1770 was advertising to sell all of his remaining interest in Atsion Forge, Etna, and Taunton.

Read's crisis came in 1773. His son was manager at Etna Furnace but the father was well aware that Charles Read, Jr. "disliked" the iron business and had no desire to carry it on. Desperate, Read sold his controlling share in Atsion Forge to Henry Drinker and Abel James, a firm of Quaker merchants in Philadelphia. In a private agreement Read also sold Drinker and James the furnace machinery and other equipment at Etna, which they then installed at Atsion. According to a letter of Drinker and James, Read felt he had not been treated fairly on the latter transaction;[4] but he was so sorely beset by mental and physical distress that after deeding the Etna lands to his son, he fled New Jersey secretly, not even resigning the public offices he held.*

Taunton Forge was the only one of his four ironworks unsold at the time of Read's disappearance. It was left, together with his other assets, in the hands of three trustees: Daniel Ellis, Thomas Fisher, and Charles Read, Jr. In 1774, they were advertising a vendue (auction) of Taunton, on June 8. There were no bidders. Later they advertised again, as follows:[5]

TAUNTON FORGE

To be sold by public vendue, on the premises, the 31st day of October next, at 12 o'clock, the forge called Taunton, situate in Burlington County, West New Jersey, within ten miles of a furnace, seven miles from a good landing, on Ancocus Creek, and 17 miles from Philadelphia. The Forge, coal houses and other buildings are in good repair, and the stream of water plentiful. The tract of land which will be sold with it contains about 1500 acres.

Any person inclining to purchase, by applying to Charles Read, he will shew the premises.

DANIEL ELLIS
CHARLES READ
THOMAS FISHER.

* Charles Read's story can be found in Chapter Three of the author's *Iron In the Pines.*

According to so-called legends—often plain misinformation—virtually every furnace and forge ever built in South Jersey supposedly made munitions for Washington's armies —even those furnaces and forges which were not established until long after the Revolutionary War was over. Taunton Iron Works, however, was one of those which actually did produce shot, shell, and even cannon for the patriot forces.

It was, in fact, the impending Revolution which made Taunton saleable. The purchaser was Thomas Mayberry of Mount Holly, who owned an air furnace near there which turned out sheet and rod iron, and during the war produced iron for camp kettles and "cast two pair of six-pound cannon in a day." Mayberry was in fairly close contact with the American high command and early in 1778 he was considered the man to revive the Andover Iron Works in Sussex County during its period of seizure by the new state government. Later that same year he bought Batsto Furnace, but resold it with a fat profit after only six months.

When Mayberry acquired Taunton, it only possessed a forge and that was in doubtful shape. Under his direction a furnace was built "with a capacity of eighty tons of pig iron a month." Soon cannon as well as other munitions were being cast, and in November 1778 his manager, John Merryman (possibly a lessee) was advertising sale of "4, 6, 8, and 12 oz. Shot and 2, 3, 4, and 6 lb. Ball." Mayberry also put the forge in order, had several workmen's houses erected and additional land acquired. Taunton now was definitely on a war footing, although Mayberry continued to make his home on his plantation near Mount Holly.

During Mayberry's ownership of Taunton he became the central figure in a rather astonishing romance. A widower of about 50 (his first wife was Cynthia Lanning), he met a pretty girl of 18 who then was working as seamstress for a Mrs. Dibley, whose husband was proprietor of a tav-

ern at Bank Alley and Chestnut Street, Philadelphia. The
girl's father, a wastrel, had been employed as an ostler for
the tavern and sought to marry his daughter to a Frenchman who kept his horse at the Dibley stable. She would
have none of that scheme. Part of what followed is told in
J. F. Watson's *Annals:*

> She was accidentally seen by Mr. M. of Mount Holly, a rich
> ironmaster. He was instantly pleased with her charm; in-
> quired into her history of the landlady, made overtures of
> marriage, and was accepted. He presented the young lady
> two thousand dollars for wedding preparations . . . and
> soon married her and took her to his home in Mount Holly.
>
> He had great entertainments at his mansion, among the
> rest a ball in which his bride danced with great grace; her
> exertions to please and entertain her guests led her into an
> unusual perspiration, and going to the entry where the air
> was cool she took a chill, and in five days after her wedding,
> died. . . .
>
> The husband was inconsolable; he fell into frequent con-
> vulsions the night of her interment; she was buried by torch-
> light after the English manner, in solemn pomp.

The bride was Mary Spring; the date of the wedding
January 31, 1780; and the "Mr. M.," of course, was Thomas
Mayberry.

A little more than two years later Mayberry took his third
wife, Mary Sinclair. They were married March 12, 1782.
Moving to Pennsylvania shortly after the wedding, Mayberry put Taunton Furnace up for sale. His advertisement
gives an idea of the establishment at that period:[7]

> 1. A Furnace now in blast . . . lying on a never failing
> stream; and erected on a plan so as to cast 80 tons of pig
> iron per month; there is a large quantity of ore near the
> works. The metal is known to equal if not excel any on the

continent for making hardware, pig iron, and especially cannon (of which sufficient proof may be had). There is a large quantity of woodland so contiguous to the works that a team may bring in six loads of coal per day. The conveying of the said iron to Philadelphia costs but 12sh per ton, it being so near a navigable creek.

2. A Forge with three fires adjoining the furnace, which also has been repaired lately, and is now in excellent order. Contiguous to said works is a good mansion house, together with several houses for workmen.

3. One undivided eighth part of Pricket's sawmill, about a mile and a half from said works, with a large quantity of timber.

Also offered for sale was Mayberry's plantation in Mount Holly, with his house, air furnace, and a distillery, plus about 200 acres of land.

Disposing of Taunton Iron Works proved no easier in 1783 than it had been a decade earlier. At the first public auction, on December 3, there were no bidders; and the same was true of a subsequent auction in 1784. Not until the summer of 1785—on July 11—was there a sale. The buyer was one George Hastings.

Soon Hastings failed to meet his payments and Mayberry was forced to bring a foreclosure suit. Now the whole auction routine had to be gone through again, with the same difficulties. On Monday, June 30, 1788, Taunton was again put under the hammer—but again there were no bidders. The same thing took place at a second sale on October 20, and at a third sale on November 29. Finally, on July 25, 1789, Taunton was sold, to Richard Edwards and Thomas Reynolds, as tenants in common. A sheriff's deed was delivered on August 15, 1789.[8]

Richard Edwards now became the manager of Taunton Iron Works. He and his wife Abigail and their numerous family made their home in the mansion on the property. Now for the first time the bright ring of children's laughter lightened life at Taunton Mansion. Meanwhile business was good. While no records of that period have been found, Edwards seems to have done quite well for some years. However, after a decade or so, difficulties increased, financial trouble followed, and the inevitable happened. John Christopher, of Hopewell, N.J., had been a major creditor, and by mid-1799 the Taunton Works were in his possession.

Christopher was not an iron man, and had no yearnings in that direction. Thus during his family's long period of ownership Taunton was run mostly by lessees. First of these was Benjamin Davis who apparently did well for awhile chiefly by operating the forge. Later, however, the property fell into neglect.

It was in 1815 that the Richards family appeared in the picture. John Christopher, on May 8, 1815, leased Taunton Works to Anthony S. Earl, familiar as a figure in the South Jersey iron business and, previously, as a manager of Speedwell Furnace.[9] This lease, with a rental of $500 a year, was for five years, with an option to renew for a further ten years.[10] Earl now divided his Taunton lease into thirds, sold one-third to Thomas Richards (later of Jackson Glass Works), and one-third to Mark Richards, Earl keeping one-third for himself.

In an agreement between the three men, dated June 6, 1815, it was provided:

> . . . that Anthony S. Earl be the Manager [of Taunton] under whose instructions a blast furnace be immediately [words illegible] and such other outworks and buildings as may be necessary to carry on an establishment of the kind . . . also to employ workmen . . . and generally to see the

Works put into operation as speedily and as economically as circumstances will permit. The forge may be carried on by the concern, or rented.

The "concern" was named the "Taunton Company."

A new furnace stack was built and the works soon put into operation. Products of the Taunton Company during the ensuing years were much the same as those of other South Jersey charcoal furnaces: hollow ware, sash weights, stoves, etc., as well as pig iron. That Taunton stoves gained something of a reputation, locally at least, is indicated by this advertisement in the *Mount Holly Mirror* of October 11, 1820:

TAUNTON FURNACE
STOVES FOR SALE
The subscriber has on hand, a good assortment of the Taunton Furnace Stoves—completely ironed and fit for immediate use—which he will dispose of on the most reasonable terms. He will also warrant them to stand the fire for a certain period of time, sufficient to determine their quality.
Mount Holly   DANIEL COPPUCK

Mark Richards eventually withdrew, with Anthony Earl and Thomas Richards carrying on between them. When it came time to renew the lease, however, they decided to abandon their enterprise. On January 15, 1820, they advertised:[11]

PUBLIC SALE
On the Premises
At Taunton Iron Works
On Monday, the 31st inst. (Jan.)
at 11 o'clock A.M.
Seven Frames of Dwelling Houses
The Stack of the Furnace.
The Frame of the Casting & Moulding House

Also the Bridge House of the Furnace.
Water Wheels and Machinery.
A pair of excellent Tub Bellows and Pipes.
                    THOMAS RICHARDS
                    ANTHONY S. EARL

The following February 7, 1821, their partnership was dissolved, an advertisement counseling "all persons having claims against the Taunton Company to present them for settlement—and those indebted to the company will please to make speedy payment to Thomas Richards, in Philadelphia, who has taken the whole concern on himself and is alone responsible for the business."

Taunton now was back in the lap of the Christopher family, and a son, Jesse, offered the property for sale on October 9, 1822. Jesse Christopher, then resident at Taunton, put up for auction:

all that messuage or tract of land called Taunton . . . about 8500 acres. There is on said premises A FORGE with two fires and one Hammer, Stamping Mill &c., in good condition, and in operation driven by a never-failing stream of water . . . A good dwelling house, barn, Coal-house, five tenant houses, together with a furnace stack and house, part of which is reasonably good, and may be repaired at small expense, as it is well known there is a sufficiency of ore on the tract to supply her yet a number of years.

Once again a public sale of Taunton failed for want of buyers. The furnace then continued in disuse but the forge was operated at least part-time by Jesse Christopher. As late as 1825 his name appears in the Batsto books as a buyer of iron. During this period, however, John Christopher died and title to Taunton became vested in his widow, Elizabeth.

Elizabeth Christopher, naturally, wanted to sell; and,

somehow, she did. On March 27, 1827, she deeded Taunton
Iron Works to Edward Thomas and John W. Cox.[12] The
price was $8,000. Barely a year later, on April 7, 1828,
Thomas and Cox sold a third interest in the property to
William F. Bladen, for $5,000. Thus far they were doing all
right.

Bladen, however, died not long afterward, so again one
finds Taunton Iron Works—a third interest this time—offered for sale by Bladen's widow, Martha. This sale was
held in the tavern of Stacy B. Campion, in Mount Holly,
on May 14, 1831, and Martha Bladen, like Elizabeth Christopher, found a buyer on the first try. On June 6 of that
year she conveyed her third of Taunton to Thomas W.
Duffield, of Frankford, for $3,750—a net loss of $1,250.[13]

Martha Bladen's advertisement stated that "the works
are in good repair and now in operation." This suggests
that the other owners—Thomas and Cox—had put Taunton
back on its feet and were in production. They also appear
to have added a steel furnace for during the middle 1830's
advertisements offered:

CAST STEEL AXES

A superior article (warranted) for sale to customers at the
Factory, at Taunton, or at the store of M. S. Powell, S.E. cor.
Arch and Front streets, Philadelphia.

About this time the firm was given a new name: Taunton
Manufacturing Company. Its line of products also was
somewhat expanded. While numerous purchases of Taunton
axes are listed in the Batsto books, on April 18, 1842, it is
stated that a dozen collier's shovels were bought for $6; a
half-dozen moulder's shovels for $4; and six long-handled
shovels at $3.75. Other purchases by Batsto from the Taun-
ton Manufacturing Company continued until mid-1844.
Then suddenly they stopped. An order for half a dozen

axes, for $15, on May 22, 1844 was the last entry. After that Batsto acquired its axes and shovels elsewhere.

These were, clearly, the last days of iron-making at Taunton. Business dwindled, and finally the plant closed, this time for good. During the hard times of 1847 the property passed into the hands of Joseph Hinchman,[14] who had a new idea for utilizing it: growing cranberries.

Whereas the iron business at Taunton always had teetered on the thin edge of trouble, the cranberry business flourished, and the Hinchman bogs developed into a substantial business over the succeeding years. Meanwhile a number of the old buildings at Taunton became sorting houses and packing sheds; the mansion again was occupied; the furnace remnants were torn down, and soon there were few signs thereabouts to link Taunton and bog iron. Sometimes the dam would be "up," sometimes "down"; and over the broad acres of the tract were cranberries, and more cranberries.

Eighty years is a long time by human reckoning. Yet so long did Taunton remain "cranberry land," a busy place in season, a quiet one at other times. Always picturesque to visitors, increasing numbers of them began to wander along "Breakneck Road" and explore the side trails and minor waterways. Later, as people began to have more leisure, this became a place for them to go on Sundays.

In turn, Hinchman—then called "Uncle Joe"—made Taunton a semi-public park in which he took special pride. He had peacocks on the lawn. A building with architecture akin to that of the present mansion stood well back behind the ice house. There, Uncle Joe kept fancy pigeons. At one period there was even a bear in a pit, which must have attracted a large influx of wayfarers and picknickers. The latter, incidentally, were encouraged, and provided with an outdoor stove near the furnace site—cookouts, after all, are very old stuff. Even visiting horses were afforded a stone watering trough which was supplied with fresh water through an underground pipe from the pond. All this in the days before motor cars prevailed. Other underground conduits fed pools of water lilies. Taunton had become, almost unwittingly, a show place.

During the boom days of the 1920's South Jersey land values increased sharply. Even Taunton, secluded as it still was, began feeling the effects of real estate speculation. Joseph Hinchman had died, and his nephew Samuel inherited the property. Meanwhile more and more people seemed to enjoy life in the woods—and Taunton had woods.

One of Taunton's visitors was aware of this fact, and particularly appreciative of Taunton. He was Edward H. Murray, Sr., of Ardmore, Pa. When Murray purchased the tract[15] in 1920, it comprised not only the immediate Taunton area but also Lake Pine, Braddock's Mill Lake, Centennial Lake, Mimosa Lake, and much adjoining acreage. The new owner's goal was real estate development, and he proposed to begin right at Taunton. A new dam was erected; some buildings repaired and renovated; others, including the "pigeon house," were torn down. A lake colony was laid out and lots offered for sale.

Murray's agent on the site was J. Lawrence Larsen, who with his family occupied the newer of the two mansions. With surprising speed a community began to develop; houses soon were ensconced in the woods around the lake, and then in the woods beyond the lake. Those who wanted a "refuge from the city" now had it. And after Larsen's death in 1946, his widow, Caro M. Larsen, became a licensed real estate broker, then realtor, and ever since has continued to operate not only in Taunton but in the other lake areas developed nearby.

Little survives of Taunton's ironworks days. Torn down in 1951 was the large, and older, house which stood close by the present mansion. One section of that house almost surely dated from the days of Charles Read* and Thomas Mayberry; and on its first floor there were three large rooms, with five on the second. As Caro Larsen, who should know, put it: "The building must have been quite a place in its day."

Near the present mansion is an ice house which is very old. According to Carter L. Larsen, who owns much of the land around the furnace site, the ice house dates from Charles Read's time. Nearby, amid a tangle of vines, brush, and trees below the dam is the location of the old furnace stack itself. There slag, chunks of charcoal, and a corner of stone foundation have been found. The latter might have been part of the furnace structure. On the same site, beside the waters spilling from the dam, once stood a "salamander," a pear-shaped mass of solid iron about two feet high. This was a relic, possibly, of the last blast at Taunton Furnace, suggesting that perhaps the fires were allowed to go out before the crucible was drained. Thus this metal, cold and solid, could only be removed by taking apart the hearth. Some years ago the "salamander" was moved near the porch of the mansion.

Yet if there be scant evidence of the iron days at Taunton there is still interest aplenty. The present mansion, dating probably from the 1830's, is of characteristic style, with its colorful cupola and happy setting. Leveled as unsafe about 15 years ago was a nearby mill, of the same period, its building surmounted by a similar cupola. This mill was run by an overshot waterwheel fed by a head-race carrying water from another lake, at a higher level farther

---

* Destruction of the "Charles Read House" at Medford Lakes (once Etna Furnace) in 1958 wiped out the last vestige of Read's original establishment.

up the stream. This mill powered the cranberry-processing machinery. There remains also the "salamander," the ice house, and, of course, "Breakneck Road," today a place for strolling and not speeding.

Beyond buildings, dams, or other specimens of human handiwork, however, is the embracing delightfulness of the natural setting; the confluence of sky, water, and woods— a setting rich with appeal at every season, especially winter, with the lake frozen, snow deep, and icicles gleaming. Some years ago, when the author was an editor of the *Courier-Post* newspapers in Camden, N.J., one of his poetry contributors, was Caro Larsen who still continues to welcome visitors to Taunton. These lines of hers were penned there, on a long-ago Christmas Eve:

"Frozen the streams, buds slumber, and birds are still,
Sentinel trees keep watch throughout the night.
In far-away towns midnight carols quiver in the air,
But here the stars chime, and birches bow before a light . . .
A tender glow from star-strewn spaces centuries remote."

Benjamin Randolph and Speedwell

Pre-Revolutionary Philadelphia was celebrated for its "remarkably beautiful signboards with backgrounds of different colors, speckled with gold and silver." Moreau St. Mery was to observe later that so accurate were these signs —unlike many in France—that from them little children might well learn how to spell.[1] With more than 275 business establishments in the Quaker City, many of which had such signboards, the streets of Penn's "green country towne" were richly attractive to strollers who took sufficient time from other affairs to contemplate them.

The general neighborhood of Third and Chestnut Streets

offered many examples along this line. "Jewels and Diamonds for Sentimentalists" proclaimed the bright signboard of Robert Bell, bookseller, auctioneer, and publisher of the first American edition of Blackstone's *Commentaries.*[2] Another book-auction house close by was in possession of the fascinating name of "Honey & Mouse." Inevitably one encountered the shop of Robert and Thomas Kennedy, known in 1770 as the "Sign of the West's Head." This "West's Head" sign bore a portrait of Benjamin West, and the Kennedys offered a fine assortment of imported paintings, prints, and maps "selected by" that famous painter. A keen competitor was William Williams, who once had been West's teacher; and at the "sign of the Hogarth's Head," he not only sold paintings but also gave flute lessons and did landscape gardening. Art was served further with the sale of oils, colors, and painter's needs at the "Sign of the Golden Ball" which, under Christopher Marshall, had become an artists' rendezvous, with Charles Willson Peale among the more regular patrons.

A particularly significant shop in that pleasant area was the "Sign of the Golden Eagle." Occupant of these premises was Benjamin Randolph, cabinet maker, and producer of some of the finest and most famous pieces of American furniture of that period. Randolph's customers included some of Philadelphia's first families, and one of his patrons was a future President of the United States—Thomas Jefferson.

Like most artisans of his day, Benjamin Randolph put his hand to any task which would earn pounds, shillings, and pence. In February 1769, for example, he gilded "a large looking glass" for Levi Hollingsworth, with whom he was to have a long business association.[3] He wholesaled shipments of mahogany. He produced wooden articles of all kinds: picture frames for his artist neighbors, particularly James Claypoole and Charles Willson Peale;

coffins for the departed; and cases for tall clocks, one of his customers for these being clockmaker Edward Duffield, and another William Connell, a clock-case dealer at Third and Spruce Streets. And in 1770 the following advertisement appeared:

BENJAMIN RANDOLPH

Takes this method to inform his customers, and the public in general, that he has for sale, at his ware room of carving and cabinet work &c., at the Sign of the Golden Eagle, in Chestnut street, a quantity of wooden buttons of various sorts, and intends, if encouraged, to keep a great assortment of them.

The People of New Jersey (in general) wear no other kind of buttons, and they say they are the best and cheapest that can be bought, both for strength and beauty, and he doubts not but that they will soon recommend themselves to the public in general.

Benjamin Randolph, of course, became famous not for his buttons, his coffins, or his picture frames, but for his superlative Chippendale furniture. A number of the chairs he made, and others attributed to him, have been discovered here and there over the years. Not until the 20th century, however, was the exceptional quality of his craftsmanship recognized and his present high reputation established.

The most spectacular "find" of Randolph chairs took place in the late 1920's, in homes of descendants of Randolph's second wife. Sold at auction in New York, one chair realized $9,500, another $15,000 and a third $32,500. This last one was purchased for the Philadelphia Museum of Art.[4] These are known as "Sample Chairs," having been models from which Randolph's custom orders usually were executed.

Today, most "Randolph pieces" are in museums and private collections—at least those of record. Some are in the Karolik Collection of the Boston Museum of Fine Arts; the Garvan Collection in the Pennsylvania Museum of Fine Arts; with several in the Winterthur Museum, including an especially endearing chair presently placed in the "Stamper-Blackwell Parlor." * This room was formerly in a house at 234 Pine Street, Philadelphia.[5]

Because so little has been published about Benjamin Randolph a few words about his family as well as his career are in order. For most of his kinsmen the name was, and still is, Fitz Randolph. Apparently Benjamin's parents dropped the "Fitz" which denotes "son of," and not, as has been said, illegitimacy.

It was in 1630 that Edward Fitz Randolph, "the Pilgrim," emigrated from Nottinghamshire, England. Settling in the area of Scituate, Mass., Edward married Elizabeth Blossom, on May 10, 1637. About 32 years later, with six of their ten children, Edward and Elizabeth moved to New Jersey. They made their home in Piscataway, but as time passed a number of their children and grandchildren gravitated to the area which would, in 1744, become Princeton.

Much of the Fitz Randolph family has been associated with that area ever since, and one of Edward's grandsons, Nathaniel Fitz Randolph (II) made a gift of the four and a half acres of land on which Princeton University (originally the College of New Jersey) was established and Nassau Hall built. In that tract was the Fitz Randolph family burial plot, and in 1909 when Princeton's Holder Hall and the great Holder Tower were erected, the graveyard was found. In consequence, the remaining bones of some

---

* These Winterthur chairs are attributed to Randolph, although not labeled with his name.

32 Fitz Randolphs were re-entombed in one of the tower walls, and among these were the bones of Nathaniel himself. A tablet now marks his memory there, with an inscription by Andrew Fleming West: In agro nostro jacet immo suo: "He rests in our ground—and yet his own." [6]

* Benjamin Randolph was named for his grandfather, the tenth and youngest child of Edward. Benjamin's father, Isaac (4/10/1701—5/-3/1750) was a cousin of the Nathaniel mentioned above, but of humbler station. Among Isaac's occupations was that of stagecoach driver for the New York-Philadelphia run. He had married Rebecca Seabrook, on November 28, 1728, and Benjamin was their sixth child, born on January 30, 1738, (1737 old style) in South River. [Isaac had 11 children in all, three by his second wife, Hannah (Dove) Lee.] [7] Of Isaac's five sons only three were to survive beyond early manhood, but those three—Benjamin and his older brothers James and Daniel—were to share with him bravery and distinction in the patriot cause during the Revolution.*

First traceable activity of Benjamin Randolph outside the Princeton area where he grew up was the buying and selling of land and the cutting of timber in the Jersey pines. How profitable these transactions were can only be conjectured. Benjamin was engaged in his lumbering activities in the early 1760's and possibly the latter 1750's,[8] and it was during this period that he acquired the lands at Speedwell, in Burlington County, where he first erected a sawmill and, much later, built a furnace. His sawmill was long known as "Randle's Mill," possibly a contraction of

---

* The family of Isaac Randolph was: by Rebecca Seabrook (1) James, b. October 1, 1730; (2) Huldah, b. March 31, 1732; (3) Daniel, b. March 7, 1833; (4) Thoda, b. April 11, 1834; (5) Rebecca, b. July 14, 1736; (6) Benjamin, b. January 30, 1738; (7) Stephen, b. July 13, 1739; (8) Ruth, b. May 20, 1741; by Hannah (Dove) Lee, widow of Joshua Lee, whom Isaac married February 17, 1745: (9) Mary, b. November 11, 1746; (10) Charles, b. 1747; (11) Issac, b. June 25, 1748.

Randolph, and until the Revolution it was operated by his next-eldest brother Daniel.

Benjamin's increasing knowledge of woods and wood-working led to his next venture, that of a "joiner" in Philadelphia. A joiner in those days was something more than a carpenter, denoting as it did a carpenter specializing in the more skilled aspects of interior wood-working. Soon he was established as a cabinet maker whose work began to attract attention; later, he signed himself, in deeds, as a "carver and gilder."

Not long after his arrival from New Jersey, in 1763 the rising young Randolph decided to take a wife. Her name was Anna Bromwich.* She was the only daughter of William Bromwich, widower and a staymaker of some means. Benjamin and Anna were married at St. Paul's Protestant Episcopal Church (then Church of England), Third Street below Walnut, on February 18, 1762. Randolph was a member of that parish.

Less than two years later William Bromwich died, and left his property to his daughter. Anna turned much of this estate over to her husband and it was a means for establishing his wood-working business on a large scale and, in 1767, acquiring the Chestnut Street shop which he called the "Sign of the Golden Eagle." Matching this expansion was the ornate business card which is illustrated in this book.

Comparing Randolph with that other famous Philadelphian, William Savery, *Antiques Magazine,* in 1925, observed that "Randolph . . . commanded a sizeable establishment and . . . thought in terms of liberal dimensions and rich decoration." It added that his advertising card, "while it was engraved by Smithers, its grandiloquence of conception must be credited to Randolph. Virtually all its

---

* So spelled by Randolph in deeds. Elsewhere her name appears as "Brummage" and in one instance as "Broomwick."

details are taken directly from the second edition of Chippendale's 'Director'—a book which only an important cabinet maker would have owned." And whereas William Savery, according to Carl Bridenbaugh, "did not possess a single carving tool," Randolph's shop was well equipped with them.

By 1767 the Randolph household had expanded a bit. Two daughters had arrived, Mary and Anna; and soon they were to acquire a close companion who became a sister in all but lineage. Above the "Sign of the Golden Eagle," on upper floors overlooking the Chestnut Street scene, were more rooms than the Randolphs required. So it was decided to take in paying guests, and the first of these arrived that same year, 1767. His name was Giovanni Gualdo, an Italian wine merchant and musician who had come to Philadelphia by way of London. A widower, he brought with him his small daughter, Frances.

John Gualdo as he came to be called was a man of rare gifts, taste, and culture. He also possessed great enthusiasm for his new-found land, and that enthusiasm was but little dampened when misfortune struck and his wine business went bankrupt. For if Gualdo had no wine, there was still music.

In February of 1769 he opened a music store on Front Street. There he sold "violins, guitars, mandolins, spinets, clavichords, German flutes and a variety of stringed instruments." He employed a staff of skilled repairmen, and also a German musician who taught violin, cello, and French horn. A servant boy was available "to copy music for anyone desiring a particular sonata, trio, duet, solo, minuet or country dance without having to buy the entire book." [9]

Gualdo was also a composer of much talent, and, later, an impresario. For him things seemed to be going very well, very quickly. At one of his concerts of "American music" the program included then-popular songs such as "Vain Is

Beauty, Gaudy Flower," works for clarinet and harpsichord as well as some of his own compositions, including a violin concerto. In their *Rebels and Gentlemen,* Carl and Jessica Bridenbaugh call Gualdo "the outstanding musical genius of pre-Revolutionary Philadelphia." He was not only able and indefatigable, but one of the best-informed musicians of his day and used in his concerts "all known instruments including the clarinet, still rarely played in Europe."

Emboldened by his initial successes, Gualdo embarked upon a second series of subscription concerts for the winter of 1770–71. These, too, were going well both artistically and financially. They came to an abrupt halt, however, on February 8, 1771. With his greatest triumphs in prospect, John Gualdo's mind suddenly gave way. Found hopelessly insane, he was put "in chains in one of the cells of the Pennsylvania Hospital."

Gualdo had lived with the Randolphs nearly five years. Long at home in Philadelphia artistic circles, Benjamin had much in common with him and the two had become fast friends. An equal bond linked the Randolph girls, especially Anna, with little Frances Gualdo, so that when John Gualdo died a dreadful death in 1772, Frances became a ward of the Randolphs, a member of the family, and as we shall see, one of Benjamin's principal heirs.

Two other lodgers soon were to find their way to the welcoming rooms above the "Sign of the Golden Eagle." One was George Washington. The other was Thomas Jefferson.

The clock of years had moved along to 1774 and America's Revolution was close at hand. Times were tense, especially in Philadelphia where colonists were gathering for the First Continental Congress.

Benjamin Randolph was an ardent and dedicated patriot who made no secret of his sympathies. He was active in Whig political circles and was an "associator" (group of patriots) and a member of the First Mounted City Troop (Colonel Randolph, they called him).[10] All this was quite enough to make him a marked man among Philadelphia's numerous Tories. That he was a "marked man" among patriots also was shown when George Washington, arriving to attend the First Continental Congress, lodged with Benjamin Randolph.

Again in 1775 Washington's diary records that he stayed at "Randolphs," and when Martha was on her way to join her husband at Morristown in the spring of 1777, she also stayed there. The latter visit is noted in a letter of May 3, 1777 from Washington to Caleb Gibbs asking that he "pay at Mr. Randolph's in Chestnut Street for the night or two she was there on her way up . . ."[11]

In the year after Washington's second visit another eminent Virginian climbed the stairs to the chambers above the "Sign of the Golden Eagle." This time it was Thomas Jefferson, who was in Philadelphia to attend the Second Continental Congress. During that visit Jefferson commissioned Randolph to make him a portable writing desk which he had designed. The original of that desk contains this note:[12]

> Thomas Jefferson gives this writing desk to Joseph Coolidge, Jr., as a memorial of his affection. It was made from the drawing of his own, by Benjamin Randolph, cabinet maker at Philadelphia, with whom he first lodged on his arrival in that city, in May 1776, and is the identical one on which he wrote the Declaration of Independence.

Joseph Coolidge, Jr., was the husband of Ellen Randolph, Jefferson's favorite granddaughter. In 1880 the Coolidge heirs presented Jefferson's original Randolph desk to the nation, since when it has been a familiar exhibit in the nation's Capital. The copy of the desk at Monticello is one of a number made during the 1876 Centennial Exposition.

With independence declared, Benjamin Randolph became increasingly active in the patriot cause. No doubt his business suffered as a result, but it would have suffered in any case since customers for luxury furniture were becoming harder and harder to find in wartime. Randolph took part in the vital battles of Trenton and Princeton. In the first, he was a member of the Philadelphia Light Horse.[13] In the second, if tradition is correct, he was a guide for Washington and his army in the night march from Trenton to a key victory at Princeton. This famous march, around the main British Army, was made over a roundabout, rough, and little-known road through Sandtown (now Mercerville) and Quaker Bridge.* Stretches of this road were stumpy and difficult, hard to follow in the dark, but it was over terrain which Benjamin Randolph had known from boyhood.

After the Princeton victory, when the Continental Army took up winter quarters in Morristown—while the British forces were rolled all the way back to New Brunswick—the records show that Benjamin was there, too, with Washington. Probably it was at this time that he became one of the Commander in Chief's secret agents. One indication of this is a letter of May 12, 1777, from Washington to the President of Congress:[14]

A Return of the Army in Jersey, as late as the 6th Inst. I transmitted yesterday morning in a Letter by Mr. Randolph of Chestnut Street; which you will probably receive today and from which Congress will be able to determine the Expediency of calling out the Militia from Delaware and Pennsylvania.**

---

* New Jersey then, as now, had two places named Quaker Bridge.
** Patriotism ran strong in the Randolph family. His eldest brother James built the Revolutionary Salt Works, at Mosquito Cove, in Monmouth County and was active in the militia. His next-eldest brother Daniel, who

Earlier, Randolph had written "Mad Anthony" Wayne, from Mount Holly, N.J., that he had captured two deserters from Wayne's corps "at a place called Speedwell Mill, of mine, with the assistance of some of my workmen." After asking pardon for the "unlucky fellows," Randolph added: "I desire no expense of mine be charged to the Country." [15]

Two months later, on May 6, 1777, Randolph had placed the following advertisement in *The Pennsylvania Evening Post:*

Holsters, pistols, carbines, swords for the Light Horse wanted immediately.

Inquire of Benjamin Randolph in Chestnut street.

That the British certainly would do once they were able to capture Philadelphia; and even then the Redcoats were on their way. By September of 1777 it was clear that General Howe and his troops as well as Joseph Galloway and his Loyalists shortly would be running the city. With discretion ever the better part of valor, Benjamin shut up his shop, bundled up his family, and sought refuge across the river in New Jersey: reportedly at what he had called "Speedwell mill, of mine." This was 23 miles from Mount Holly, and as a place for his family to hide out Benjamin could hardly have found one more inaccessible.

There is in the Historical Society of Pennsylvania an old survey map which makes this very clear. Although of a later period, it shows the "mansion house" at Speedwell, the pond, the dam, the West branch of the Wading River

had run the Speedwell sawmill, was a magistrate in Freehold. As one of the defenders of the Toms River Blockhouse, he was captured, put in the shocking Sugar House prison along with Captain Joshua Huddy, and exchanged at the time Huddy was murdered. A cousin, Nathaniel, was a Captain of militia, captured, spent two years in the Sugar House, was exchanged, and soon afterward was killed in the Battle of Springfield.

and its tributary, Tranquility Branch. Only two other houses appear on the map and the nearest to Speedwell was a mile away. As for roads there were only two: a wagon track to Jones Mill (just south of present Chatsworth), and a wavy winding route through the woods labeled "Speedwell to W. Horse." The White Horse referred to has long been known as Paisley which at present is marked by a bend in the Tabernacle-Chatsworth road.

What was there at Speedwell in 1777? Most important, there was a "good new two-story house, framed and covered with cedar, good cellars walled up with stone, good brick hearths and oven." There was also a "good log house for the sawyer, a large commodious barn and stabling for sixteen or eighteen horses." The mill "goes with two saws, newly repaired." There were on hand four horses, 30 head of cattle, a peach and an apple orchard. This information comes from an advertisement in which Randolph offered the property for sale.[16] Mentioned also were "two hundred acres of iron ore."

Benjamin himself was not spending much time at Speedwell. In November of 1777 he was in Burlington. During the battle for Fort Mifflin he had been assigned to carry a flag of truce to General Howe. Howe had refused to receive it and Randolph wrote directly to Washington. In his letter was the following information he had gleaned:[17]

The officer of the Friggot told me they had just been sending two floating Batteries down the Schuylkill with four 32 Pounders on board to assist against our fort. They were in want of provisions but expected their Shiping up in two or three days. He wanted to no whether General Putnam was likely to Join your Excellency soon or not.

Hardly had the British evacuated Philadelphia in June of 1778 than Benjamin Randolph was back at his old address "in Chestnut street," his family with him. But things had changed. A conqueror had come and gone; the city was dirty and battered; and much destruction had been left in the wake of the departing British and Loyalists. Damaged more than most was the "Sign of the Golden Eagle" judging by an inventory of property loss. Benjamin indeed had been a marked man and his Tory enemies had made the most of their brief glitter in the sun. The inventory, made in 1778, showed that when the damages to the Randolph premises had been totted up, the total was 2,811 pounds, ten shillings, more than most for comparable establishments.[18] It is not surprising, therefore, to find Benjamin as a signer of the new Whig Association "to support each other in disclosing and bringing to justice all Tories within their knowledge." The more conspicuous Tories had left on Lord Howe's ships; but quite a few remained. General Benedict Arnold, in fact, was soon to marry one of them.

These were particularly distressing times for Randolph personally. His wife had died and was buried in St. Paul's Episcopal Churchyard, in the lot where his brother Stephen had been interred in 1763. Characteristically, Benjamin made for Anna a carved mahogany grave marker. Also there were the three girls—Mary, Anna, and Frances —to look after, and with diminished income. All city shops had been ordered closed when General Arnold first took the city in charge after the British evacuation; but even when those shops reopened, Benjamin's particular business was slow. The real money then was in merchandizing necessities. Congress offered to appoint Benjamin "to superintend the making of paper for loan-office certificates and bills of exchange." That was July 31, 1778. On August 8 he declined.[19] He had other plans.

To his roles as lumberman, joiner, cabinet maker, carver and gilder, and soldier, Benjamin Randolph soon would add another—merchant. Such was the trend of the times. Other patriots were making money. Some were getting rich. Benjamin, himself, would not do too badly.

First step in the new direction was the following announcement in three successive issues of the Pennsylvania Packet in November 1778:

TO BE SOLD AT PUBLIC VENDUE

On Thursday the nineteenth instant, at the Ware Room of Benjamin Randolph in Chestnut street.

A Quantity of Carvers and Cabinet makers Tools, consisting of planes, saws, gouges, chissels, work benches &c, &c with a variety of carved mahogany brackets, figures, carved and gilt girandoles, with sundry other furniture of different kinds, and a small quantity of mahogany. The sale to begin at Nine o'clock in the morning, and continue till all are sold.

BENJAMIN RANDOLPH

The sale was held as scheduled. It was conducted by John Ross, an auctioneer, or in the term of the times, a "vendue merchant." Ross's account book shows that some 536 pounds ten shillings was realized for "Mahogany Stuff. Furniture, Brassware &c Sold at his [Randolph's] Ware House in *Chesnut* street," and "paid in full." Later on Randolph was to have other dealings with Ross in his role as "merchant," which was his designation on a 1780 tax list.[20]

One of Randolph's first mercantile ventures was in privateering. Quite a few of his friends had put money in privateers and some were doing all right; one heard little about the ones who lost, as many did. Financial details of the privateering venture are lacking, but it is more than probable that some of his cargoes were put up at auction by John Ross. Two entries in his account particularly attract attention: a realization of 738 pounds paid to Randolph on June 13, 1780, and another of 303 pounds, 15 shillings, on April 17, 1782. There was other merchandizing, too. How remote his new endeavors were from his old ones under the "Sign of the Golden Eagle" is indicated by his sale, on October 31, 1781, of "six pieces of Died Jerminey Linnens," at one pound six pence per piece, to William Richards at Batsto, a transaction noted in Richards' diary.

If Randolph had had enough of cabinet making, he also had had enough of Speedwell Mill, his sawmill in the pines. Twice during 1779 he advertised it for sale. The notice advised persons interested to apply to John Jacobs, overseer on the premises, or the owner in Philadelphia. In another advertisement he merely offered to lease the place.

But if Benjamin had had enough of Speedwell, Speedwell had not had enough of him. The mill was finally sold on April 24, 1780, but the buyer quickly defaulted and by December of that year the property was back in Randolph's hands. On February 11, 1781, Speedwell was sold again, to Thomas Dungan and Jacob Hufty, but Randolph's luck was still bad, and after foreclosure proceedings the property was deeded back to him by the Sheriff, on December 4, 1783.[21]

For Benjamin Randolph 1784 was an eventful year. Forty-six years old, still vigorous, his sights remained focused on the future. He had little apparent desire to engage in the political maneuverings in Philadelphia. Many of his Revolutionary War associates were, for a time anyway, out of the national picture. Perhaps he felt as many did then, that it was up to the states which had won their independence to make up their minds what to do with it, and that with trade reviving after a post-war slump, it was time for him to recoup his family fortunes.

That spring marked a second break in the Randolph family circle. This time it was Mary. While there is no direct evidence, one senses vaguely that Benjamin was not too happy over her decision to marry his "cutter" and overseer at Speedwell. In any case, the ceremony took place on May 11, 1784, at St. Paul's Episcopal Church in Philadelphia.[22] The name of the groom was John Jacob Sluyter, and he had been in charge at Speedwell from 1779 onward. It was there that the couple now went to live, and where their two children—Randolph and Anna Frances—were born.

After the wedding Benjamin took two decisive steps on his own account: he moved his residence to Burlington, N.J.; and he began construction of a furnace at Speedwell. On September 1, 1784, Randolph took title to a dwelling at Fourth and Pearl Streets, Burlington, with a large lot which fronted also on the Delaware River.[23] In the deed Benjamin is described as "formerly of Philadelphia but now of the City of Burlington." This disposes of any thought that he might have been buying the property for speculation. With him in the new home, of course, were the two girls, Anna and Frances Gualdo, now well up in their teens.

Some may wonder that Randolph could move so far from all his associations in the Quaker City, from its cultural and social activities, and, even granting his disinterest, from the excitement of those days in which a new nation was being built. Everything indicates, however, that Benjamin's motives now were primarily economic. His sale advertisements had made plain that the Speedwell tract contained "two hundred acres of ore" with rights to about 700 additional acres. So if he could not sell his property, with its sawmill, it is not too surprising that he should try his hand at smelting the iron. Originally he did not contemplate living at Speedwell, but with a proper home in Burlington, he could keep close watch on his managers.

It could also be questioned why Randolph should have

chosen to go into the iron business at that particular time. Activity in the field had been sluggish. Both Batsto and Taunton furnaces had gone begging for buyers for several years and it was only a few months earlier that William Richards had decided to take Batsto off the tired shoulders of Charles Pettit and his co-owners. Randolph, however, may have been influenced by the lush prosperity of one of his former customers, Colonel Isaac Zane, who owned the successful Marlboro Iron Works near Winchester, Virginia. Zane's great stone mansion was surrounded by gardens, fish ponds, and fountains, and the interior was "filled with superb furniture made by Benjamin Randolph of Philadelphia." [24] Zane lived in style, even on the frontier; perhaps Speedwell, much less remote, could match Marlboro as a money-maker.

Not only did Randolph build a furnace and its satellite installations at Speedwell, he also erected a second and sizeable dwelling house (the first one was occupied by the Sluyters). This construction seems to have been completed before the winter of 1784 set in. Sluyter was made manager of the furnace as well as the sawmill, and business was soon under way. The earliest record located to date is a letter of February 5, 1785 to Levi Hollingsworth in Philadelphia, signed by "Jno Cooper, Ck. for Speedwell Furnace." In the following December there was another order to Hollingsworth to "let the bearer, Richard Sexton, have five hundred wt. Bar Iron at the cash price." This letter was signed "B. Randolph, Speedwell Works." [25] Beyond doubt, the cabinet maker had become an ironmaster.

Randolph apparently was uncertain of the extent of his lands at Speedwell. Many early surveys were roughly made, vaguely described, and filled with exceptions and allowances for overlapping boundary lines. In the fall of 1784 Randolph had a new survey made, and with 522 additional acres taken up on November 3rd of that year his holdings then ran to a total of 1,717 acres.[26] Dating from that survey is a large boundary stone, still standing, marked "B.R./1785," at a corner "where formerly stood a pine tree thus lettered."

As a furnace Speedwell may be judged moderately successful. In iron production it probably was not in a class with Batsto, Martha, and Weymouth. But from the fragmentary evidence available (no account books or other records have come to light), it made money for Randolph during the few years he lived to operate it; and his successors, chiefly lessees, found it a worthwhile operation for a good many years. The principal product was pig iron, sold at first in city markets, and later to such nearby forges as Union (at Chatsworth), Stafford Forge, and the Wading River Forge and Slitting Mill nearby at what became Harrisville.

Surviving relics of Speedwell are few. Charles Boyer found "a cast iron hearth and iron lintel" which had been made there. Existing is a pig with the name "Speedwell" upon it in raised letters. Except for a few other minor relics—all, of course, undated—there remain only portions of the furnace base, bits of slag here and there, and the above-mentioned "B.R." boundary marker. One of the two Randolph houses was standing until the 1920's, but finally it had to be torn down.

Part of the furnishings of the Randolph house in Burlington were the already-noted "Six Sample Chairs," prime examples of his craftsmanship. They were about all he had saved from his days at the "Sign of the Golden Eagle." Today's romantic aura did not hang about them then; they were furniture, to sit on. Thus no special significance was attached to their removal, in 1788, to a new domicile.

Reason for this removal was Benjamin Randolph's decision to marry again. During his years in Burlington he had made many friends—they were to speak in his behalf after his death—and in the pleasant social circles of the West Jersey provincial capital he encountered a young and attractive widow. She was Mary Wilkinson Fenimore, daughter of Nathaniel Wilkinson. Her husband, William Fenimore, had died in 1785.

A strange romance was that of Benjamin and Mary, at least in retrospect. It was a romance beset with obstacles which ardor seems to have been insufficient to overcome. The first obstacle was religion. Both the Wilkinsons and the Fenimores were prominent Quaker families in Burlington County. There had been Quakers here and there in Benjamin's family, but he was not one of them. This problem was solved by Mary, who married Benjamin regardless, and in consequence was disowned by the Burlington Friends Meeting on September 1, 1788.[27]

More difficult was the problem involving their children. Mary Randolph had five of them by her first husband: John W. Fenimore, Priscilla, Nathaniel, Rachel, and William F. Benjamin had Anna and her foster sister Frances Gualdo. Two estates also were involved: that of Anna Bromwich Randolph on the one hand, and that of Nathaniel Fenimore on the other. To meet these issues practically, according to Benjamin:

There was a verbal agreement between me and my wife Mary previous to our marriage that neither of us would claim or demand any right, title and interest whatsoever in or to any part of the property or Estate of the other during the Coverture or at any other time.

After the wedding the Randolph family appears to have moved into the Fenimore menage in Springfield Township. This, too, seemed like a practical step. Mary's was an established household in which she felt at ease and where Benjamin naturally expected to find love, comfort, and happiness. It may be doubted, however, that his children —Anna and Frances—felt as free of misgivings as did Benjamin. They were then in their early twenties, a difficult age to be shifted from the first fiddle section to the second in their father's household. And while Mary's children were younger, they probably found adjustment difficult, too; especially if they inherited their mother's rather decisive temperament.

How long did the honeymoon last? The facts are these: In 1789 Randolph conveyed title to Speedwell Furnace to his daughter Anna, ostensibly in return for her having given him title some years earlier to Philadelphia property "which vested in her in fee by descent as heir-at-law of her deceased mother." [28] Randolph began spending more and more time at Speedwell, less and less in Burlington, and by 1790—only two years after the wedding—was giving Speedwell as his address.

Also in 1790, Benjamin Randolph made his will, which is noted below. And Frances departed for Morristown. (That same year Frances Gualdo married Gabriel Ford, of Morristown. Gabriel was one of the sons of Col. Jacob Ford, Jr., who built the historic Morristown mansion known as "Washington's Headquarters"; and it was there that Frances and Gabriel went to live.) After Frances left there are strong indications that Anna was living at Speedwell.

On December 21, 1791, Benjamin Randolph died. The circumstances of his death are unknown. When his will was read it was found that he had made the following bequests: to his niece, Margaretta Robbins (of Freehold) fifty pounds; to his widow, Mary, "the sum of twenty pounds and no more." The residue of the estate was left two-thirds to his daughter Anna, and one-third to his

foster-daughter Frances Gualdo Ford. The token legacy to
his wife was "explained" in the will as a consequence of
the pre-marital agreement, Randolph declaring that "I
have in no wise intermeddled with the Estate either real
or personal which belonged to her previous to our union." [29]

Randolph's executors were his "esteemed friend, Joseph
Pascal, my daughter Anna Randolph, and my esteemed
friend Joshua M. Wallace." Mary was "included out" again.
Thus it was not surprising that nine days after her husband's death Mary Fenimore Randolph moved to block
probate of the will. She filed the following caveat:

> I Mary Randolph, Widow of Benjamin Randolph late of the
> township of Northampton, Burlington County, deceased—
> do object and caveat against the probate of the last will and
> testament of the said Benjamin Randolph, or any writing
> pretended to be his said last will until I am heard against
> the same in common law.

There was a hearing in Orphans Court (which has wide
jurisdiction in family matters). Unfortunately there is no
record of the testimony. Mary was heard, and so were a
procession of witnesses summoned by William Griffith,
then Burlington County surrogate. Among the latter were
the executors, numerous friends, and acquaintances of the
deceased, and the Fords, who came down from Morristown to testify.

Mary Randolph lost her case. The will was probated on
February 14, 1792, and the bequests were subsequently
distributed. Failure of Randolph to mention his other
daughter, Mary Sluyter, in the will suggests that she
had been advanced her share of his estate upon her marriage. And nothing is more characteristic of the warmth
and benevolence of Benjamin Randolph than his legacy
to Frances Gualdo Ford, daughter of his old friend whom
he had raised and loved as his own.

There is nothing to show the total value of the Randolph estate. Without doubt it was considerable, or Mary probably would not have challenged the will. Yet while she never knew it in her lifetime, she may well have had the most precious legacy of all: those "Six Sample Chairs" which had remained in her home after his death. Perhaps they had been a wedding gift from Benjamin. But there they were, presumably unnoticed and taken for granted. "Used furniture" then, the chairs had no great monetary value in contemporary scales of worth. And had anyone suggested in 1791 that three of those six chairs someday would fetch over $50,000 at auction—such a person would have been pitied as a bit more than "teched." *

An empty home Speedwell must have seemed to Anna after her father's death; especially with Frances gone also. True, the Sluyters were there, but most evidence suggests that Benjamin and Anna had not had too much in common with them.

As an executor, Anna Randolph stayed on at Speedwell until the estate was settled, and was giving the furnace as her address as late as the winter of 1792–93. Clearing of the furnace tract title took a bit of doing. On October 27, 1792, she purchased from Thomas Cooper and John Butterworth some additional land—1,273 acres less various exceptions—for 300 pounds.[30]

After Randolph's death the furnace operations were continued, under lease, to Sluyter. He carried on until January 14, 1797, when according to Boyer, he failed. Then with Mary and their children Sluyter went to live in Augusta, Ga.

Anna Randolph was to retain ownership of Speedwell

---

* Mary Randolph's will, dated June 1, 1816, and probated July 22, 1819, distributed her estate among her five children, with Nathaniel as executor and residuary legatee, and thus inheritor of the household goods including the "Six Sample Chairs," and also three Negro slaves, Robert, Lydia, and Fanny, who were to be "sold by my Executor for his own benefit. . . ."

Furnace for 44 years, a long time. Perhaps she inherited some of the fascination which the primitive locale had for her father. Most women would have sold the property as quickly as possible after settlement of the estate; instead, Anna acquired that additional land. Yet even so, Speedwell was no place for a young unmarried woman to live, however, worthwhile it might be as an investment (her rentals averaged about $500 annually for nearly three decades). There was no social life. It was a long trip to Philadelphia and she had few friends there. So shortly after the estate was settled, Anna went to live with her foster-sister, Frances Ford, and her husband, in the Morristown mansion. Anna never married. She lived in Morristown the rest of her life, and died there on February 28, 1835.

Speedwell's fortunes thereafter, with one exception, were chiefly the humdrum routines of a small furnace village. On July 14, 1798, Anna Randolph leased it to Joseph Walker and John Youle, who in 1802 acquired the Wading River Forge and Slitting Mill, and in 1808 purchased the Stafford (or West Creek) Forge near Manahawkin. Youle, listed in deeds as an "iron founder of New York," seems to have spent quite a bit of time at his South Jersey ironworks. And for a while, he lived in the attractive old mansion at Stafford Forge, which is still visible from the Garden State Parkway. After Walker's death Youle took a lease on Speedwell for a further term of seven years and became sole owner of the other properties.[31] After the Wading River Works burned down, about 1810, much of Speedwell's iron went to Stafford Forge for refining.

Following expiration of Youle's lease, Speedwell Furnace was operated by Mark Richards, already mentioned in this book as an associate of but not a relative of the family of William Richards. During part of this period, Anthony Sykes Earl is mentioned as manager, a post he also held at Taunton Furnace. Later in 1827 Richard Campion was the manager. In 1829, however, Mark Richards ceased operations at Speedwell, and at Anna Randolph's request installed one of his employes in the dwelling as a rent-free tenant, the purpose being to protect the property from vandals and the land from squatters. The furnace was idle.

One break in those dull days at Speedwell made big headlines in the newspapers. This was in March of 1827, and one press account ran as follows:[32]

STOP A MURDERER

A man named John Kross, charged with a most cruel, inhuman and outrageous outrage upon Rebecca Kross, his wife . . . lately absconded from Speedwell Furnace (where he was employed). One hundred dollars is offered by the people of the neighborhood for his apprehension . . . He is about six feet high, large and robust, dark hair and small black whiskers . . . had on when he went away, a blue coat and pantaloons, red flannel shirt, and a half-worn hat. He is supposed to be between 40 and 50 years of age.

The *Mount Holly Herald* seems to have outdone all competitors in explosive phraseology:

The circumstances attending this murder, the expressions of this demon in human shape, and the manner in which his shocking purpose was effected, are too horrible to be related —and have no parallel in the catalogue of barbarities. To conceive, much less execute so brutal a crime would, we should suppose, have been impossible for any mother's son however wickedly inclined.

The manhunt was state-wide. Indignation ran high. Far to the north, in Hackettstown, one Nathaniel Allen Rand was suspected of being "the murderer Kross." He was arrested, taken to Mount Holly, put in jail, examined, and released—after Manager Campion, of Speedwell, had traveled to Mount Holly, seen the prisoner, and assured the authorities that he was not the man. There this tale ends, for the author's searching disclosed no account that "the murderer Kross" was finally brought to justice.

On December 23, 1833, Anna Randolph, "of Morristown," then well in her sixties, decided to sell Speedwell. Now it passed into the Richards family. The purchaser was Samuel Richards, highly successful operator of Martha, Atsion, and Weymouth ironworks.[33] Repairs were made, the furnace stack refinished, gangs of ironworkers employed, and Speedwell once again was back in operation.

Just as the best days of the bog iron business were waning, so the best days of Speedwell had long since passed. Even Richards, a master at the iron business, could not turn Speedwell Furnace into a money-maker. Soon operations were off-and-on, then more off than on; and long before Samuel Richards' death in 1842 he had virtually abandoned the works. Speedwell was not even a specific bequest in his will, being lumped with his properties "not specifically devised."

A quiet coda often brings a stormy musical composition to a close. So the closing chapter of the Speedwell story matches in mood the waters of the nearby and aptly-named Tranquility Creek. For eight more years the property lay idle. Long gone was the old sawmill. In ruins was Benjamin Randolph's furnace. Speedwell had about reverted to its original status: it was simply real estate.

Settlement of the Samuel Richards estate was slow, perhaps difficult. Finally, on June 30, 1850, for a mere $1,750, Stephen Colwell, Richards' executor, sold the property to James McCambridge, who had been acquiring other lands in the vicinity.[34]

McCambridge had been proprietor of the Eagle Tavern,

not far to the southwest. Dating as far back as 1798, when Gideon Pharo was host, this tavern had been drinking headquarters for Speedwell's workmen.[35] A wriggling line on an old map is marked "to Barnhart's Tavern" which was the name from 1810 when Jacob Barnhart acquired it until 1826 when he sold it to McCambridge. Then it became the Eagle Tavern. Its cellar hole may still be seen by the observant explorer who follows the old road north from Green Bank, past the corner where the old Washington Tavern once stood. Eagle Tavern probably was abandoned in the late 1830's, about the time Speedwell's operations had finally ceased.

Meanwhile, cranberries—and later blueberries—were replacing iron as the chief product of the area. On August 28, 1868, McCambridge sold the Speedwell Furnace site and some additional lands—a total of 2,007 acres—to his brother-in-law, Stephen Lee.[36] The price was $8,000. Today, almost a century later, Speedwell is still in the Lee family. Its present owner is another Stephen Lee who loves his lands, cherishes Speedwell's historic background, and is gracious in the matter of informing lost wayfarers where they are, where the furnace once stood, and where, until comparatively recent years, Randolph's old dwelling house was to be seen.

Finding Speedwell today is not difficult. It is marked on most maps although it is no longer a village. Easiest route to follow is along the macadam highway a bit more than three miles south from Chatsworth on the road to New Gretna. Suddenly a little road comes in from the right. This road leads to old Speedwell and the modern home of Mr. and Mrs. Stephen Lee. Another route, some-what wilder and more venturesome, leads from Tabernacle east, past "Hampton Gate," on beyond the Carranza pine-land memorial, over the tracks of the Central Railroad of New Jersey, on to the Friendship Bogs with its neat cluster of houses and buildings, left to a winding road and then —Speedwell.

One final note. There is in Morristown, N.J., a "Speedwell Avenue." It has been theorized that this was named by or for Anna Randolph—a gracious thought. But actually it was once the road to another Speedwell Iron Works —New Jersey had two—which was built along the Whippany River shortly before the Revolution. This Morris County Speedwell consisted of a furnace, forge, and slitting mill, a full scale enterprise. Some of it was in operation as late as 1850.

By a striking coincidence, one of the owners of this Speedwell was Dr. Timothy Johnes; Dr. Johnes was a brother-in-law of Col. Jacob Ford, Jr., who built the Morristown mansion; and thus an uncle-by-marriage of Gabriel Ford, who married Frances Gualdo, foster-sister of Anna Randolph.

It was a further coincidence that Anna Randolph should leave the shadows of one Speedwell Furnace to live close to those of another. This time, however, she found peace and happiness. Frances was closer to her than any other being on earth; and if one Speedwell sometimes sparked memories of another, they were moments which the daughter of Benjamin Randolph was proud to recall.

Railroad to Nowhere

"Who would want to take a ride to nowhere?" "What's the sense in a railroad with only one end?" So scoffed "experts" when it was proposed to build a railroad from Camden to a desolate ten-mile stretch of seashore, a great sandy island on which were scattered but seven cottages. This island was to become Atlantic City.

Railroading was high adventure in the mid-19th century. Lines across southern New Jersey had been championed for many years before any were built. In 1836 a railroad was proposed along a route from Camden to Tuckerton, via Quaker Bridge, Harrisville, and Bass River. Such a route had at least a long-established seaside resort as its eastern terminus; sea-bathing at Tucker's Beach had been popular for more than half a century. But a railroad to what then was "Abseekum Island" was something else again. Only sand and those few cottages lay at its far end. One observer called it "a lonely region, inaccessible and remote."

Despite scorn and scoffing, the railroad to "Abseekum Island" was built. Its founder was Samuel Richards of Jackson Glass Works—nephew of Samuel Richards of Atsion, son of Thomas Richards, and grandson of Batsto's William Richards. Samuel was also the dynamic leader in establishing Atlantic City, in transforming "nowhere" into the "Playground of the World."

The Book of Proverbs tells us that "where there is no vision, the people perish." Samuel Richards possessed vision in abundance. When he gazed at "Abseekum" Island he did not see its vast stretches of sand; he saw a great resort city with imposing hotels, a city rivalling Long Branch to the north and Cape May to the south. Both had prospered despite the slow access of water transportation. Atlantic City—Richards coined the name—would be reached in less time and by far more people. Samuel Richards was able to command the capital, determination, and energy needed to build the railroad which would transform "Abseekum Island" into Atlantic City.

It has been said that Samuel Richards looked like a bank president and worked like a horse. For all his handsome appearance and meticulous dress no task was too small, no problem of construction too intricate for him to tackle personally. He enjoyed working with his hands, and displayed a special interest in machinery: he was responsible for a number of inventions, including a railroad snow plow.

More than once Samuel Richards took personal command of his railway construction gangs; and the railroad and Atlantic City, itself, were both laid out partly under his direct supervision. His interest was so persistent that some complained that it seemed difficult to lay a rail, drive a spike, or raise the rafters of a hotel without Samuel breathing down the workers' necks. Charles R. Colwell, of Weymouth, who knew him well, stated it this way:[1]

> One of Mr. Richards' marked peculiarities was his inability to look at the doing of any difficult piece of work without showing a disposition to assist in, as well as direct it—a disposition he not infrequently indulged.

The "daddy" of the Camden & Atlantic Railroad was once cited as Dr. Jonathan Pitney, of Absecon, a distinguished physician who was one of its first directors. But when that attribution appeared in a *History of Atlantic City*, by A. L. English, it was hotly disputed by the late General Elias Wright, engineer and land developer. Wright declared that Samuel Richards was not only the pioneer in building the railroad but also the real founder of Atlantic City.

General Wright's story, based on his personal knowledge, appeared in the *Atlantic City Press* in 1895. Wright declared that he knew Dr. Pitney and "never heard of him claiming to be more than he was." He also did not think Pitney ever contended that he had started the railroad or founded the city. Wright stated: "Mr. Samuel Richards was an incorporator of the Camden & Atlantic, a director from its organization, and for 24 years an active officer either as Director or Assistant President." His letters to Richard B. Osborne, chief engineer in charge of plans and construction, "show that Richards was the active businessman on the board, and the officer who secured the chief part of the right-of-way, and practically its pioneer. I know this from my official position with the company."

Samuel Richards was also the early advocate of a bathing resort on "Abseekum Island" and Wright declares that he had proposed the name "Atlantic City," remarking that it had a national appeal and that "there was much in a name." Largely through Richards' influence, according to Wright, "the Camden & Atlantic Land Company was organized, the lands purchased, and the charter of the land company obtained on March 10, 1853."

As far back as 1714 the sandy island had been called "Abseekum." Three hundred acres of it, more or less, had been sold to one John Scott. By the 1830's about 1,225 acres of beachfront was in the name of Jeremiah Leeds, some of whose descendants lived in the seven little houses which dotted the island. Leeds died in 1839, and by 1853 his heirs were happy to sell more than a thousand acres of that beachfront for an average price of one dollar per acre. It was almost as good a deal as the purchase of Manhattan from the Indians. Buyer of the beachfront was Richards' aforementioned Camden & Atlantic Land Company.

In an address to the stockholders of that company, Samuel said: "The principal portions of the lands now in possession of the company and contracted for by them lie in intermediate sections along the beach. They comprise about one thousand acres at the average cost of $1.00 an acre."

Ridiculous as this price seems today, more than a few thought it was no bargain then. There was no convenient way to reach those acres of sandy beach. As for the proposed railroad, it was considered a wild gamble and not an investment. For example, railroads were deep in monopoly politics in those days, and the Camden and Amboy Railroad seemed, literally, to own the State of New Jersey. But neither the bosses of that road nor their paid politicians raised any objection to a charter for the Camden & Atlantic. When they thought about it, they only laughed. Who would buy stock in such a wild scheme as a railroad to nowhere?

They reckoned without Samuel Richards. The stock issue was $500,000. In a surprisingly short time it was all sold. Original subscribers were: Colwell & Ball, 400 shares; Thomas Richards (Samuel's father), 200 shares; Joseph Porter, 200; Andrew K. Hay, 200; Enoch Doughty, 100; W. W. Fleming, 100; William Coffin, 100; Jonathan Pitney, 20; Jesse Richards, 20; Thomas H. Richards, 20; John Lucas, 50; John H. Doughty, 1; Daniel Doughty, 1; Robert B. Leeds, 5; James Leeds, 5; John Leeds, 5; Chalkley S. Leeds, 5; Richard Hackett, 5; John C. Da Costa, 40.

Influence of the Richards family is quite evident by the names of the stockholders. And from 1855 to 1857 the president of the Camden & Atlantic was George Richards, one of Samuel's uncles. Also, of 1,477 shares, the Richards family controlled 740, a majority.

Minutes of the company for a meeting of June 25, 1852 show election of the following directors: Stephen Colwell, Samuel Richards, W. W. Fleming, Thomas H. Richards, William Coffin, Joseph Porter, Jonathan Pitney, Enoch Doughty. Hay was elected chairman, Samuel Richards secretary, Coffin treasurer. Colwell, Fleming, and Samuel Richards were named a committee to draft by-laws. On July 1, 1852, Thomas H. Richards, who had been ill, offered his resignation and John C. DaCosta was elected director and president of the company. The following December DaCosta resigned and Hay was chosen president. In 1854 Hay was taken ill, and Samuel Richards was made acting president.

After numerous construction difficulties—the roadbed over the Atlantic City meadows was washed away twice—the railroad was finally ready for operation. Meanwhile the directors had acquired an interest in the Cooper's Point Ferry, thus assuring a connection with Philadelphia. The route was complete.

Formal opening day for the Camden & Atlantic Railroad

was July 1, 1854.[2] For many—spectators as well as riders—it was a thrilling occasion. The first train, an official special, consisted of nine passenger cars drawn by an engine named "Atsion," for the furnace town then owned by Director Fleming. Crowds milled about the Cooper's Ferry terminal as the steaming engine seemed impatient to get going, and a slow procession of VIP's filed into the nine cars. Each boat from Philadelphia seemed to bring more guests, each with a printed invitation, and more and more curiosity seekers crowded around to see the first iron horse take off for the seashore.

Finally, a bit after 9 A.M., the engine whistle sounded, the iron horse belched a great cloud of black smoke, there was a grinding and creaking—and the train got under way. It was the beginning of a triumphal journey. The cheering crowds in Camden gave only a foretaste of the accolades to come. Once out of the city the train gathered speed, and soon the excitement of accelerating motion, the rhythmic click-clack of the rail-joins, and the now-joyous whistle of the train were delighting the throng of notables aboard.

In Haddonfield there was a brief halt as a crowd-pleaser. At Junction (as Atco then was called), Samuel Richards' glassworkers were lined beside the tracks. There was a long stop at Waterford. Judge Joseph Porter, one of the directors, owned the glassworks there and his workmen turned out not only to see but to celebrate. There was a loud gun salute. The judge bowed from a car platform. Flags were unfurled, and finally the ladies of the town marched over to the train, presented bouquets, and handed the judge a wreath of laurel on which flowers spelled out the words: "Welcome to Waterford." [3] Another director, Andrew K. Hay, lived just below at Winslow; and while the train paused, crowds cheered, and Hay took a bow—after Waterford it was rather an anticlimax. It also was the last stop.

South Jersey's new iron horse thereafter rolled swiftly
down the straight-away to Absecon, mostly through woodlands broken only by the railroad itself. Many months
earlier, surveyors had cut the path and built the bridges
amid the shadows of the pines through which the six hundred were now riding. Towns familiar today—Hammonton, Elwood, Egg Harbor—were not there then. To some it
may have been a dull ride, but it impressed a contemporary reporter who wrote:

> It was a distance of twenty-five miles without the slightest
> curve, the rails resembling a piece of ribbon stretched far
> away in the distance beneath the o'ershadowing of primeval
> forests.

Despite this lyric note, the actual ride was far from idyl-
lic. The seats in the cars were plain boards—not even
cushions were provided. The engine was a wood burner
and great clouds of smoke descended impartially upon
the humbler passengers and the VIP's. The bridge across
the thoroughfare was not finished, so the passengers had
to get off the train and were taken over the waterway in
boats. As for the ride itself, in addition to the smoke, the
progress of the cars—on a roadbed which consisted of iron
rails spiked to planks resting on cross-ties in the sand—
was far from smooth, thus offering the passengers little in
either ease or comfort. The road, of course, was single-
track, with no signals of any sort. James M. Pettit, first
conductor on the road, has told that to stop the train it
was necessary for him to traverse its length "and attract
the engineer's attention by striking him with a piece of
wood," and by holding up his forefinger tell him a passenger was to get off at the next station.

Finally the 600 passengers and their hosts found themselves in "Atlantic City." Their reactions doubtless were
mixed. A big dinner awaited them at the United States Ho-

tel, a huge four-story structure intended to accommodate four thousand guests. At that time, however, only one wing of the place was up, and even that was not completed. After dinner the 600 either sat it out at the hotel or strolled on the beach where some of them enjoyed counting the remains of six shipwrecks.[4] There was nothing else to do, save gaze at the ocean which then as now rolled and thundered in mighty majesty.

One reporter, however, found nothing boring or dull. Said he: "The unremitting attention of Mr. DaCosta [John C.] President of the Company, to the comfort and enjoyment of the guests entirely obliterated any note of time, and he was ably sustained by Messrs. Richards, Hay, Fleming, Judge Porter and the gentlemanly conductors and attaches of the road."

Clearly, the bar at the United States Hotel was open.

After this dramatic debut it only remained to open the Camden & Atlantic Railroad to the public. This was done on July 4, 1854. Trains were scheduled to "run daily, Sundays excepted, between Camden and the village of Absecon." It was some time before the problem of the meadows was conquered and passengers could ride directly into the new city by the sea. After that, Sundays were to be the big days for C. & A. passenger traffic.

Curiously, none of the earlier engines of the Camden & Atlantic were named for the Richards family. Samuel is said to have made objection. Other directors, however, had no such inhibitions. Thus engines were named for Enoch A. Doughty, Andrew K. Hay, DaCosta, Charles Freeman, Rufus Hill, Charles P. Frazier and John Lucas, of Lucaston. Names of other locomotives were: Atlantic, Pacific, Arctic, Camden, Oriental, New Jersey, Sea Gull, Petrel, Tempest, Curlew, and John Brodhead.[5] The author has no record as to when many of these engines were

in service. Also it is possible that these were not all different locomotives, but, as is the way with ships, the same
engine may have had different names at different times.

Commuter service was one of the first considerations of
the original Camden & Atlantic directors. On November 9,
1855, a committee consisting of Directors Coffin, Porter,
and Samuel Richards was named to work out commutation
rates and as early as May 9, 1856, commuter tickets were
issued at the rate of 24 coupons for $12, good for a four-
month period. Over the years, however, commuters became a secondary consideration of the railroad. Time and
again commuter trains would be shunted on sidings to let
a shore-bound express roar by. On holiday weekends the
"accommodation train" as it was euphemistically called
would sometimes wait for two expresses to pass before
crawling along to the next station. Business, after all, was
business; and the shore was the big business.

Samuel Richards and his colleagues, however, had en-
visioned Atlantic City not only as a resort but as a freight
terminal. At considerable expense they built a wharf more
than one hundred feet long at Absecon Inlet, where the
water was 16 feet deep.[6] Their first idea proved right; their
second wrong. Passenger travel came up to expectations,
but the freight terminal did not.

Due partly to this fact, and partly to other considerations, C. & A. earnings soon became insufficient to carry
the road's indebtedness. In addition to the original stock issue, $1,000,000 of seven percent bonds had been issued,
and a floating debt of $400,000 had been incurred.[7] The
capital cost of building the railroad had turned out to be
considerably greater than original estimates, and this despite the fact that the road was for the most part straight
and level. As the C. & A. continued to run in the red, it
was forced into bankruptcy during the panic of 1857. Several directors of the railroad were also directors of the

Camden & Atlantic Land Company and gave the railroad financial assistance—to prevent a halt in the train service —but even this outside help was not enough.

After the Camden & Atlantic was reorganized and fresh capital acquired, a sharp increase in traffic soon made it comparatively prosperous. In 1862 came the tie-up with the Raritan and Delaware Bay Railroad at Atco, affording direct New York-Philadelphia travel by the two lines. It was a short-lived venture but it looked good then. That same year it was proposed to build a branch to Mays Landing, but that never materialized. By 1871, however, the C. & A. was showing a profit of $180,379, with a total of 366,818 passengers carried and 66,543 tons of freight.[8]

It is worth noting that of the original directors of the road, before bankruptcy, a number were still on the board in 1871: Andrew K. Hay, Walter D. Bell, Enoch A. Doughty, and Samuel Richards. Of interest also is that year's report on the locomotives:

CAMDEN	Received	May 1871: condition good.
PETREL	”	July 1869: requires general repairs.
ATLANTIC	”	May 1868: in fair condition.
SEA GULL	”	June 1866: very good condition.
JOHN BRODHEAD	”	July 1863: in shop under repair.
CURLEW	”	1855: in very good condition.
TEMPEST	”	Dec. 1853: in shop; needs repairs.
SURF	”	1854: old and unreliable.
LITTLE GIANT	”	requires repairs very much.

As to cars, in 1871 there were 19 first class cars; 24 second class cars; 4 baggage cars; two mail cars, and one smoking car. That year, too, a "waterhouse with a windmill attachment" was erected at Hammonton.[9]

Atlantic City, meanwhile, was expanding rapidly. Real estate prices and more than a few family fortunes were made in that era. By 1872 the population had grown from seven families to three thousand people. More and more hotels were constructed; hundreds of summer cottages went up; and slowly, all-year-round dwellings were being built. Old "Abseekum" Beach was becoming a city in fact as well as name. A boardwalk had been erected from the Inlet to Missouri Avenue. It was eight feet wide and three feet above the sand; its sections were taken down in winter and stacked for protection against the weather. But it was a boardwalk, and forerunner of the world-famous structure of today.

Bearing in mind that the Camden & Atlantic, after 20 years, was still a single-track railroad, it is not surprising that Samuel Richards should put up a fight for better rail facilities. Some of the directors, like more than a few railroad directors of later years, apparently felt that anything was good enough for passengers. Had not the notorious Jim Fisk observed that passengers were as useless to a railroad as mammaries to a man! A struggle followed, and four directors resigned: Richards, Charles R. Colwell, Walter Dwight Bell, and William Massey. The "sit-tighters" had won. They were content with poor schedules despite increasing business. They were satisfied with obsolete equipment. As late as 1871 the greater part of the track consisted of the old flat rails.

A man of Samuel Richards' aggressive temperament would scarcely allow his enemies to think they had won a real victory. He swiftly organized a new company, and acquired the capital necessary to build a narrow-gauge railroad from Camden to a point slightly south of the then growing Atlantic City. Nine months from the date of ground-breaking, the first train was put into operation and carried a delegation of officers, directors, stockholders, and friends.

It was a tremendous victory for Richards in more ways than one. The Camden & Atlantic had put every possible obstacle in his path. When he began construction from both ends of the line simultaneously, the C. & A. directors refused to let the construction engines be taken over its tracks or its cars to be used for shipment of supplies. The Baldwin Locomotive Works sent its construction engine by water, around Cape May and up the thoroughfare. Ties were brought in by water from Baltimore. And Richards won a hectic right-of-way battle in Atlantic City with his former colleague, Enoch Doughty, who had remained as a C. & A. director.

Meanwhile Richards had purchased several buildings from Philadelphia's 1876 Centennial Exposition. The State Building was used for offices at the Camden terminal. The Finance Building was transformed into the station house in Atlantic City. A third building intended for an excursion station at the foot of Florida Avenue was washed away in a storm.

Competition of the "Narrow Gauge" as it came to be called soon made itself felt. Round-trip fares had been three dollars; soon they were cut as low as a dollar. New throngs poured in; new hotels went up; new capital was attracted; and Atlantic City was launched upon a new boom which was to make it far and away the most popular New Jersey seashore resort.

Commerce in many of the way-station towns was stimulated, particularly in lumber, glass, and agriculture products. New development sprang up all along the route of the railroads; land speculators profited most of all especially in the shore areas.

Phenomenal now was the rise in Atlantic City real estate values. A lot purchased in 1856 for $1,500 was sold for $225,000 not long after the "Narrow Gauge" began operation. A tract near the inlet was bought for $21,000, sold two years later for $63,000, and five years after that realized over $1,000,000. Countless similar stories could be told: Atlantic City was growing with a speed which even astonished its founders, and those persons with much nerve and a little capital often found themselves wealthy overnight.

A device which packed the shore trains on weekdays as well as weekends was the "dollar excursion," no matter that the cars were the dregs of the car yards. Few seemed to care that the windows were open wide so that smoke and cinders poured in and that those women dressed in white for a shore parade might arrive a sooty mess. For a dollar what could one ask? Unfortunately, the more expensive regular rides were only a little better, although in the Pullmans, when they came along, screens were installed, and later this "modern convenience" was even extended to the excursion trains.

Paradoxically, the railroads, which made so much prosperity possible, were to wind up sharing it least. At first things seemed to go well for Samuel Richards' "Narrow Gauge": opening year profits were $50,000, above expectations. In 1880, however, the Pennsylvania Railroad controlled West Jersey & Atlantic Railroad built a third line to Atlantic City, by way of Mays Landing and Newfield. Three years later the "Narrow Gauge" was sold in foreclosure proceedings, and acquired by the Philadelphia & Reading Railroad which converted it into a standard gauge, double-track, railroad. To meet that progressive competition the Camden & Atlantic and West Jersey &

Atlantic were consolidated under one management and given the name West Jersey & Seashore Railroad. Not until the 1890's, however, was the C. & A. made into a double-track railroad in the same year that the railroad bridge was built over the Delaware River at Delair.

Thus at the turn of the century Atlantic City was served by two first-rate railroad systems. Both roads acquired new engines designed for those high-speed runs to the shore which made railroad history. Of these, the train called "Nelly Bly"—running direct to New York—became nationally famous.

Samuel Richards was gifted with great foresight. Yet he almost surely would be astounded to see what has happened to the railroad systems he did so much to establish. Once human beings jammed and crammed themselves into buses—and either liked it or tolerated it—the breathing space of a railroad car became old-fashioned to some. True, the railroads did little enough to fight the bus competition, and appeared quite content to cut off more and more passenger trains. As time passed, the Reading and West Jersey & Seashore lines were consolidated; and now it is not unlikely that all passenger service along the route of the old Camden & Atlantic Railroad will go the way of the stagecoaches it supplanted. Faded into memory already are the way-stations where ticket agents once seemed so important at their desks behind green-shaded lamps. Lost in the past, too, is the old "midnight train," famous for inspiring poets and awakening light sleepers.

Residents of the many towns which owed their birth to the C. & A. will miss not only the commutation trains but also the once-glamorous expresses with their long strings of Pullman and dining cars. Dim, too, the day when townsfolk turned out to see packed holiday trains roar by, chortling with glee when one of the "Western Trains"— with differently colored cars—streaked past the stations which today seem candidates for firewood. There was a time when direct service to Atlantic City—over the C. & A. tracks—came from such "far-off" places at Chicago, Minneapolis, and Denver.

Yes, Samuel Richards would be amazed. The diesel has replaced the iron horse. The old familiar whistle has given way to the deep snort. The passenger may give way entirely to freight, so that only cattle will be able to ride the rails to the "World's Playground." How long the freight train itself will last is further conjecture, with trucks becoming bigger and bigger. In another century all of us will have moved along; and our descendants, reading a nostalgic story like this, may decide they "haven't missed a thing." They could not be more wrong. But we won't be on hand then to explain why.

Appendices

Genealogical Sketch of the Richards Family

William Richards, of Batsto

Born September 12, 1738; baptized St. Gabriel's Episcopal Church, Douglassville, Pa.; died Mount Holly, N.J., August 31, 1823.

Married: In 1764, Mary Patrick (6/24/1745–11/22/1794), daughter of John and Anna (Dunklin) Patrick. Their eleven children were:

1 *Abigail:* (6/1/1765–5/14/1794); buried Pleasant Mills, N.J.
2 *John:* (6/1/1767–11/30/1793); buried Pleasant Mills, N.J.
3 *Samuel:* (5/8/1769–1/4/1842); buried Laurel Hill, Phila., Pa. Married (1) Mary Morgan (nee Smith); (2) Anna Maria Witherspoon (nee Martin).
4 *Elizabeth:* (8/21/1771–9/24/1857); married the Rev. Thomas Haskins; buried Pleasant Mills, N.J.
5 *Rebecca:* (8/7/1773–5/10/1809); married John Sevier, Jr.; buried Pleasant Mills, N.J.

6   *William:* (7/1/1775–12/21/1796); buried Pleasant Mills, N.J.
7   *Joseph Ball:* (10/6/1777–3/26/1797); buried Pleasant Mills, N.J.
8   *Thomas:* (2/10/1780–10/16/1860); married Anna Bartram.
9   *Jesse:* (12/2/1782–6/6/1854); married Sarah Ennalls Haskins; buried Pleasant Mills, N.J.
10   *Charles:* (8/8/1785–5/11/1788); buried Pleasant Mills, N.J.
11   *Anna Maria:* (2/8/1789–5/2/1816); married John White.

Mary Patrick Richards died November 22, 1794, and was buried at Pleasant Mills. On January 18, 1797, William Richards married Margaretta Wood (6/6/1772–12/21/1850), daughter of Isaac Wood, of Moorestown, N.J., at St. Andrews Episcopal Church, Mount Holly, the Rev. Andrew Fowler officiating. The eight children of William and Margaretta Richards were:

12   *Benjamin Wood:* (11/12/1797–7/12/1851); married Sarah Ann Lippincott; buried Laurel Hill, Phila., Pa.
13   *Charles Henry:* (4/9/1799–4/26/1802); buried Pleasant Mills, N.J.
14   *George Washington:* (5/5/1801–6/23/1802); buried Pleasant Mills, N.J.
15   *Augustus Henry:* (5/5/1803–2/17/1839); married Rebecca McLean; buried Laurel Hill, Phila., Pa.
16   *William:* (1/16/1805–4/19/1864); married Constantia Marie Lamand.
17   *George Washington:* (5/3/1807–4/22/1874); married Mary Louisa LeGuen.
18   *Joseph Ball:* (11/9/1811–1/30/1812); buried St. Andrews Episcopal Cemetery, Mount Holly, N.J.
19   *Mary Wood:* (3/6/1815–9/19/1860); buried St. Andrews, Mount Holly, N.J.

The Family of Samuel Richards [3]

Samuel Richards was born May 8, 1769, probably at the family home "near Warwick Furnace." He died January 4, 1842, at his Philadelphia home, 357 Mulberry (Arch) street. On November 18, 1797, he married Mrs. Mary Smith Morgan (?/?/1783–3/1/1860), daughter of William T. Smith, of Philadelphia, and widow of John Morgan, son of Gen. Jacob Morgan. The eight children of Samuel and Mary Richards were:

1 *Mary Smith:* (9/18/1798–7/17/1799); buried Christ Church graveyard, Phila., Pa.
2 *William Smith:* (12/3/1799–1/23/1803).
3 *Joseph Ball:* (12/18/1800–9/7/1801).
4 *Samuel Patrick:* (2/19/1802–9/?/1803).
5 *Thomas Smith:* (10/14/1803–11/4/1839); married Harriet Nichols, daughter of Gen. Francis Nichols. Their four children were: (1) Samuel (2/4/1826–2/16/1852); (2) Henry K. (12/12/1828–9/22/1866); (3) Mary Smith (7/15/1832–10/19/1904), married Tinsley Jeter; they had four children, one of them Harriet Richards Jeter Robeson; (4) Susan (?), married William L. Dungleson, of Bethlehem.
   NOTE: Thomas Smith Richards, who learned the iron business at Batsto, was long a half-owner of that furnace, and also a partner with his cousin, John Richards, in Gloucester Furnace, near Egg Harbor. He was active in his father's store at 111 No. Water St., Philadelphia, and lived at his home, 357 Mulberry Street.
6 *Sarah Ball:* (7/20/1805–2/21/1888); married Stephen Colwell (see chapter on Weymouth). Their three children were: (1) Samuel Richards Colwell (3/24/1839–8/29/1873), married his cousin Anna Maria Richards (see 11 below); (2) Edward Stephenson Colwell (4/12/1841–3/8/1864), killed when thrown from a horse during a parade in Washington, D.C.; (3) Charles Colwell (1/21/1844–?/?/1901), married Laura Ritz.
7 *William Smith:* (11/11/1806–?/?/?); died in childhood; second son of this name.
8 *Elizabeth Ann:* (1/17/1810–7/20/1848); married Walter Dwight Bell. They had one child, Mary (11/?/1844–5/?/1865).

Mary Richards died on May 3, 1820. On October 8, 1822, Samuel Richards married Anna Maria Martin Witherspoon (?/?/1783–7/1/1860), widow of Thomas Witherspoon of New York and daughter of Burling Martin, of that same city. The three children of Samuel and Anna Maria Richards were:
9 *Mary:* (6/23/1824–9/10/1824).
10 *Maria Lawrence:* (9/2/1826–12/21/1899); married William Walton Fleming. Their two children were: (1) Clarissa Wal-

ton Fleming (?/?/?–10/1/1854), died in childhood; (2) Samuel Richards Fleming (4/27/1850–9/26/1886).*

11 *William Henry:* (1/25/1828–1/19/1863); reputedly married Mary Thorne; their "reputed daughter," Anna Maria, (?/?/1852–?/?/?).

The Family of Elizabeth Richards Haskins [4]

Elizabeth Richards was born August 26, 1771, and died September 24, 1857. She married, in 1799, the Rev. Thomas Haskins, a Methodist minister (11/7/1760–6/29/1816) who was born in Dorchester, England. She was Haskins' second wife, his first being Martha Potts Haskins (1/25/1764–7/20/1797). The three children of Elizabeth and Thomas Haskins were:

1 *Mary Richards Haskins:* (6/1/1800–?/?/?); married John DuPuy, in ceremony performed by the latter's brother, the Rev. Charles Meredith DuPuy, rector of St. Luke's Episcopal Church, Germantown. Their children were: (1) Thomas Haskins DuPuy (6/25/1821–5/15/1890), married Martha Allen; (2) Charles Meredith DuPuy (12/14/1823–10/7/1898), married Ellen M. Reynolds, one of their children was Herbert DuPuy, distinguished metallurgist and DuPuy family biographer; (3) Horatio Alfred DuPuy (1/31/1826–8/28/1875), married Marie Wilder; (4) Emma Louisa DuPuy (3/15/1828–1/2/1896), married Enoch Courtney, of Balto., Md.; (5) Elizabeth Haskins DuPuy (8/17/1830–12/19/1907), married Thomas Graham; (6) Clara Augusta DuPuy (9/4/1832–?/?/?), married Samuel Blythe Rogers; (7) John Daniel DuPuy (2/12/1835–12/29/1837); (8) Mary Haskins DuPuy (5/7/1837–?/?/1838); (9) Gertrude Ellen DuPuy (6/27/1841–6/?/1902), married Henry S. Sanford.

2 *Martha Potts Haskins:* (8/30/1805–1/8/1853); died at Nice, France; married John Wurts, attorney and Pennsylvania State Senator. Wurts died in Rome, Italy. Both he and his wife are buried at Pleasant Mills.

3 *Elizabeth Richards Haskins:* (?/?/?–10/14/1828). Her stone at Pleasant Mills reads "erected by a bereaved sister."

* Maria Lawrence Fleming, her husband, son, and mother—Samuel's widow—are all buried in Brussels, Belgium.

The Family of Rebecca Richards Sevier [5]

Born August 7, 1773; died May 10, 1809, at Batsto; married in 1794 to John Sevier, Jr., son of the first governor of Tennessee. She is buried at Pleasant Mills. The children of Rebecca and John Sevier, Jr., were:

1 *William Richards Sevier:* (12/17/1794–?/?/?).
2 *James Richards Sevier:* (11/27/1796–?/?/?); he was living as late as 1830; the name of his wife does not appear, but the names of their five children were John, Mary Eliza, Joseph, Rebecca, and Susan.
3 *Mary Eliza Sevier:* (4/2/1797–?/?/?); married Joseph Throckmorton; their children were: (1) William Richards Throckmorton (12/6/1822–?/?/?); (2) Anna Maria (12/21/1824–2/18/1831); (3) Joseph W. (3/4/1827–?/?/?); (4) Rebecca (8/30/1831–?/?/1833); (5) Sarah Richards (8/30/1831–?/?/?).
4 *Sarah Brown Sevier:* (?/?/1801–?/?/1802).
5 *Samuel Richards Sevier:* (3/30/1803–?/?/?); married, had one child, Mary Eliza; was living in 1823.
6 *Thomas Richards Sevier:* (3/19/1805–?/?/?); living 1830.
7 *John Marshall Sevier:* (5/18/1807–?/?/?).

The Family of Thomas Richards [6]

Born February 10, 1780, near Warwick Furnace, Penna.; died October 17, 1860. Married, on October 18, 1810, Ann Bartram (3/15/1787–8/?/1865), granddaughter of the famous botanist. Their children were:

1 *William Bartram:* (9/18/1811–4/?/1875).
2 *John M.:* (2/25/1813–4/29/1849).
3 *Elizabeth Bartram:* (11/28/1814–2/8/1865).
4 *Mary:* (8/10/1816–5/2/1818).
5 *Samuel:* (8/15/1818–2/21/1895); married Elizabeth Moore Ellison; their children were: (1) Mary (11/5/1850–8/25/1851); (2) Thomas John (4/24/1853–7/28/1937), married Elizabeth Winn; their four children were: (a) Bartram; (b) Annabella; (c) Elizabeth; (d) Winifred, married Arthur Devan (children Richards, Thomas, Christopher, Roger, Winifred, Mary Augusta); (3) Samuel Bartram (7/2/1855–5/15/1946), married Mary Dorrance Evans; their two children were: (a) Meta Ellison (3/23/1882–), married (1) Edmund Cooper

Hoyt; they had one son, Samuel Bartram Richards, and (2) Louis Bosdevex Taylor (Hoyt son changed name to Taylor); (b) Natalie (9/4/1890–), married Joseph Brevett Townsend, has two sons: Joseph Brevett, Jr., married Annie Lee Furness; and Benjamin Richards, married Ethel Husband.

6 *Anna Bartram:* (12/23/1820–7/7/1906); married Benjamin J. Crew.

7 *Mary:* (5/20/1823–8/21/1832).

8 *Rachel Bartram:* (11/23/1825–?/?/1907); married the Rev. Thomas Erskine Souper.

9 *Thomas:* (4/29/1828–1/18/1910); married Deborah Milhouse Kimber.

10 *Rebecca Say:* (8/8/1831–9/24/1901); married Walter Newbold; their two children were: (1) Elizabeth; married Samuel Mickle Fox and had two children: (a) Samuel Mickle Fox, Jr., married Francenia Randall; (b) Elizabeth, married Reginald Forbes, and had one daughter, Patricia Newborn, married Bernard S. Dempsey; (2) Anna Bartram; married Remson Bishop, and had five children: (a) Newbold; (b) Mildred; (c) Remson; (d) Anstice; (e) Isabel Bishop, the famous artist.

The Family of Jesse Richards [9]

Born December 2, 1782; died June 8, 1854; married, on September 20, 1810, Sarah Ennalls Haskins (12/19/1788–10/14/1868), daughter of his brother-in-law, the Rev. Thomas Haskins by his first wife, Martha Potts. All are buried at Pleasant Mills. Their children were:

1 *William R.:* (8/22/1811–4/1/1813); buried Pleasant Mills, N.J.

2 *Thomas Haskins:* (12/12/1812–1/28/1873); buried at Pleasant Mills.

3 *Samuel Patrick:* (10/19/1814–12/?/1901); married Sarah Lippincott; their one son was named Jesse.

4 *Elizabeth Haskins Richards:* (11/13/1816–7/1/1909); married George Augustus Bicknell at St. Andrews P.E. Church, Mount Holly; both buried at New Albany, Indiana. Their children were: (1) Martha Haskins Bicknell (4/10/1842–?/?/?); (2) Emma Valeria Pintard Bicknell (12/12/1843–?/?/?); married the Rev. George Madden Love, in St. Paul's Episcopal Church, New Albany, Indiana; (3) George Augustus Bicknell, Jr. (5/15/1846–?/?/?); became Rear Adm. U.S.N.; (4) Rev. Jesse

Richards Bicknell (11/13/1848–?/?/?), rector St. Paul's P.E. Church, Balto., Md.; he assisted at the marriage of his sister Emma.

5 *Anna Maria Richards:* (?/?/1819–?/?/1890); buried Pleasant Mills; married Maj. Lachlan McIntoch of Georgia, an officer in the Confederate army.

6 *Sarah:* (10/14/1821–4/27/1873); blind for a number of years before her death; buried Pleasant Mills.

7 *Jesse:* (8/3/1831–6/26/1889); buried Pleasant Mills.

The Family of Anna Maria White [11]

Born February 8, 1789, at Batsto; died May 2, 1816; married in 1810, John White, of Delaware; their three children were:

1 *Mary R.:* (?).

2 *Elizabeth D.:* (?); married Alfred Horner; their three children were: (1) Alfred, (2) Inman, (3) Mary. Elizabeth D. White died prior to 1876.

3 *John R.:* (3/20/1815–3/1/1874); left two children: (1) William W., (2) Ella.

The Family of Benjamin Wood Richards [12]

Born November 12, 1797, at Batsto, first child of William Richards by his second wife Margaretta Wood; died July 12, 1851; married on January 10, 1821, Sarah Ann Lippincott, daughter of Joshua L. and Sarah (Wetherill) Lippincott. Their children were:

1 *Sarah Lippincott:* (9/7/1823–4/3/1894); married James Constable, of New York; three of their children were Stevenson, Howard, and Anna.

2 *Selina Margaretta:* (12/21/1824–11/26/1902); married James Ricketts Lawrence, of New York; they had two sons (1) Benjamin B. Lawrence; (2) George F.

3 *Louisa Leamy:* (6/18/1826–7/20/1852).

4 *Augustus Henry:* (4/14/1829–3/25/1880); married, (1) Mary Canby; their children were (1) Arabella (9/19/1833–7/9/1836), (2) Louise L. (?), married William Bradford; (3) Edward Canby (1/?/1857–8/11/1857); married, (2), a widow Mrs. Jane Hicks Sharpless, and they had a daughter, (4) Mary Lippincott; married Dr. J. Gurney Taylor, of Overbrook, Pa.

5   *Benjamin Wood:* (8/9/1831–12/16/1908); married Mary Oakley; lived in Hammonton, N.J.; had St. Memin plate of William Richards of Batsto; buried Laurel Hill, Phila.

6   *Howard:* (10/31/1837–1/12/1921); married Harriet Mayo, daughter of Edward and Adeline (Marx) Mayo, in Christ Church Chapel, Elizabeth, N.J., their children were: (1) Adeline Mayo (12/4/1871–1/3/1914); (2) Sarah Lippincott (1/30/1875–9/13/1939); (3) Howard, Jr. (6/27/1877–9/25/1940), married Maud Ashurst (baptized Emma Matilda) at Holy Trinity P.E. Church, Phila.; their children were: (a) Howard Ashurst (6/14/1914–); (b) John Ashurst (8/15/1915–); married (1) Monaise Adelaide Jones, and (2) Nada Jones Young; (c) Owen (6/17/1918–); married Frances Bedell; (4) Edward Carrington (9/23/1886–); married Elizabeth Veech Coan, daughter of Rev. and Mrs. Frederick Coan; their children were: (a) Frederick H. (11/6/1919–); married (1), Marjorie Louise Jeanne, (2) Jennifer Osgood-Edwards of England; (b) William Lippincott (1/26/1931–); married Jean Gillanders; (c) Elizabeth Spear (5/22/1922–); (d) Annette (?), married Hiram L. Parent.

7   *Charles Everett:* (3/7/1841–7/15/1911).

8   *Meredith:* (9/4/1843–4/3/1845).

The Family of Augustus Henry Richards [15]

Born May 5, 1803, at Batsto; died February 20, 1839; buried at Laurel Hill, Philadelphia; married Rebecca E. McLean, daughter of John McLean, of Ohio; their children were:

1   *John McLean:* (6/?/1834–1/19/1839).

2   *Rebecca McLean:* (2/8/1836–?/?/?).

The Family of William Richards III [16]

Born January 16, 1805, at Batsto; died April 19, 1864; buried St. Andrew's Cemetery, Mt. Holly, N.J.; married, February 6, 1831, Constantia Marie Lamand, daughter of James Louis Lamand, of Trenton; civil ceremony performed by George Haywood, magistrate of Mt. Holly; their children were:

1   *Mary Louisa:* (12/29/1831–?/?/?); died in childhood.

2   *William Louis:* (6/26/1833–?/?/?); died in childhood.

3   *George:* (5/2/1835–?/?/?); living in the 1860's.

4 *Margaretta Francis:* (5/30/1836–?/?/?); died at an early age.
5 *John Oakman:* (10/16/1837–?/?/?); died in childhood.
NOTE: All the children except George are buried in St. Andrew's cemetery, Mt. Holly, "before 1850" according to the records.

The Family of George Washington Richards [16]

Born May 3, 1807, at Batsto; died April 22, 1874; married, on May 21, 1829, to Mary Louisa Le Guen, daughter of Louis and Josephine Le Guen, formerly of Bordeaux, France, at St. Stephen's Episcopal Church, Philadelphia, the Rev. James Montgomery, rector, officiating. Their children were:

1 *Louis Henry "Harry":* (4/7/1831–?/?/?); married, (1) Margaret Starr, daughter of Isaac Starr, (2) Mrs. Caroline Harlan, in Cleveland, Ohio. The children of the first marriage were: (1) L. Harry (3/14/1855–3/3/1857); (2) Mary Louisa (9/5/1856–?/?/?), married Howard Butcher, and had three children: (a) Mary Louisa; (b) Margaret, married Abram G. Tatnall; (c) Theodora; (3) George Washington (5/16/1858–7/?/1932), married Sallie R. Taulane, and had one child, L. Harry II (5/2/1890–3/20/1944), married Emily C. Kimball, and their daughter Emily Louise, married Harold Atlee Haines; (4) Isaac Starr (1/25/1861–?/?/?), married May Fletcher Kuner, had one daughter, Dorothy F. (?); (5) Margaret (4/5/1863–?/?/?), married J. Dandridge Murdaugh; (6) Lydia Duconing (6/25/1865–?/?/?), married 1892, A. Hays Compton; (7) Theodora (6/19/1867–8/27/1936), married Charles J. Green, had one daughter Theodora S. The children of Louis Henry Richards by his second wife, Caroline, were: (8) Helen Richards (7/5/1880–?/?/?); (9) Le Roy (2/14/1883–5/21/1936), married Grace Pessano and had two sons (a) LeRoy Jr. (3/31/1912–), married Jeanetta Burpee, had two children; (b) William Pessano Richards (5/20/1915–).
2 *Emily Richards:* (10/15/1832–?/?/?).
3 *Josephine R.:* (8/?/1833–3/7/1835).
4 *Mary Louisa:* (8/15/1835–1/10/1836).
5 *George William Hylton:* (6/4/1837–?/?/?); married children: Mrs. Henry A. Breckenridge, Mrs. A. J. Doggett, William Hylton, Jr.
6 *Eugenia Victoria:* (12/3/1838–9/14/1839).

William Richards, of Batsto

Owen Richards

He emigrated to Pennsylvania from Merionethshire, North Wales, at some time before 1718. On December 22 of that year he purchased three hundred acres of land in Amity Township, now Berks County. Owen Richards was married twice. There are no records concerning his first wife. In 1727 Owen married, in Christ Church, Philadelphia, Elizabeth Baker. She survived him and died in 1753, when she was about eighty years old without having had any children; she was buried in the graveyard of St. Gabriel's Episcopal Church, at Douglassville, Pa., earlier known as "St. Gabriel's of Morlatton." The date of death of Owen Richards is not known but it was after 1734. The four known children of Owen Richards by his first wife were:

1 *James Richards:* (?); nothing is known of him except that he purchased 150 acres of his father's farm in 1729.
2 *William Richards (I):* (?/ab. 1705–1/?/1752); probably born in Wales, in 1735 bought a 150-acre farm adjoining that of his brother James, mentioned above; his will is on file in Philadelphia; his wife's Christian name was Elizabeth, but her maiden name is not known; for his family, see below.
3 *John Richards:* (?), his wife's name was Sarah; their two children were: (1) Edward, baptized St. Gabriel's 1737, (2) Susannah, baptized same church 1739; a third child, supposedly an infant, was buried in 1736; John Richards reputedly moved to Virginia.
4 *Elizabeth:* (?); nothing is known about her.

William Richards I [2]

Father of William Richards of Batsto. The first name of his wife was Elizabeth. They had seven children:

1 *Mary Richards:* (?); married John Ball of Douglas Township, Berks County. One of their children was Joseph Ball (?/?/ab. 1748–4/28/1821), ironmaster and financier, whose background is below.
2 *Owen Richards, Jr.:* (?/?/?–?/?/?); baptized St. Gabriel's Church; a soldier of this name is listed as a private in Cap-

tain Gray's company, Fourth Pennsylvania Regiment, Continental Line. The name of his wife does not appear. His children were: (1) William, (2) John, (3) Mary, (4) Elizabeth (Barr), (5) Eleanor (Hamilton), (6) Jane (Stevens), (7) Sarah (Roberts).

3   *James Richards:* (?/?/1722–?/?/1804); a farmer; served as sergeant in Captain Tudor's company, Fourth Pennsylvania Regiment, Continental Line, having enlisted May 10, 1777. His wife Mary's maiden name is not known, they had the following children: (1) William; (2) Frederick; (3) Elizabeth (Rutter); (4) James; (5) Owen; (6) Mary (Fox); (7) Sarah (Schmale), Of these children William (1/27/1754–?/?/1786) married Mary, daughter of John and Elizabeth Miller; their four children were: (a) William, died in childhood; (b) Elizabeth, also died in childhood; (c) James (3/27/1782–9/21/1828), married Ann Hunter Smith, daughter of John Smith of Joanna Furnace; (d) John Richards (6/5/1784–11/29/1871) whose background is below.

4   *Ruth Richards:* (?/?/?–?/?/?); married Daniel Kunsman; their children were: (1) Rebecca (Hoffman); (2) Elizabeth (Miller); (3) Mary (Seiler); (4) Catharine (Canstatter); (5) William.

5   *William Richards II:* (12/12/1738–8/31/1823); manager of Batsto, who with his family is the subject of the first portion of this book.

6   *Margaret Richards:* (?/?/?–?/?/1793); married Cornelius Dewees; their children were (1) William; (2) Owen; (3) David; (4) Cornelius; (5) Mary (Patterson); (6) Samuel.

7   *Sarah Richards:* (?/?/?–?/?/ab. 1825); married James Hastings; their children were: (1) Howell; (2) William; (3) John.

Joseph Ball

Because of their close association with the Richards enterprises in New Jersey, the following notes are given on members of collateral lines.

He (?/?/1748–4/28/1821), was the first son of Mary Richards (daughter of William I) and John Ball of Berks County, Pa. He married Sarah May, the daughter of Captain George May for whom Mays Landing, N.J. was named. Their only child, Mary Ball (4/23/1778–6/21/1800), married Robert Frazer, son of Gen. Persifor Frazer.

Little is known of Joseph Ball's youth. It was spent, in all probability, in the iron furnace area of Berks County where he was born and where so many of his relatives lived. In 1754 his father, a road supervisor, is recorded as buying land nearby.

Joseph Ball's name has not been found in any of the records of the Berks County furnaces. But he must have gained some knowledge of that business since he was able to manage Batsto Furnace so successfully during the most difficult days of the American Revolution.

Ball was introduced to Batsto by his uncle, William Richards II, who was employed there for varying periods from 1768 onward. Ball was in his middle thirties when he became Batsto's manager under Col. John Cox. And it was under his direction that cannon as well as shot and shell were produced in large quantities for the Continental armies. Ball became the key partner in the works in 1779, in close association with Cox, Charles Pettit, (both Assistant Quartermasters General of the Army), and General Nathanael Greene, then Quartermaster General.

Some years later Ball was a partner in the Weymouth and Martha Furnaces; an extensive investor in real estate, owning the Pleasant Mills plantation prior to its absorption into the Richards domain, as well as many other tracts of land in New Jersey, Pennsylvania, Delaware, Ohio, Kentucky and the District of Columbia, the last-named holdings creating lengthy legal difficulties after his death.

Joseph Ball was a founder-director and president of the Insurance Company of North America, in whose board room his portrait hangs; the Pennsylvania Company for Insurances on Lives and Granting Annuities; and, in 1791, a director of the Bank of The United States. He was a close associate of Robert Morris (American financier and statesman) and Stephen Girard (businessman and philanthropist), moved in top Philadelphia circles, and on February 18, 1797 dined with President George Washington. Ball served as an Alderman, and for a time as a member of the Pennsylvania Assembly.

In later life Ball made his home at 349 Arch street, Philadelphia, and had a country place on the Point-No-Point road, near what is now Port Richmond. He died one of the wealthiest men in the United States. Surprisingly, he left no will. Because of this there was much litigation lasting more than half a century—over some of his properties. Ball's funeral took place May 1, 1821, at the Second Presbyterian Church, Philadelphia, of which he had been an elder. He was buried in the graveyard of that church.

John Richards

He (6/5/1784–11/29/1871) married Rebecca Ludwig, daughter of Michael and Susanna Ludwig, and then Louisa Silvers, daughter of Ephraim and Elizabeth Silvers. There were six children by the first marriage, including Rebecca and Jesse, who died in 1824. One child of his second marriage was Louis Richards (5/6/1842–5/2/1924) a Reading, Pa. attorney who in 1882 wrote "A Sketch of Some of the Descendants of Owen Richards." Louis married Minerva Elizabeth Hoff, and their two children were John H. (4/3/1878–4/28/1955) an executive of the Bethlehem Steel Corporation, and Susan Richards of Reading, Pa.

According to a memorial tribute by Louis Richards, John Richards went to Batsto in 1807 to visit his great uncle William and there became fascinated with iron as had so many members of his family before him. Shortly afterwards, he was given a position as assistant manager at Weymouth, then owned by Samuel Richards and Joseph Ball. In 1810 John went to live at Green Bank, N.J., where he kept a store and served as a Justice of the Peace. During this period he met his first wife, Rebecca Ludwig. On May 30, 1811 they were married in Reading and after the ceremony rode on horseback to their home in Green Bank.

Two years later John Richards bought a tract of cedar timber at Bridgeport, on Wading River, N.J. There he built a store, a home, and constructed a bridge across the stream. In 1816 he was employed by Jesse and Samuel Richards to superintend Washington Furnace, in Monmouth County (see chapters on Weymouth and Washington). Less than three years later he moved back to Bridgeport, but in 1819 he was employed by Samuel Richards as superintendent at Atsion, and a year later as resident manager at Weymouth.

In 1830 John Richards joined his cousin Thomas S. Richards—son of Samuel of Atsion—in purchasing Gloucester Furnace, on the south shore of the Mullica River near Egg Harbor, N.J. He was manager at the works, and Thomas S. represented the firm in Philadelphia. During this period John Richards was elected (1836) to a term in the New Jersey Assembly; and in 1841 married his second wife, Louisa Silver. Their only child, Louis Richards, was born at Gloucester Furnace.

After Gloucester Furnace shut down about 1848, John acquired the Carbon Furnace at Mauch Chunk, Pa. In 1854, near seventy, he decided to retire, sold Carbon Furnace, and bought an estate called

"Stowe" near Pottstown, Pa. He lived there for eighteen years, and died at eighty-seven.

Mary Patrick

In the historic cemetery at Pleasant Mills, N.J. is a gravestone inscribed: "Mary Patrick: d. Sep. 18, 1795, age 24 years, three months."

Obviously this Mary Patrick is not the first wife of William Richards, for her stone, correctly inscribed, is nearby. Some have believed this to be the grave of an otherwise unrecorded child of William and Mary Patrick Richards. The fact that none of their eleven listed children was named for their mother lent some support to this conjecture. Calculation of dates, however, shows that William and Mary were having children so regularly that the birth date of this "Mary Patrick" simply does not fit. She may have been a twin, but surely that fact would have been recorded.

Likely explanation for the mystery is that Mary Patrick Richards had a brother, Samuel, of whom she and her husband both were fond. (She also had a sister, Esther, born in 1747, who married Ezekiel Leonard.) Brother Samuel Patrick, like William Richards, was an iron founder, worked at Warwick Furnace where William had worked, and later at the Forest of Dean Iron Works. No statistics on Samuel's marriage are available, but his wife's name was Rebecca, they had two children, one named "Hons" and the other almost certainly Mary —the Mary buried at Pleasant Mills.

The Batsto Diary of William Richards 1781-84

Note Tucked in a Pocket of the Booklet

This pocket book was given J. Harry Richards by his grandmother, Margaretta, the 2nd wife of William Richards.

It was made by Mary, his first wife and had originally worked upon it in worsted—

WM RICHARDS

1781

April 17, 1781	Batsto Furnace. House Ex. To cash for fish	12 doll
the 19th	Left Batsto to go to Pena to see my family Shall leave 2 half Joes with W. Lash and two of State [N.J. State currency] Wm. Loviman for the Hay.	
	Cash. Gave to Robert Lusk 40 Dolls to go to Atsion	£0–4–0
	Omitt going home Till 20th	
20	Expenses House at Wm. Murnell	44 Dol
21	In Philadelphia at Black Horse Saty 18–6	
	On the Road &c.	4–
22	Sent By Mr. John Jacoby for fish State Exp atsunder 1781	4–2–6
April 26	Left home for Batsto	
27	Wm. Roggins Dr. to Cash—Eight Dollars State	£3–0–0
May 7	Cash Paid Hugh Lusk	£3–0–0

12	Cash Paid Charles Loveland £ 2 half Jose and four £ Hard Dollars	£7-10-0
	Borrowed of Mr. Joseph Ball, Nine Pounds in Gold—to Pay—for baking £9.0.0	
	Negros	
16th	Mr. Lusk went to Lebennon. H. Lusk and wife to Phila. the g. on the Day preceeding	
May 25	Mr. Robert Lusk returned from Lebennon. Mrs. G & Mrs. R—to Batsto same day.	
28	Mr. H. Lusk returned with his wife	
29th	Mr. Jacobs went Flora. A. Crooks with him	

June 9th 1781	Returned from going after—Mrs. Ried went home. Expenses to Hedingfield and home again to Batsto	8.6
June 25th 1781	Wm. Crooks began to—the Forge Timbers with his two sons—	

By Letter from Col. Charles Pettit—Mr. Joseph Ball has Received £9–10 Hard Money which I Borrowed of him some time ago. Letter dated June 26th 1781

June 29, 1781	Cash Paid—Smith's wife at his house 0.17.6		
	Expenses at the—after Hay—on Joseph Estols 0.2.8		
	Cash Paid Mr. Robert Lusk		
	for Smith's Hay—Settled this	2	6
	2/6 Toward his Expenses	2	6
	at the Ferrey 2/		

Received June 28, 1781 of Mr. William Read for six Kittles —£6.0.0 and there remains Nine Pounds un Paid Which is to be Paid by the first of September.

June 30th 1781	Cash Paid Samuel Ball for my own use	£1.7.6

July 4	Left Batsto to go Home	
	Cash gave Jos. Hugh his Expenses with this sum	0–20
	Cash Laid out at Samuel St—for 2 Dear skins for my own use.	
5th	Cash laid out for dinner and Callico in Philadelphia	£9.15.0
	Expenses at the Wagon homewards	0 17:10
		1.2

Springdale July 7th 1781

	old Mrs. Leonards Mother to Half Bush salt which she says I. Jonas is to Pay for a 20/	
5th July	Bought of Col. Charles Pettit	
	1 Box of Sugar 375 1 six pense	
	Same said to be 2 th	
July 16th	portrage	9.9–0
	Cash taken from home. Ent in Batsto Book When I set off for Batsto	£1.63
	arrived safe at Batsto 17th	
July 23d 1781	gave Mr. Robert Lusk £0.15.0 to go after teams.	
July 28th 1781	Batsto	
	Settled with Mr. Robert Lusk to this time his Expenses since he was in Phild.—all Pd.	
Aug. 8th	Expenses at Olliphants Loading Timber	3.9
	at Haneses the same time and next day for Carting and Loading	12.4
	at Shinns same time	3.0
	Cash for Mic—of Mr. Jacobs	£1.13.9
Aug. 28th	Received of Col. Charles Pettit Twenty Half Johannes and Sixteen Hard Dollars—amounting to	£66.0.0
	Gave Mr. Robert Lusk to buy Beever seven Half Joes and four Hard dollars amounting to	£22.10.0
29th Aug.	Sett off to go home. Took with me seven half Joes and four dollars. gave one of the above	

	Dollars one out of the Desk to Ch. More.	
Aug. 29th 1781	Left Batsto to go home. Returned 8th Sept.	
	James Greay Paid for him in Joes for—	12.6
Sept. 13th	Lett Mr. Joseph Ball have three half Joes	£9.0.9
Sept. 17th 1781	Received of John Fassman 29 Hard Dollars to keep for him. gave him one of the above Dollars.	
26th	Went to Mount Holley. Back the next day. Expenses there and Back	
	to get Dementions for forge Plates Pattrons	£13.4
Oct. 3d	Received of Mr. Garden	£9.0.0
1781	which Mr. Ball got of	
	Received of Charles Pettit, Esq. the same day	£50
	Settled Cash acct at this time.	

	I gave Mr. Richards Price an order to receive nine Pounds Hard Money of W. Read and twelve Hard Dollars of Capt. Shaner.	
Oct. 11	Settled the Cash acct. to this day and is due	
1781	Batsto Coy.	£23.5.6
Oct. 31st 1781	Cash Paid Thomas Regroary for a box of Candles not Charged.	
Oct. 31st 1781	Bought Col. Benj. Randolph six pieces of Died Jerminey Linnens	
	at £1.6.0 per Piece part of a Dubble Ball Containing 40 Tins which I was to have at first cost. Cash pd. for the above.	
	Lent a stub Pensil not Returned to Mr. Wescoat. Present.	
Nov. 1th	gave the Carters at Longacoming not charged	4.6
1781		
	Paid for Carting	5.3
Nov. 21th 1781	Returned after being absent 18 days.	
	Companeys Business—	
	to my Expenses for the above 2 days Ent nd in going from Home to glaser forge and to the Bellows Maker, Kinnerd, Esq.	£1.5.0
	gave Joseph Ball five bushels of Mault in Exchange for Ten Bushels of Rye and Cash	£0.7.6

Dec. 10th 1781	Received of Mr. Gardiner 4 dollers when going to Meriland to buy Pork for Batsto	

Expenses at Longacoming

Dec. 10. 1781	£ 0.2.0
at Hedenfield	6.9
14—at the ferrey	4.0
at Buck	2.0
at Mathers	2.0
19—Left home to go by the Bellows Maker	
Expenses to Philad.	£ 0.10.0
23. Expenses to Batsto	
at the ferrey	0.15.0
at Longacoming	7.6
Total Ent/rd	£ 1.12.6
in Cash Book	£ 3.5.3

14th of Dec. 1781	Received of Mr. Joseph Ball 50 Dollars	£ 18.15.0
April 26th 1782	Left the mana/mint of Batstoworks to Mr. J. Ball	
26th	Cash on hand £ 26.10 got of Mr. J. Ball for a Sulkey sold to Saml* Cupper—Sundereys other Moneys on hand at this date	

	£ 9 26.10
	9
	£ 35.0.10

1782 April 28	Sent by Saml. Suves 28 shillings to buy fish and Salt.	
30th	Received 25 Shillings	
	Paid Michael Rogers 4 / 2	
June 3 1782	Agreed with Timothy Leach for four thosand three foot shingles at £ 6.10.0 to have *aflorien* at 20s to sink the Cask on Midlings at 16s and pay 3s for Cask.	
June 29th 1782	Cash Paid Daniel Morrison in full.	£ 0.17.1
Sept. 27 1782	I gave a note Israel Whelen for £ 3.17	
	The Last Week in July 1782 David Howel worked 4½ days at Quarrey's stone with	

*   Samuel Cooper

Intent of Building to the 12th of August.
David Howel worked four days.

Oct. 27th 1782	Received of Mr. Charles Pettit twenty-five Dollers on acct. of J. Ball	
	Six Dollers left. Isrel Whelton for Spirits.	
Nov. 7th 1782		
	Cash paid for oxen	£ 16.7.6
	Expenses after ditto	9.0
the 9th	Paid Equilea Jones, the Miller	1.10.0
	Nathiel Jones, son Quilea for Boarss ver	1.17.6
	Capt. Anderson to pay	3.2
the 9th	Paid the Scool master Mathers	1.17.6
June 17th 1783	Wm. Stepleton Dr. c/o Cash paid his Boy	8.4
	Unpaid	3.11
18th	Two men came here to tend Mason to begin work Tomorrow.	
Aug. 20th 1783	Isseree Whelen Dr. to an order in favour of him on Charles Pettit, Esq. for Eleven Pounds 1st 8sh 20 days sight.	
	Cash Paid James Dunwoodey in part for lotes 21st Aug t. 1783	£ 12.0.0
Aug. 25th 1783	Sent by John Newland 20 Bus/h Lime to the Meeting House. 1	£ 0.15.0
	Took with my team before then 25 Bus of lime	£ 1.5.0
	Acct. of Cash Received since Settlements. . . .	
Nov. 27th 1783	of Charles Pettit Esq. in Philadelphia 25 Dols	£ 9.7.6
March 27th 1783	of Mr. Ball being Exchanged for state money	£ 3.0.0
April 10th 1783	By Cash Received of Mr. Joseph Ball	135 Dolls.
		£ 50.12.5
Aug. 19th 1783	By an Order Mr. Pettit in favour Is Whelen	£ 11.1–8
Nov. 23d	Left Timothy Leach acct. with Mr J. Ball to Collect	£ 3

Nov. 25th 1783	gave Capt Anderson 6 french crowns	
Dec. 2nd 1783	Sent John Mellon three Hides	
Dec. 27th 1783	Settled with Capt. Even Anderson.	£1.0.0
	Had to pay for a barrel	7.6
	By an order of Mr. J. Carson for 200 Dollers Nov. 23d Rec.	£37.10
Feb. 21, 1784	Sent Capt. Anderson one french crown	
	Received of Mrs. Margaret Paschel 12 dollers and a note for five	£6.7.6
June 18th 1784		
Oct. 8, 1784	Expenses after Forge Men at Hanes. 2/ at the Buck, 3/ at the Ferrey, 2/6 the 9th & the 10th, 5 the 10th at Home 12th at Red Lion 5—at Black—4.2 at Pott House.	

An acct. of Piggs Made in Blast
Ending Nov 30th 1775

1344 Tons   Piggs
82.16.1   Contry Casting
16.10.0.11 forge   do
   8.3.1   pottiware
besides ore taken up and shott

NOTE: This Diary believed to be in the handwriting of William Richards is a booklet about four inches by six inches, with a covering of green, rose and brown worsted, and lined in dark green. It is a "purse-type" volume.

George Washington's Cypher

Nearly a century ago a letter was sent to the New Jersey Historical Society by Thomas H. Richards, one of its members. That letter posed what Sherlock Holmes might have called "a three pipe problem." At the time Richards was active head of the Batsto Glass Works, in the South Jersey pines; but his letter concerned the earlier days of the Batsto Iron Works, industrial predecessor of the glass factories. That ironworks, famous from pre-Revolutionary times, had closed down in 1848.

Richards' letter, addressed to the Corresponding Secretary of the Society, follows:

Batsto, May 28, 1864

Dear Sir:

I take the liberty of sending to you a rude and somewhat mutilated casting made at this place during or soon after the war of the revolution. An iron blast furnace was established here in 1762,[1] and was kept in continuous operation until 1846.[2] During the war of independence many cannon, mortars, shot and shell were cast, of which I have seen many rejected pieces, but of this casting neither my late father[3] nor any of the oldest residents of the place can give any explanation. It is probably intended to represent the coat of arms of General Washington, and is very similar in design to the escutcheon of the English Washington family represented in Lossing's Field Book of the Revolution. Shortly before the commencement of this civil war, Col. Lewis Washington was at this place, and upon seeing this casting took a seal ring from his finger upon which was engraved the same design with the exception of the cypher (G. W.).

I have understood that it is a custom in monarchical coun-

[1] Correct date 1766.
[2] 1848, according to Batsto records.
[3] Jesse Richards, son of William Richards.

tries of Europe to place the arms of the ruler, with his or her cypher on the walls of stores, hotels, and other public buildings, and having seen in the Danish West Indies plates so placed, very similar to this, I have thought that this was intended for a similar purpose—to indicate the era in which some building was erected. Whatever may have been the design of the making of the casting, I send it to the New Jersey Historical Society, hoping it may interest its intelligent members.

Very respectfully, your obedient servant,
T. H. RICHARDS.

Wm. A. Whitehead, Esq.

This letter was not news when it first came to the author's attention about eight years ago. Several New Jersey historians had known of it, and all had tried in vain to locate the mysterious casting and discover an explanation of its purpose. The writer was assured that further effort would be a "wild goose chase."

A "wild goose chase" is better than no chase at all. So, despite the fact that searches at the Society's headquarters had drawn a blank each time, it was decided to try once more. Formal inquiry was made, indexes combed, records consulted, but no such chunk of iron could be found listed among the Society's possessions. That seemed to be that.

Some months later, the author visited Mount Vernon and inspected the interesting firebacks there, particularly one in the West Parlor. This fireback bore Washington's "crest and cypher," with an italic "*G.W.*" A handbook disclosed that this was "one of four firebacks purchased in Philadelphia." A request to the Mount Vernon Ladies Association of the Union, which maintains the Washington shrine, brought the reply that the firebacks had been purchased from a Charles Pettit in Philadelphia. Reference to Fitzpatrick's *Writings of Washington* next yielded this fascinating correspondence:

To Charles Pettit
> Philadelphia, Sept. 7, 1787
> Sir: Having received the dimensions of three more of my Chimneys for which I want castings, I have to request them as follows [then follow the details of measurement].
> The mould already made, may subserve for the above Castings reducing it first to the largest of the above chimneys,

then to the second size, and lastly the smallest, the crest and Cypher to each.
I should be glad to receive them as soon as possible and the money shall be immediately paid for them.

On October 2, 1787, Washington sent Pettit "by the *Charming Polly* . . . . patterns for the hearths of Chimneys which I beg may be cast and sent to me by the first conveyance to Alexandria . . . ." And in a later letter, to Clement Biddle, Washington asks Biddle "to pay Mr. Charles Pettit's bill for 4 Backs and 8 Jambs sent to me, which amounts to 18 pounds, five shillings, one pence."

This, clearly, was pay dirt. Charles Pettit[4] not only was Philadelphia agent for the Batsto Iron Works at that time; he had long owned a substantial interest in that enterprise. It was inconceivable that Pettit would have had Washington's order executed at any ironworks save Batsto, which then was managed and also partly owned by William Richards, founder of the South Jersey industrial dynasty.

It seemed time to make one last effort to locate that casting donated to the New Jersey Historical Society back in 1864. Now there was available not only a description of the firebacks and the crest and cypher at Mount Vernon (illustrated in the author's *Iron in the Pines*); but the photographic evidence and the description in the Richards letter were suspiciously similar.

Luck came at last. With those clues to go by, Howard Wiseman, of the Society's staff, made a search not only of the Society's index but of the shelves in the basement. Then he reported a piece of iron, partly broken, which did indeed bear the initials "G.W."

Illustrated here, that casting is beyond doubt the one from which the Mount Vernon firebacks were made. The design is identical, and either it is the mould mentioned in the letter from Washington to Pettit, or a replica, and almost surely the former. A precious possession, by any reckoning!

Reprinted by permission from the
Proceedings of the New Jersey
Historical Society.

[4] Charles Pettit had been Secretary of the Province of New Jersey prior to the Revolution and split with Governor William Franklin to join the patriots. Later he became part owner of Batsto Iron Works, Deputy Quartermaster General under Nathanael Greene, and after the war an important financial figure in Philadelphia and one of the founders and first president of the Insurance Company of North America.

Chapter Notes

Abbreviations

In the Bibliography and Chapter Notes the following abbreviations have been used:

AC — Atlantic County deeds and wills, housed in Mays Landing.

BC — Burlington County wills and deeds, housed in Mount Holly.

CC — Camden County deeds and wills, housed in Camden.

GC — Gloucester County deeds and wills housed in Woodbury.

MC — Monmouth County deeds housed in Freehold.

NJ — Deeds and other records of the State of New Jersey housed in Trenton.

BCHS — Burlington County Historical Society

HSP — Historical Society of Pennsylvania

NJA — New Jersey Archives

PMHB — Pennsylvania Magazine of History and Biography.

WCL — William L. Clements Library, Ann Arbor, Mich.

1. William Richards

1 Coventry Furnace Books, HSP; 2 Warwick Furnace Books, HSP; 3 Letters to William Richards, HSP; 4 Philip Vickers Fithian, *Journal 1775–1776*, ed. by Robert Greenhalgh Albion and Leonidas Dodson (Princeton: The Princeton University Press, 1934), p. 255; 5 Original in HSP; 6 DuPuy Genealogy; 7 Original in HSP; 8 *Pennsylvania Packet*, June 26, 1783; 9 Greene-Pettit Letters, WCL; 10 *Ibid.* 11 *Pennsylvania Packet*, April 15, 1784; 12 St. Andrew's Protestant Episcopal Church records; 13 BC wills, Liber C, p. 342.

2. Samuel

1 The Atsion silk mill was in operation 1839-1850, Atsion books, BCHS;   2   GC wills, Liber D, p. 341;   3   BC wills, Liber K, p. 157.

3. Rebecca

1 Letter of Washington to Pickering, September 9, 1798;   2 Richards papers;   3   Washington Township records;   4   BC wills, Liber K, p. 157.

4. Thomas

1 GC deeds, Liber AA p. 708; BC deeds, Liber W, p. 64;   2 CC, Surrogate's records;   3   E. M. Woodward, *Bonaparte's Park and the Murats* (Trenton, N.J.: MacCrellish & Quigley, 1879), p. 93; 4 *Ibid;*   5   Woodward & Hageman, *History of Burlington and Mercer Counties, N.J.*, Philadelphia: Everts and Peck, 1883;   6 *West Jersey Press*, December 19, 1883;   7   *The Atco Argus.*

5. Jesse

1 BC wills, Liber C, p. 342;   2   *National Gazette & Literary Register*, October 18, 1824;   3   BC deeds, Liber B3, p. 16;   4 *Mount Holly Mirror*, February 6, 1834;   5   GC mortgages;   6 N.J. Census data.

6. William III

1 St. Andrew's Protestant Episcopal Church records;   2   BC and AC deeds;   3   GC deeds, Liber B4, p. 341;   4   St. Andrew's Church records;   5   *Ibid.*

7. Benjamin

1 Letters, Yale University Library;   2   George Wilson Pierson, *Tocqueville in America*, abridged by Dudley C. Lunt from *Tocqueville and Beaumont in America* (New York: Doubleday & Co., 1959), p.

310-11;   3 Louis Richards, *Sketches of Some Descendants of Owen Richards,* Philadelphia: Collins, printer, 1882.

8. Weymouth

1   Henry Van Dyke, *Days Off* (New York: Charles Scribner & Sons, 1927), pp. 163-67;   2   NJ deeds, Liber AV, p. 68;   3   Day Book of Jos. M. Paul;   4   Charles S. Boyer, *Early Forges & Furnaces in New Jersey* (Philadelphia: University of Pennsylvania Press, 1931), p. 251;   5   Day Book of Jos. M. Paul;   6 Weymouth Furnace Book: 1808-10;   7   Bathe G.: Oliver Evans; 8   Andrew Stewart papers;   9   *Ibid;*   10   *Ibid.*

9. Weymouth

1   Henry C. Carey, *A Memoir of Stephen Colwell,* Philadelphia: Collins, printer, 1871;   2   *Ibid;*   3   *Ibid;*   4   Directory 1866: (Talbot & Blood, publishers);   5   AC deeds, Liber 180, p. 89;   6   AC deeds, Liber 180, p. 91.

11. Jesse's Folly

1   MC deeds, Liber X, p. 287;   2   MC deeds, Liber X, p. 282; 3   MC deeds, Liber X, p. 284;   4   Account Book, State of N.J.; 5   MC deeds, Liber V2, p. 244;   6   MC deeds, Liber E, p. 221; 7   Charles S. Boyer, *Early Forges and Furnaces in New Jersey* (Philadelphia: University of Pennsylvania Press, 1931), p. 245.

12. Three at Hampton

1   BC deeds, Liber E, p. 3;   2   BC deeds, Liber F, p. 206;   3 BC deeds, Liber E, p. 6;   4   Charles S. Boyer, *Early Forges and Furnaces in New Jersey* (Philadelphia: University of Pennsylvania Press, 1931), p. 86;   5   *National Gazette & Literary Register,* January 22, 1825;   6   BC deeds, Liber R2, p. 534;   7   Atsion Furnace Books, BCHS;   8   NJ, Wharton Tract records;   9 BC deeds, Liber V2, p. 77.

13. Breakneck Road to Taunton

1 BC deeds, Liber C, p. 12; 2 NJ deeds, Liber AB, p. 68; 3 Original in BCHS; 4 Drinker Letter Books, 1773, HSP; 5 NJA 1st Series, Vol. 29, p. 482; 6 *Pennsylvania Packet,* November 24, 1778; 7 *Pennsylvania Packet,* November 29, 1783; 8 BC deeds, Liber C, p. 12; 9 BC deeds, Liber M2, p. 112; 10 GC deeds, Liber AA, p. 708; 11 *Mount Holly Mirror,* January 15, 1820; 12 BC deeds, Liber U2, p. 80; 13 BC deeds, Liber D3, p. 135; 14 BC deeds, Liber Y6, p. 352; 15 BC deeds, Liber 575, p. 295.

14. Benjamin Randolph and Speedwell

1 Kenneth and Anna M. Roberts, trans. and ed., *Moreau St. Méry's American Journey* (New York: Doubleday & Co., 1947), p. 176; 2 Carl and Jessica Bridenbaugh, *Rebels and Gentlemen: Philadelphia in the Age of Franklin* (New York: Oxford University Press, 1962), pp. 162, 166; 3 Hollingsworth Papers, HSP; 4 George De Cou, *Burlington, A Provincial Capital* (Burlington, N.J.: The Library Company of Burlington, 1945), p. 187; 5 *Joseph Downs, American Furniture: Queen Ann and Chippendale Periods in the Henry Francis du Pont Winterthur Museum,* New York: The Macmillan Company, 1952; 6 V. Lansing Collins, *Princeton Past and Present* (Princeton, N.J.: The Princeton University Press, 1946), section 7; 7 Fitz Randolph-Snowden Genealogy, HSP; 8 NJ Wharton Tract papers; 9 Bridenbaugh, *Rebels and Gentlemen,* pp. 157, 159; 10 *PMHB,* Vol. 56, pp. 119, 125; 11 John C. Fitzpatrick, ed., *The Writings of Washington from the Original Manuscript Sources: 1745-1799,* Vol. VIII (Washington, D.C.: United States Printing Office, 1931-1944), p. 11; 12 Marie G. Kimball, *The Furnishings of Monticello* (Charlottesville, Va.: Thomas Jefferson Memorial Foundation, 1954), pp. 27, 28; 13 William S. Stryker, *The Battles of Trenton and Princeton* (Boston: Houghton, Mifflin & Co., 1898), p. 250; 14 John C. Fitzpatrick, ed., *Writings of Washington,* Vol. VIII, p. 46; 15 Logan Papers, HSP; 16 *New Jersey Gazette,* February 17, 1779; 17 *PMHB,* Vol. 19, p. 362; 18 J. Thomas Scharf and Thompson Westcott, *History of Philadelphia, 1609-1884,* Vol. I (Philadelphia: 1884), p. 387; 19 *Journal of Congress,* July 31, 1778; 20 John Ross, Day Book, HSP; 21 BC deeds, Liber G3, p. 402;

22 St. Paul's Protestant Episcopal Church records; 23 BC deeds, Liber A, p. 74; 24 Carl Bridenbaugh, *The Colonial Craftsman* (Chicago: The University of Chicago Press, 1961), p. 25; 25 Hollingsworth Papers, HSP; 26 BC deeds, Liber G3, p. 402; 27 Burlington Friends Meeting records, BCHS; 28 Charles S. Boyer, *Early Forges and Furnaces in New Jersey* (Philadelphia: University of Pennsylvania Press, 1931), p. 203; 29 BC wills; 30 BC deeds, Liber G3, p. 399; 31 Boyer, *Early Forges and Furnaces in New Jersey,* p. 206; 32 *The Woodbury Herald,* March 27, 1827; 33 BC deeds, Liber G3, p. 402; 34 BC deeds, Liber C5, p. 48; 35 Charles S. Boyer, *Old Inns and Taverns of West Jersey* (Camden, N.J.: Camden County Historical Society, 1962), p. 77; 36 BC deeds, Liber W7, p. 469.

15. Railroad to Nowhere

1 Richards papers; 2 *West Jerseyman,* July 5, 1854; 3 *Ibid;* 4 *Ibid;* 5 Camden & Atlantic R.R., *Annual Report for 1871;* 6 Wheaton J. Lane, *From Indian Trail to Iron Horse* (Princeton, N.J.: The Princeton University Press, 1939), p. 399; 7 *Ibid;* 8 Camden & Atlantic R.R., *Annual Report for 1871;* 9 *Ibid.*

Bibliography

MANUSCRIPTS

Atsion Furnace Books: Burlington County Historical Society.
Atsion 1819 Furnace Book: Owned by the Author.
Batsto Store Books: Owned by the State of New Jersey.
Batsto Furnace Books: Property of the Author.
Batsto Letter Book of Jesse Richards: Owned by the Author.
Coventry Furnace Books: Historical Society of Pennsylvania.
De Tocqueville–Benjamin Richards Correspondence: Yale University Library.
Henry S. Drinker Letter Books: Historical Society of Pennsylvania.
Fitz Randolph-Snowden Genealogy: Historical Society of Pennsylvania.
Hollingsworth Papers: Historical Society of Pennsylvania.
Logan Papers: Historical Society of Pennsylvania.
New Jersey Papers: Historical Society of Pennsylvania.
Joseph Paul Account Books: Historical Society of Pennsylvania.
Charles Pettit–Nathanael Green Correspondence: The William L. Clements Library.
Benjamin Randolph Diary Extracts: Historical Society of Pennsylvania.
William Richards Batsto Diary: Historical Society of Pennsylvania.
Richards Family Papers: Courtesy Mrs. Louis B. Taylor.
Samuel Bartram Richards Papers: From Benjamin Richards Townsend.
Benjamin Richards Papers: Mrs. Maud A. Richards.
George W. Richards Bible Record: Mrs. Harold A. Haines.
Samuel Richards Papers: Historical Society of Pennsylvania.
Richards Papers: The late Harriet Richards Jeter Robeson.
John Ross, Vendue Merchant, Account Book: Historical Society of Pennsylvania.
Warwick Furnace Books: Historical Society of Pennsylvania.
Washington Furnace Books: The State of New Jersey.

Weymouth Furnace Books: 1808–1811: Owned by Mr. and Mrs. Arthur Becker.
Weymouth Furnace Book: 1820: The Atlantic County Historical Society.
Weymouth Furnace Books: 1813–1829: Owned by the Author.
Weymouth Papers: Andrew G. Stewart.
Joseph Wharton Records: The State of New Jersey.

PRINTED SOURCES

Ball Estate Association. *Ball Family.* Mansfield, Ohio: R. J. Kuhl, 1900.
Barber, John W. and Howe, Henry. *Historical Collections of the State of New Jersey.* New York: S. Tuttle, 1844.
Bining, Arthur C. *Pennsylvania Iron Manufacture in the Eighteenth Century.* Harrisburg, Pa.: Pennsylvania Historical Commission, 1938.
Boyer, Charles S. *Early Forges and Furnaces in New Jersey.* Philadelphia: University of Pennsylvania Press, 1931.
——— *Old Inns and Taverns in West Jersey.* Camden, N.J.: Camden County Historical Society, 1962.
Braddock–Rogers, K. "Fragments of Early Industries in South Jersey," *Journal of Chemical Education,* Vol. VIII, Nos. 10, 11 (October, November 1931).
Bridenbaugh, Carl and Jessica. *Rebels and Gentlemen: Philadelphia in the Age of Franklin.* New York: Oxford University Press, 1962.
Bridenbaugh, Carl. *The Colonial Craftsman.* Chicago: The University of Chicago Press, 1961.
Carey, Henry C. *A Memoir of Stephen Colwell.* Philadelphia: Collins, printer, 1871.
Christian, Louise Aymar and Fitz Randolph, Howard Stelle. *The Descendants of Edward Fitz Randolph and Elizabeth Blossom, 1630–1950, and Supplement.* n.p. privately printed, 1950.
Collins, V. Lansing. *Princeton Past and Present.* Princeton, N.J.: The Princeton University Press, 1946.
Cushing, Thomas and Sheppard, Charles E. *History of the Counties of Gloucester, Salem and Cumberland.* Philadelphia: Everts and Peck, 1883.
De Cou, George. *Burlington: A Provincial Capital.* Burlington, N.J.: The Library Company of Burlington, 1945.
——— *The Historic Rancocas.* Moorestown, N.J.: Printed by the News Chronicle, 1949.

Downs, Joseph. *American Furniture: Queen Anne and Chippendale Periods in the Henry Francis du Pont Winterthur Museum*. New York: The Macmillan Company, 1952.

Eberlein, Harold D. and Hubbard, Cortlandt V. *Portrait of a Colonial City*. Philadelphia: J. B. Lippincott Co., 1939.

Fithian, Philip Vickers. *Journal 1775–1776*. Ed. by Robert Greenhalgh Albion and Leonidas Dodson. Princeton, N.J.: The Princeton University Press, 1934.

Fitzpatrick, John C., ed. *The Writings of George Washington from the Original Manuscript Sources: 1745–1799*. 39 vols.; Washington, D.C.: United States Government Printing Office, 1931–1944.

Gordon, Thomas F. *A Gazetteer of the State of New Jersey*. Trenton, N.J.: D. Fenton, 1834.

Hall, John F. *The Daily Union History of Atlantic City and County*. Atlantic City, N.J.: The Daily Union Printing Co., 1900.

Hartley, E. N. *Iron Works on the Saugus*. Norman, Okla.: University of Oklahoma Press, 1957.

Heston, Alfred M. *South Jersey: A History*. New York: Lewis Publishing Co., 1924.

Kimball, Marie G. *Furnishings of Monticello*. Charlottesville, Va.: Thomas Jefferson Memorial Foundation, 1954.

Lane, Wheaton J. *From Indian Trail to Iron Horse*. Princeton, N.J.: The Princeton University Press, 1939.

Lundin, Leonard. *Cockpit of the Revolution*. Princeton, N.J.: The Princeton University Press, 1940.

McCormick, Richard P. *Experiment in Independence: New Jersey in the Critical Period, 1781–1789*. New Brunswick, N.J.: The Rutgers University Press, 1950.

Overman, Frederick. *The Manufacture of Iron In all Its Various Branches*. Philadelphia: Harry C. Baird, 1850.

Pierson, George Wilson. *Tocqueville in America*. Abridged by Dudley C. Lunt from *Tocqueville and Beaumont in America*. New York: Doubleday & Co., 1959.

Prowell, George R. *The History of Camden County, N.J.* Philadelphia: L. J. Richards & Co., 1886.

Richards, Louis. *Sketches of Some Descendants of Owen Richards*. Philadelphia: Collins, printer, 1882.

Ritter, Abraham. *Philadelphia and Her Merchants*. Philadelphia, privately printed, 1860.

Roberts, Kenneth and Anna M., trans. and ed. *Moreau St. Mery's*

American Journey, 1793–1798. New York: Doubleday & Co., 1947.

Scharf, J. Thomas and Westcott, Thompson. *History of Philadelphia, 1609–1884*. 3 vols., Philadelphia: 1884.

Shinn, Henry C. *The History of Mount Holly*. Mt. Holly, N.J.: *The Mount Holly Herald*, 1957.

Stewart, Frank H. *Notes on Old Gloucester County, N.J.* Camden, N.J.: Sinnickson Chew & Sons, 1917.

Stryker, William S. *The Battles of Trenton and Princeton*. Boston: Houghton, Mifflin & Co., 1898.

——— *The Capture of the Blockhouse at Toms River*. Trenton, N.J.: Naar, Day and Naar, 1883.

Swank, James M. *The History of the Manufacture of Iron in All Ages*. Philadelphia: American Iron and Steel Association, 1892.

Van Dyke, Henry. *Days Off*. New York: Charles Scribner & Sons, 1927.

Watson, John F. *Annals of Philadelphia and Pennsylvania in the Olden Time*. 2 vols., Philadelphia: E. S. Stuart, 1898.

Woodward, Carl R. *Ploughs and Politicks: Charles Read of New Jersey and His Notes on Agriculture*. New Brunswick, N.J.: The Rutgers University Press, 1941.

Woodward, E. M. *Bonaparte's Park and The Murats*. Trenton, N.J.: MacCrellish & Quigley, 1879.

Woodward, E. M. and Hageman, John F. *History of Burlington and Mercer Counties, N.J.* Philadelphia: Everts and Peck, 1883.

Index